Michael L. Chyet

مایکل

Berkeley, July 29, 1987

NUBIAN CEREMONIAL LIFE

NUBIAN CEREMONIAL LIFE

Studies in Islamic Syncretism and Cultural Change

Edited by John G. Kennedy

The University of California Press
and
The American University in Cairo Press

1978

Standard Book Number: 74-77726
Library of Congress Card Catalog Number: 0-520-02748-5

The University of California Press
  Berkeley   Los Angeles   New York

The American University in Cairo Press
  113 Sharia Qasr El Aini, Cairo

Photoset and printed in Malta by Interprint (Malta) Ltd.

Contents

v

List of Photographs

Acknowledgments

Robert Fernea, director of the Nubian Ethnological Survey, and Laila Shukry al-Hamamsy, as well as the other senior researchers of the Nubian project, Theodore Thayer Scudder, Peter Geiser, and Charles Callender, and their assistants deserve much credit for any success our projects may have had. They provided background work, contact with informants, and all the assistance we asked for. All these people have my profuse thanks, as does the Social Research Center of the American University in Cairo and the Ford Foundation, who made the research possible. I am particularly grateful to my own field assistants Hussein Fahim, Omar Abdel Hamid Miseemi, Samiha al-Katsha, and Sohair Mehanna, and to Fikry Gamil M.D., who was the resident medical doctor in the village during most of our stay. They were as fine a research team as any social scientist could ask. Zeinab Gamal and Bahiga Haikal, who assisted us on our last trip to New Nubia, were also very helpful.

Of course, a great deal of what we regard as success in this research was due to the cooperation of the Kanuban villagers, and indeed all Nubians treated us with great consideration. We were the beneficiaries of their justly proverbial hospitality, and no thanks are enough to express our gratitude.

My wife Sylvia again proved a great psychological resource to me in the field, in addition to her customary efficiency in carrying out all her research tasks and daily sustenance activities. Her contribution here is considerable. My children Janua and Sian managed to maintain their usual optimistic outlook under some occasionally stressful conditions of village life, and they gave me no cause for regret for having them in the field.

I want to thank my excellent secretaries Sandra Lipshultz and Ruth Marx whose patience, persistence, and good sense have enabled this work to go through the several drafts which were necessary. I am also profoundly grateful to Marilyn Neuhart for the proofreading and editorial comments that allowed the manuscript to reach the printer at last.

I cannot fail to mention the assistance given me by Hamza al-Din, the great Nubian musician. He corrected many of my errors regarding Nubian words and concepts. His recorded music brings back the Nubia that is gone forever.

Preface

How is mankind to live with the Nile? In closing the gap between the granite walls of the valley at Aswan with the tons of rock and concrete that constitute the High Dam, modern Egypt addressed itself to a challenge that had confronted all preceding generations in this ancient land. Though it created a rich, fertile valley in the northeast corner of the barren Sahara, the Nile never permitted its beneficiaries to forget their debt. No matter in how many successive seasons the river rose peacefully to water the land and deposit its renewing silt on the shores, years would come when a flood would ravage the habitations and farmlands that were the products of its generosity or when the river would fail to rise in sufficient supply, thus causing drought and famine instead of ample harvests. The mystery of the Nile's unpredictable performance became a transcendental preoccupation with ancient Egypt, the focus of myth and ceremony. It infused with meaning a pattern of life in which the prosperity of one generation had to become some assurance against the devastation which might fall the lot of the next.

As essays in this volume suggest, the Nile remained an important element in Egyptian Nubian beliefs and ceremonialism despite centuries of Christian and Islamic influences. But modern science and technology, in providing the means to conquer the Nile, has removed the ancient homelands of the Nubians themselves from the river.

They are resettled today in New Nubia, near Kom Ombo, and the waters of the Nile come to them through canals, released by fiat from the man-made lake which covers their ancient home-land. At last the Nile must tamely do the bidding of a country which seems to have wrested from the unpredictable will of nature this once volatile source of supernatural belief. Science has cast the final spell. Looking into the now clear waters of the silt-less river, only the reflection of our wan faces may be seen; we each may perceive for ourselves that the inhabitants have fled.

Yet in this reflection, which should mirror the triumph of man ascendant, traces of anxiety remain. The press warns of negative consequences from the High Dam, all phrased in technical terms: the loss of water through leakage underground or through evaporation from Lake Nasser; changes in the climate; declining soil fertility because of the loss of silt; destruction of fishing grounds in the Mediterranean because of higher water temperatures. Each frightening report may be answered with explanations and technical counter-measures; they may not be cause for substantive concern when compared with the great material benefits which construction of the High Dam has already brought to the people of the lower Nile. Why then do these worrisome omens persist in the clear waters of the domesticated Nile? Can they be related to the concern for the past which prompted archeological excavations and ethnographic studies before the construction of the High Dam? On first examination the parallel may not seem unwarranted, but to seek human understanding of a region, and to feel uncertainty about the future may in fact be complementary concerns. Both are products of unprecedented technological innovation.

Archeologists and Egyptologists from around the world successfully awakened international concern for the artifacts and monuments of ancient cultures which appeared doomed to destruction in Nubia by the construction of the High Dam. The most spectacular result of this concern may be seen today, high above the banks of the Nile where it was fashioned: the now reassembled colossi of King Ramses II and his family viewing the watery burial grounds of less monumental evidence of human endeavors. Another Nubian temple rests behind the glass walls in Central Park, New York. But most of what remained of the past in Egyptian Nubia must now be studied in photographs and drawings and through the descriptions and analyses of those who rushed to Nubia before the inundation.

The Ethnographic Survey of Egyptian Nubia in the early sixties, of which the essays which follow are one of the results, was also an effort to salvage something threatened by destruction. Of course the government of Egypt accepted full responsibility for resettling all the residents of Nubia who lost their homes and villages under the reservoir created by the High Dam. But the way of life of these communities could not, like the temples, be reassembled far from the banks of the Nile where they had developed. Therefore, we the contributors to this volume and many others, attempted to record the culture which was about to disappear.

Ample scientific and pragmatic justification existed for salvage ethnography in Old Nubia. The project proposal stressed such issues as ecological adaptation and labor migration. We offered to be of help to those responsible for planning Nubian resettlement by providing information about the characteristics of Nubian society; we became a means of communication between administrators and administered. The more general humanistic issue — that a unique human culture should be described before it radically changed or disappeared — was perhaps less successfully communicated. Nevertheless, important contributions to ethnology, such as these essays, have also come out of the project. We think it significant that a record now exists of the culture and society of Egyptian Nubians before the High Dam, and, like the historical documentation from the sites and antiquities of the area, will become part of the common human heritage.

However, more than a decade later, as I recall the conditions under which the ethnographic research in Nubia was conceived, I recognize that the prospect of the High Dam engendered in me, and perhaps also in my friends and colleagues of those days, many of the same conflicting emotions of admiration and concern which are increasingly recognized to be associated with each great advance in human control over nature. The ritual behavior described in *Nubian Ceremonialism* is a form of human action which attempts to bridge the gap between certainty and uncertainty, but, so also our ethnographic studies among the Nubians were a form of ceremonialism. They were attempts to reduce uncertainty about ourselves and the consequences of man's brash technological endeavors through studying the behavior of others. The rites of research and analysis must be our response to the image we see in the Nile, the reflection of ourselves and our own responsibilities. The studies so well presented in this volume reveal some of the perceptions the Nubians had about themselves and the world they occupied. Implicitly, we are invited to think about the meaning of our own ceremonialism, and the authors of these essays with their Nubian informants, earn our gratitude and admiration.

Robert A. Fernea
Austin, Texas

Introduction

The High Dam at Aswan erased innumerable historic treasures, and it also forever obliterated the ancient land of a living people, the Nubians. About 50,000 Egyptian Nubians were collectively uprooted and removed to an area selected by them near Kom Ombo, in Aswan Province. In the Sudan almost as many Nubians were relocated at a site near the Ethiopian border called Khashemengerba.

In 1961, prior to this massive resettlement, Laila Shukry al-Hamamsy, Director, and Robert A. Fernea of the Social Research Center at the American University of Cairo recognized the immensity of the social changes which were about to occur. They therefore decided to attempt to salvage some of the cultural heritage of the Egyptian Nubians before their removal. This book is a result of the work on one segment of the project which they initiated and carried through in pursuit of this goal. It attempts to bring together material on the subject of religion and ceremonialism which was gathered by myself and several assistants during our work on one part of the larger Nubian ethnographic survey. For several reasons we are presenting our data on ceremonialism separate from other material on Nubian culture.

First, though there is very little information available on Nubian culture, in the data that do exist there are scant references to ritual and religion. Of all the aspects of their cultural inventory, this is the one most seriously in need of documentation.

Second, this information is of particular usefulness in understanding the dynamics of Nubian life in previous days, and for purposes of comprehending the responses of these people to changed conditions. Its special utility in this respect derives from the fact that, even up to the recent resettlement, life in Nubia was oriented by a continuous round of ceremonial activities. The amount of time, effort and money spent upon ceremonialism was so great that it is no exaggeration to say that ritual activities dominated Nubian cultural life. It is also apparent that adaptation and modification of ceremonialism have been features of Nubian life for centuries, and that these people have been extremely receptive to ideas and practices from elsewhere. This tendency towards syncretism and assimilation in ceremonial customs reflects the intense involvement of Nubian action and thought with the supernatural, and it is my opinion that if one does not understand this complex ritual system one can make no beginning at the comprehending of Nubian behavior and culture, or of the changes occurring in them.

Finally, even though the main thrust of our field study in Kanuba was directed to the question of cultural change and innovation, we gathered a great deal of material on religion. My own endeavor to understand Nubian religion was greatly enhanced by the fact that three of my field assistants were especially interested in ritual, and two of them have since produced Masters' theses on aspects of Nubian ceremonialism. Parts of their work are included in the present book (chapters 2, 3 and 7).

I also had the good fortune to provide some guidance for data collection to Nawal al-Messiri and to direct her M.A. thesis even though she worked in a different sub-project of the Nubian ethnographic survey. The part of her thesis that is included in this book as chapter four is a particularly important contribution because it deals with the Kenuz district of Dahmit, while most of the other material relates more directly to the Fadija section of Nubia (see "Note on Nubian Ethnic and Language Names," below).

Additional data specific to the Kenuz are presented in Fadwa al-Guindi's chapter and in the chapter by Armguard Grauer and myself. These describe the system of beliefs and rituals relating to the spirits of the Nile. However, it should not be thought that this description of Kenuz ceremonial is unrelated to the rest of the material of the book. Even though the customs relating to Saints' tombs as described by al-Messiri were particularly strongly developed among the Kenuz, they were also typical of the Mahas-speaking region, and were numerous in the Arabic-speaking Aleqat people living between the two major Nubian groups in Egyptian Nubia. Other data on the Kenuz are presented in descriptions of Kanuba, where a section of the village consists of Kenuz from the district of Abu Hor.

With the exception of the introductory chapter and that on death rituals (chapter 11), my own work in this volume has previously appeared in several journal articles. However, I have added data and discussions to most of the chapters, and in particular the description of the zār has been augmented. I am thankful to the following journals for permission to reprint material: *American Anthropologist* for "*Mushāhara*: A Nubian Concept of Supernatural Danger and the Theory of Taboo", *Human Organization* for "*Zār* Ceremonies as Psychotherapy", *Man* for "Circumcision and Excision in Egyptian Nubia", *Journal of American Folklore* for "*Aman Doger*: Nubian Monster of the Nile".

This book is primarily ethnographic. Although I am fond of theoretical formulations, I also believe strongly in the obligation of all anthropologists to present descriptive material on the cultures they study as a first order of business. I owe this orientation to my former teachers Walter Goldschmidt, William A. Lessa, and Ralph Beals, all of whom have made lasting contributions to the ethnographic literature. The longer I work in this field the more convinced I become of the value of substantive data. Looking back over the history of anthropology, it is apparent that ethnographic facts generally have been of far more lasting significance than the great bulk of theoretical formulations, no matter how brilliant the latter seemed at the time of their currency.

Though here there is an emphasis upon the presentation of data, there is also considerable analysis and interpretation. The chapter on the *ṣalāt al-jūm'a* by Fahim, the one on the *dhikr* by Fahim and myself, and that on marriage by al-Katsha each have analytical discussions relating the described rituals to changing conditions in the resettled village of Kanuba. These interpretive analyses have some pertinence to understanding change in Nubian culture generally. My chapters on the *mushāhara* concept and circumcision ceremonies also have relevance for wider theories of taboo and initiation rituals. That on funeral customs may illuminate some aspects of the relationship of the psychological and social processes relation to death.

The chapter on Nubian *zār* contains an assessment of the therapeutic effectiveness of this type of treatment ceremony which may be of interest to those concerned with transcultural psychiatry. If any theoretical framework characterizes this book, it is a general structural-functional mode of looking at things.

The Ethnographic Survey of Egyptian Nubia

In the original overall research for the Ethnographic Survey of Egyptian Nubia, three districts in Nubia were chosen for intensive community studies, one from each of the major linguistic areas. Dahmit was selected in the Kenzi-speaking section of Nubia (Aswan to Sebua), Malki in the Arabic-speaking section (Wadi al-Arab to Korosko), and Ballana in the Mahas-speaking area (Korosko to Adendan). No work was possible in the Sudan at the time due to political conditions. In addition to community studies, an ecological survey of resources and their uses in Nubia was designed and a survey of Nubian architecture was formulated. Two other studies of urban Nubians in the cities of Cairo and Alexandria were also planned, since it is well known that great numbers of Nubians have spent their entire lives outside of Nubia, even though maintaining life-long ties with their native villages. Thus, as the designers of the larger project recognized, no study of Nubian culture and society could be comprehensive which neglected its migratory and urban aspects. A final unit of the Survey was added later. This was a study of a previously resettled Nubian community north of Aswan in the vicinity of the new resettlement area, part of which is reported in this book.

Despite considerable administrative problems and other vicissitudes, most of the units of the Ethnographic Survey were completed. Robert Fernea, director of the project as a whole, completed a community study in the Fadija (Mahas-speaking) district of Ballana near the Sudanese border. He was assisted by Karim Durzi, Afaf al-Dib, and Bahiga Haikal of the Social Research Center staff (see Fernea 1967). Charles Callender executed a community study in the Kenuz district of Dahmit with the assistance of Fikry Abdul Wahab, Fadwa al-Guindi, and Nawal al-Messiri (see Callender 1967 and Callender and al-Guindi 1971).

After a failure of health by a senior researcher, a graduate student was assigned to the district of Malki in the Arabic-speaking area of Nubia, but he was unable to complete that study. An economic survey of Nubia was carried out by Theodore Thayer Scudder with the assistance of Abdul Hamid Zein (Scudder 1966), and the urban survey of Nubians in Cairo was completed by Peter Geiser with the assistance of Nadia Hagag (Geiser 1967,a,b). In 1963, Abdul Hamid Zein also made a field study oriented to the *sāqia* irrigation system in the southernmost Egyptian Nubian district of Adendan (Zein 1967).

The Kanuba Study

The final segment of the Ethnographic Survey of Egyptian Nubia was added in 1962, when I was engaged to study one of the Nubian communities that had been previously resettled between Aswan and Luxor as a result of the prior raisings of the Aswan Dam. After a survey of these communities, I selected one which, to protect its identity, has been named Kanuba. It is located in Aswan Province, in the vicinity of Kom Ombo, not far from where the rest of the Egyptian Nubians were settled in 1963–64. Kanuba is a community which contains members of both of the linguistic groups of Old Nubia. I directed a field study in this community during 1963–64 for a total period of about fourteen months with the able assistance of Hussein Fahim, Omar Abdel Hamid Miselemi, Samiha al-Katsha, and Sohair Mehanna.

Before relocation, the same research team made three survey trips of several weeks each to Nubia. The main purpose of these trips was to become acquainted at first hand with the districts from which the people of Kanuba migrated after the flooding of their lands in 1933–34. We gathered data in the Kenuz *'omodiyyas* of Dahmit and Abu Hor, the Arab Nubian *'omodiyya* of Malki and the Fadija *'omodiyyas* of Korosko, Diwan, Ballana and Adendan. Most of our time was spent in Diwan and Abu Hor, due to the fact that the majority of people in the village of Kanuba, which we were studying intensively, had migrated from these two districts. However, about two weeks altogether on two of these trips were spent in Dahmit, where we benefited from the generous hospitality and help of Callender and his research team. About ten days were also spent in the areas of Ballana and Adendan. On these later visits Zein was of great help, particularly in Adendan, where he was working at the time. In Ballana the previous informants employed by Fernea and his group were very hospitable, since his ethnological field crew had left a very good impression there.

After the resettlement of the Nubians had been completed in 1964, I also made several trips to New Nubia, near Kom Ombo. On one of these visits, involving a survey of traditional medical practices, our group had the able extra assistance of Zeinab Gamal and Bahiga Haikal, both of the Social Research Center.

Our survey visits to Nubia, brief as they were, proved to be extremely important to our understanding of the community of Kanuba, and to the comprehension of Nubian culture generally. It was mainly due to the consequent revelation concerning the actual conditions of life in Old Nubia, in contrast to the Kanuban emigrants' reports of that life, that convinced me during the visits that much of the traditional culture might well disappear. I feel that many aspects of the Nubian heritage may now be lost. Time exacerbates the problem and has spurred me to gather the data collected fere for the record.

Our field methodology in the village of Kanuba employed a number of strategies. First, we relied primarily upon participant observation methods by all members of our research team for several periods totaling about thirteen months. The indepth immersion in village life, which provided our most satisfactory and abundant data, was supplemented by several focussed-interview schedules, and other data gathering methods.

The longest schedule was administered to a random sample of 60 percent of the adult women of the village during the final month of our stay. It took more than two hours to administer, and gathered information on 106 items relating to education, degree of participation in life outside the village, knowledge of the outside world, marriage and family, pregnancy history, travel history, social participation and visiting patterns within the village, and economics. Other shorter schedules were administered earlier in the study. One of these schedules, administered by Fahim, gathered information in some depth on the work and migration histories of men, and on their future aspirations. Another short schedule administered by Omar Abdel Hamid was aimed at securing information about land holdings, field sizes, agricultural technology, houses, and the changes in these in the relatively short history of the village. A third, devised by al-Katsha, focussed upon the activities and attitudes of unmarried girls of marriageable age.

A method for checking questionable data and for filling gaps was devised, which proved quite effective. By the end of our study we had involved the village in our enterprise to a fairly high degree, and many of the villagers, in keeping with their strong motivation to secure benefits to Kanuba, were convinced that it was necessary to present an accurate picture of the village to the world. This desire was of course complicated by wishes to appear in the best light possible. About two weeks before the conclusion of field work we therefore informed the men that we wanted to go over certain points with them, and arranged an evening meeting in the mosque. We then conducted group sessions on Nubian culture and village life which were recorded on tape for several days. Fahim led the discussions with my assistance, and due to his skill in handling it, they proved extremely fruitful.

The fact that this method was used late in the study was, I think, critical to its success. By that time, we were well known and the hostilities and suspicions which we had first encountered were largely dissipated. The villagers knew that we understood a great deal about the village and the few attempts at concealment that were made by some visiting men at these sessions were laughed down by the majority, who knew that we were well aware of the true situation. Another interesting feature of the method was the fact that, being in a group, each man was aware that what he was saying was perceived by others. Since men were present from both the religious factions in the village and from all age groups, this method enabled elicitation of nuances of interaction that were very revealing in themselves. In general, the collective effort to recall events of the past, the inter-stimulation of memory with regard to past customs, and the collective response to the presentation of any inconsistencies in the data were tremendously valuable. But it should be re-emphasized that the success of the method was based upon the fund of knowledge we had built up by living in the village. At an early period it would have elicited nothing but guarded responses.

A word should be said about the virtues of team participant-observation. Our group lived together in a house in the village. The research household consisted of my family and four research assistants, plus a cook. We ate our meals together and usually wrote up our notes in the evening, sometimes around the same table. This provided an atmosphere of maximum participation through discussion, exchange of information on events and village personalities, and collective planning of data-gathering strategies. The living arrangement of what seemed an optimum number of researchers allowed flexibility, feedback and reformulation of problems and tactics as fieldwork proceeded. It allowed a goal-directed camaraderie to develop that was invaluable. At all times we were aware of what was going on in the village, what had happened, what was planned, and what the attitudes of various individuals were towards these phenomena. I cannot recommend this mode of work highly enough.

Kanuba

Since several of the chapters in this book describe events and behaviours in the village of Kanuba, its major features will be outlined here. Kanuba, which has about five hundred inhabitants, is not a result of the most recent relocation of Nubians. It came into existence in 1933–34 when the Aswan dam was last raised. The site of the village is about twelve kilometers south of Kom Ombo, forty kilometers north of Aswan, and three kilometers south and east of the market center of Daraw, a town of some thirteen thousand people under the jurisdiction of the Kom Ombo *markaz*. However, with the great resettlement of the Nubians in 1963–64 near Kom Ombo, the Kanubans saw an opportunity to rejoin the rest of the Nubians and in this way secure some advantages which the government was giving to this group. They petitioned strongly to be a part of New Nubia, and their request was eventually granted. They were thus able to get out from under the jurisdiction of the Upper Egyptian officials who dominate Daraw, and in terms of building new houses and other advantages, to be treated like the newly resettled Nubian villages. At the same time they socially and psychologically rejoined their Nubian kinsmen. Kanuba is now included as part of the Markaz al-Nasr, the new administrative division created for the resettlement area. This development was quite an upturn of fortune for the Kanubans who, since their migration in 1933, have waged a difficult struggle in Daraw both economically and as an ethnic minority.

The first group of settlers at Kanuba came from the district of Diwan, which was just North of the Old Nubian capital of Derr in the Fadija (Mahas-speaking) area of Egyptian Nubia. The Egyptian government made some monetary compensation at the time, but it was only a pittance. However, a group of men from Diwan put their savings together with this compensation money and, after looking at several sites, selected the area where Kanuba now stands to found their new village. They purchased 426 *feddans* (a *feddan* is approximately the size of an acre) for agriculture and an additional 64 feddans on which to build houses, a school, and a mosque. This purchase was made from the Kom Ombo Valley Company, a corporation that owned and operated the large sugar mill at Kom Ombo and was dominated by wealthy landowners, including Aboud Pasha, then Prime Minister of Egypt.

According to the elders of Kanuba, one condition of the purchase was that the company would build a canal from the Nile, so that the fields around the village might be irrigated. This part of the agreement was never fulfilled and at the time of our study in 1963–64 Kanuba was still surrounded by desert. There were two wells that produced somewhat brackish water, but only about ten *feddans* were under cultivation at the time we initiated our research. The people were very bitter about the failure of the company to fulfill its commitment.

In the first days of village construction, several men spent all of their savings and compensation money to dig deep wells and to build *sāqias*; and during the early 1940s a man who had relatives in the village moved from Cairo to try farming with more modern methods. He bought a gasoline pump with his savings from working with the British army and hired men to dig some canals, but within a few months the pump broke down. It proved too expensive to repair. The water was very deep and saline; and within a couple of years attempts to irrigate the land through the villager's own efforts eventually foundered and resulted in the loss of what little capital they had.

Their dreams of carrying on an agricultural life being frustrated, the Kanubans were forced to seek their livelihood in other pursuits. In the early years many of them migrated to the cities to take jobs in service occupations, following the long-standing traditions of Nubia. Others sought employment in the vicinity — in Daraw, Kom Ombo, or Aswan. During the first decade, urban migration is reported to have produced an imbalanced sex ratio comparable to that of Nubia. However, as the years went on, some of the children of men who had migrated returned to the village. Some older men also came back to retire, but the majority of returnees were young people educated in Cairo or Alexandria who had become disenchanted with the city for one reason or another, and had elected to take up a more rural existence. By the time of our stay the sex ratio was still somewhat imbalanced, fluctuating at an index figure of around Seventy (i.e., seven males to ten females). This was a much better figure, however, than the fifty-six that was typical in Nubia at the same time (Geiser 1967, p. 169); it may be attributed to the greater opportunity for urban-type employment in the Aswan region than was available in Nubia. This high proportion of literate men with extensive urban experience is a major reason for the fact that the village of Kanuba is quite atypical in many ways in comparison with both the Upper Egyptian peasant villages surrounding it, and with other Nubian villages as well.

In fact, a major reason for selecting the village to study was this atypicality, though I was not aware of the depth of the uniqueness on my first survey visits. At that time, I perceived only that the outlook of this village was quite different from others I had seen. The air of progressiveness and optimism and a kind of sophistication were quite striking in spite of the many economic handicaps that were evident. The people had no fields and little water. Many houses in certain parts of the village were abandoned, either because the termites (*gourda*) had eaten all wooden parts or because a kind of oily saline substance (called *al-nazz*) had seeped up through the ground, destroying the walls and making the area unlivable. In spite of this, the Kanuban people had an attitude of hopefulness and many signs of productive activity were visible.

It turned out that a major reason for the progressive, forward-looking attitude of this village was that the people had been able to find viable solutions to their economic problems. These consisted mainly in the fact that, having more education than the surrounding Upper Egyptians, the Kanubans were able to secure many of the white-collar and public-service jobs in this part of the economically expanding Aswan province. They did not get jobs at the Kom Ombo sugar company, few became tradesmen, and most of them did not work as servants, as had been their ethnic tradition. Instead, they took over jobs as clerks in hospitals, telegraph and post offices, and became teachers, social and recreational workers, and so on. A few became shopkeepers and some had enough training to take skilled technical jobs in such facilities as pumping stations and the weather station at Aswan. About 40 percent of the men were in occupations of this kind at the time of our study. Since many of these men worked at some distance, they returned only on weekends and holidays. They were called the "people of the weekend" by the others. It is clear that the village of Kanuba has played a vital role in filling the growing need for skilled and educated individuals in the province.

The Aswan area has always been considered a hardship post for urban Egyptian officials and technicians and it is difficult to get them to serve there. However, these Nubians preferred the Aswan region to the city, where competition, discrimination, and rapid social change often made them very unhappy. Of course, the sense of vitality and optimism that we noted in 1963 was enhanced by the general high level of activity, by the euphoria created by the building of the High Dam at Aswan, (which was then going on) and by the impending relocation of all the Egyptian Nubians into the Kom Ombo vicinity. Both these interrelated sets of events had brought thousands of workers into the area from other parts of Egypt and had created a tremendous economic upsurge. The government had built a large chemical fertilizer plant in Aswan and was widening many of the towns' streets, erecting hotels, and in general attempting to promote tourism. All of these happenings contributed to a general optimism and sense of change in the province. Yet Kanuba stood out, even in this general climate of rapid social change, and on our trips to Nubia in 1962 and 1963, it was referred to again and again as a kind of model of progress that other Nubian villages wished to emulate.

Kanuba is a conglomerate village made up of fragments of villages from several districts of Nubia, and this circumstance has produced some of the problems of factionalism and lack of integration that it has experienced. The main group of inhabitants, about half the population, come from the Fadija district of Diwan. This group generally has controlled the politics of the village, even though there is a factional split among themselves on religious grounds. (This split will be explicated further in a number of chapters.)

Apart from this dominant Diwan group, there are Fadija families from the closely situated Old Nubian districts of Derr, Tongala, Abuhandl, Tomas, and a group of Kenuz families from the district of Abu Hor. Most of the Abu Hor people came to Kanuba in 1937, some four years after the initial settlement. They built houses on both the north and south sides of the village center. These groups of houses are called Kenuz *bahari* and Kenuz *gibli* by the people, and each is separated by several hundred yards from the main Fadija section. The Kenuz houses are quite distinctive in that they have preserved the vaulted-roof style famous in their part of lower Nubia. This makes quite a contrast with the Fadija section, where the older houses are a mixture of the spacious flat-roofed mudbrick structures found in the northern Sudan, with the addition of some urban-like features.

In 1963 the village petitioned the government to be included in the rebuilding activity it was carrying out to resettle the Nubians from behind the dam, and asked for redress of certain former injustices. Their pleas were finally heard, and after a number of starts and delays, most of the Diwan families were offered new dwellings of approximately the same concrete-and-stone style as those made for the large resettlement near Kom Ombo. The Kenuz refused the new houses, preferring to remain in their own much more spacious dwellings of traditional construction. This response is generally typical of the greater cultural conservatism of the Kenuz, which can be seen in many areas of life. The dominant Fadija group in the village is called the *Nūbiyyīn* or the *kushāf* (the Turkish term for district governors) by the Kenuz and by the other Upper Egyptian groups of the surrounding area.

Education

In both groups the men speak fluent Arabic and use it interchangeably with their own Mahas or Kenzi according to their ethnic group and as the occasion demands (see "Note on Nubian Ethnic and Language Names," below).

Many women, on the other hand, particularly those of the older generation, have very limited Arabic, and a few speak none at all. About 77 percent of the women are illiterate. However, most of the younger women speak Arabic very well, and about 13 percent can read and write it with the capability gained from attending primary school up to the sixth grade, the level at which it has been traditional for them to be withdrawn from school.

About 90 percent of the adult men of Kanuba are literate and many of them have 'had advanced schooling beyond the secondary level. The literacy rate of this village is thus far above that of the country of Egypt as a whole, which at the time of study was around 30 percent for males and far less for females. Since the 30 percent figure includes the cities, it can be seen how Kanuba stands out among the peasant villages of the surrounding region.

A government primary school was established in the village in 1937. There is an intermediate school nearby in Daraw, but for secondary school the children must travel to Kom Ombo by bus. Those older villagers who had attended school in Nubia before 1933 had all gone to *kuttābs*, the traditional religious primary schools run by old sheikhs who taught the boys to memorize the *Qurān*. The people of Kanuba believe strongly that education is the way to success, and they frequently visit the school to check on their children's progress. Again, the attitudes and behaviors are atypical for the area.

Social Organization

A medical clinic was established in Kanuba in 1963. It serves several villages in the vicinity and only through their energetic lobbying with officials were the Kanubans able to get it placed in their village. According to the local doctor, who has had wide experience in Egypt, this clinic has a relatively high rate of use, indicating a greater awareness of modern medicine than is generally found in rural Egypt. This, of course, is in keeping with the unusually urban-like character of this village.

The social organization of Kanuba rests on nuclear family households which are integrated at the village level through the village association and the village club. These are democratically organized groups and all important village affairs are handled by them. In Old Nubia the *sheikh al-qabīla* (tribal leader) and later the *'omda* and *sheikh al-balad* were important traditional, government-appointed leaders. In Kanuba the traditional *sheikh al-balad* post exists, but its aged incumbent at the time of the study was bypassed by the young men of the association, who dominated village affairs.

This more democratic type of organization was much more possible in Kanuba than it was in Old Nubia due to the lack of the strong lineage groups, which had been traditional basis of social organization. It has been fostered by the shifts in the occupational structure to wage and salaried work. Such transformations have created nuclear family independence based on the modern western model, as opposed to the extended kinship groups that were adaptive to the economic system of *sāqia* agriculture in old Nubia.

Another change of circumstances that is having an effect on village organization is the fact that Kanuba is much more a part of the state administrative structure than were the more autonomous Nubian villages before 1933. In this century there was a continuous trend on the part of the central government to bring Nubia more and more within the orbit of the Egyptian administrative system, but the area was remote from the urban centers of power and was therefore left largely alone. Consequently, local leaders and structures were more free and at the same time more responsible in carrying on many decision-making functions than is presently the case in Kanuba. Now the police force of Daraw and Kom Ombo and the judicial structure of the Markaz handle crimes and litigation of all types, while the Arab Socialist Union of the region handles relationships with the Central Government. Thus much of the old political autonomy has been lost. However, the Nubians hate to take their disputes and problems to an outside source and still try to resolve most issues within the context of village organization.

Social life in the village is best conceived as consisting of a dual social world, with sex differentiation constituting a major social dichotomy. As is typical of this part of the world, women are regarded as being mentally quite inferior to men and as having naturally more passionate natures. They are therefore carefully watched, since premarital chastity and postmarital promiscuity are matters of male and family honor.

Women who are married or are of marriageable age wear black transparent garments over their cotton dresses when they leave the house. Around the village men dress in *jalabeyas* of various colors, but many of them wear Western style suits for their clerical occupations outside. In public social activities women sit together in an area apart from men and their daily activities, revolving around household and neighborhood, are almost wholly spent in the company of other women. As girls approach the age of puberty they are more and more segregated from boys; and in school, which in the recent past was exclusively a male domain they are seated separately.

Inasmuch as the activities of the sexes are largely separate, with women being a kind of subordinate caste excluded from village political decisions and public religious participation, it is not surprising that there is a separate female social structure in Kanuba. This structure is founded upon neighborhoods with overlapping networks related by dyadic ties between pairs of women. For example, each neighborhood generally has two or more cliques in which each member owes to other members obligations of visiting, service, and goods for any special or ritual occasion or time of need. Every woman is obligated to visit and provide labor and gifts in major village events such as wedding feasts and funerals, but the major responsibilities generally fall upon one or two of the clique groups that are most closely related to the protagonists.

Religious Life

Although many aspects of the religious life of Kanuba are discussed in the following chapters, some general observations will help the reader to understand the descriptions of changes in ritual in those chapters. There is a good-sized mosque at the edge of the village which serves as the center of the religious life of the people — and, like all Nubians, the Kanubans are Sunni Muslims of the Malikite persuasion. They observe all the major Islamic holidays and believe in the practices codified as the Pillars of Islam.

In Kanuba some of the rich symbolism and traditional practices of Old Nubia, described in several chapters of this book, have been abandoned. For instance, circumcision has lost the elaborate ritual formerly associated with it, the Nile spirits and *mushāhara* beliefs are minor and unimportant, there are no sheikhs' tombs in the village (there are important shrines in Daraw, but these are not Nubian and have attracted little veneration from the Kanubans), and *dhikr* ceremonies are rare and have completely changed in quality and meaning.

The most important overall change is a drastic reduction or purging of traditional Nubian ritual practices. As will become evident in later chapters, the reasons for such changes in religion as have occurred are largely the result of several conditions. Major among these have been the secular ideas emanating from the city and the reformative influence of the village representatives of the conservative Ansār al-Sunna sect. Without anticipating the later discussions too much, I should say that it is our conclusion that these two opposing trends, one hyper-religious and one anti-religious, have tended to work conjointly (though in different aspects of the system) toward the same end — a streamlining of Nubian ceremonial practices and a general dampening of religious enthusiasm in the village. The favorable setting for these influences to operate was established by the relocation of the village in a new environment.

These same forces were also at work in many parts of Old Nubia, but the circumstances of resettlement provided the opportunity of starting anew without much of the old cultural baggage that tends to accrete gradually in the lives of most groups and becomes ever more burdensome to people as time goes on. Along with this, the resulting shifts in political leadership, the economic hardships, and the hard problems of existence in the immediate years after resettlement drained energy away from ritual and absorbed much of the money and time that in Old Nubia was channeled into the ceremonial cycle. By the time the Kanubans were economically on their feet in the 1960s, the old ceremonial impetus had been eroded away. This erosion was due not only to the secularization pervading the cities of Egypt, but also to rigidly simplifying doctrines of the Anṣār al-Sunna. Such changes were not easy transitions. They have involved social conflict and mental turmoil.

Recent Conditions

By September 1971, the time of my last brief visit to Kanuba, the economic picture had changed radically for the better. Since the government was building canals to irrigate the land of the newly resettled Nubians, officials had finally complied with the insistent requests of the village leaders. A feeder canal had been constructed from the large canal carrying water to New Nubia to the fields surrounding Kanuba. On my visit I was overwhelmed by the transformed appearance of the area. Large stands of sugar can extended south from Kanuba for almost a mile, while to the East the green of the vegetables and *durra* reached out into what until 1970 had been open desert.

Although we did not have an opportunity to document adequately the many profound changes that have occurred as a result of this improved economic picture, several things were apparent. Only two Kanuban men had become full-time farmers; the rest had carried on their salaried jobs. The village had organized a co-operative society to handle agriculture. The society had hired a group of *Saīdīs* from nearby to do the actual farming, while it organized marketing, book-keeping, and the purchases of seed. It is too early to know how these economic changes will affect the village, but there is no doubt that the effects on all aspects of social and cultural life will be profound.

It does not seem unlikely to us that many of the changes which have occurred in Kanuba may be prototypical of what will occur among the large groups of resettled Nubians near Kom Ombo who have more recently been wrenched from their isolated traditional homeland. Thus this book may be of use in understanding this transition by providing detailed baseline data on the background of traditional Nubian ceremonialism and by describing some changes experienced by Nubians who were earlier projected into similar circumstances by the forces of history.

Note on Nubian Ethnic and Language Names

The section of the Nile Valley known historically as Nubia stretched from the first cataract at Aswan, Egypt, into the Sudan just beyond the fifth cataract near the beginning of the great curve of the Nile. The peoples living in this narrow strip of land, which extended some five hundred miles along the great river, spoke languages of the category known as Nile Nubian, a subdivision of Nubian within the larger Eastern Sudanic language subfamily (Greenberg 1963).

The two major subgroupings of the Nile Nubian 'omodiyyas extending from Daboud to Sebu'a was made up of villages whose inhabitants were speakers of Kenzi. The people themselves were called Kenuz (sometimes Kenuzi or Kunuzi) and in local parlance, particularly among the Mahas-speaking Nubians, the Kenzi dialect of Nubia was known as Metoki. Just south of the Kenuz from Wadi Sebu'a to Korosko was a group of villages whose people were racially and culturally Nubian, but who spoke only a dialect of Arabic. These Nubians identified themselves as belonging to the Aleqat tribe. South of this short break, the speakers of Nile Nubian continued with the Mahas speakers. They began at Korosko and occupied the banks of the Nile in an unbroken sequence southward to a point almost a hundred miles into the Sudan. The southernmost Egyptian Nubian 'omodiyya was the Mahas-speaking district of Adendan.

To the south of the Mahas-speaking districts in the Sudan were the Dongolese speakers. Their language is nearly identical to that of the Kenuz; these two languages are linguistically so close that they are regarded, for most purposes, as dialects of the same language (Stevensen 1956 and Bell 1970). There has been considerable speculation as to how the populations representing these two branches of the same language became geographically separated (eg., Millet 1966, and Bell 1970), but no solid evidence is yet available.

Another label in common use in the area, but whose precise meaning is somewhat nebulous, is *Fadija* (variants in the literature are *Fadicca*, *Fadiga*, *Fadidja*, *Fadika*, *Fadicha*). In our experience this was a somewhat pejorative word among the Kenuz, but it was also used by Mahas people farther south in the Sudan to designate the northernmost group of Mahas speakers (from about Korosko to Ballana or perhaps Adendan). Some of the connotations which we, as non-linguists, got from Kenuz for the term *Fadija* were "slavelike," and "push him and whip him". On the other hand, many people living within this particular area seemed to use the term simply descriptively and neutrally to designate this northern group of Mahas speakers. Those farther south (from about Wadi Halfa to the area of the Dongolese speakers) called themselves the "Mahas" as a name for their ethnic group, in addition to speaking the language of the same name. Therefore I believe that "Fadija" does not primarily designate a dialect, but more meaningfully refers to an ethnic subgroup. As far as I know, evidence is not available upon which to base either cultural or linguistic distinctions of conclusive fineness. Nevertheless, utilizing the peoples' own usage, I will call the group of Mahas speakers in Egypt (i.e., north of the second cataract) the Fadija and I will reserve the term Mahas for their language. The group in the Sudan calling themselves the Mahas also speak this language.

A final language reference that should be mentioned is the word *roṭān* (or *riṭāna, raṭāna, riṭāna*). This is the general colloquial term in use in the region for all the Nubian languages. The Arabic meaning is "non-Arabic language". However, the Nubians themselves use *roṭān* as the most broad category for their own language, i.e., as a word embracing both Kenzi and Mahas dialects.

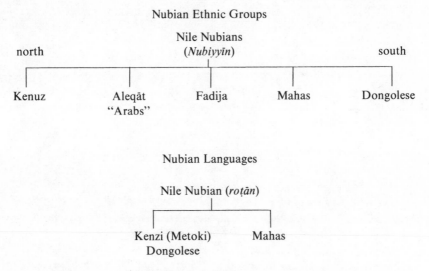

Nubian Ethnic Groups

Nile Nubians
(*Nubiyyīn*)

north				south
Kenuz	Aleqāt "Arabs"	Fadija	Mahas	Dongolese

Nubian Languages

Nile Nubian (*roṭān*)

Kenzi (Metoki)   Mahas
Dongolese

All male Nubians speak fluent Arabic as a second language. Most women can also communicate in Arabic and women of the younger generations are fluent.

Chapter 1

Nubia: History and Religious Background

JOHN G. KENNEDY

It is perhaps indicative of the attitudes of our times that, with the building of the High Dam at Aswan, Egypt generated a worldwide movement to save the ancient monuments of Nubia, but stimulated practically no effort to document the culture of the living Nubians. Yet approximately 50,000 Nubians in Egypt and another 50,000 in the Sudan were suddenly uprooted from the lonely quietude of their isolated Nile villages and transplanted into prepared compact settlements of stone houses far removed from the great river. The consequent profound impact of this upheaval on the people's lives seems just as important a topic of attention as the losses to knowledge of ancient history.

The Nubian part of the Nile valley is under the water now backed up behind the 225-foot High Dam at Aswan. It is estimated that Lake Nasser, which extends to the south almost three hundred miles behind the dam, will have a surface area of more than 2000 square miles. It was hoped that the water from the lake would increase the productive area of Egypt by more than 30 percent and that the turbines at the dam would provide significant amounts of electric power for the country.

Part of the price for this huge attempt to solve Egypt's economic problems and to move towards modernity was the drowning of much of the cultural history of the area and the removal of the Nubian peoples from their traditional homeland. This great price was partially offset by the efforts of archaeological expeditions sent by nations of the world to recover all that was possible of historical importance before the waters irrevocably rose. The Nubians were provided with new communities, in addition to being compensated financially to some degree for their losses. In spite of the intensive archaeological efforts prior to the completion of the dam, it is certain that much important evidence in this historically significant battleground of the ancient world has been irretrievably lost beneath the water. The loss of information with regard to the living Nubian peoples has been even more severe: it has been the loss of living culture.

1

It is surprising, but true, that the culture of the Nubians is practically unknown. It was only in 1957 that Rolf Herzog published a book, *Die Nubier*, that first put some solid information into the informational vacuum that then existed. Herzog's book provides many useful facts about Nubian culture, but it is principally culture-historical in approach and does not rely upon intensive field work. A fine book, with a series of photographs accompanied by an excellent ethnographic essay, is *Nubians in Egypt* by R. Fernea and G. Gerster (1973). This book goes some way towards filling the gap and makes a good introduction to the culture. Besides these two works, however, anyone wishing to learn something of Nubian life must rely on obscure articles and the reports of travelers, most of whom made trips through the area in the nineteenth century. Burckhardt, the famous Middle East traveler who in 1813 spent only six weeks in the region, is still one of the best sources on old Nubian culture, although others such as Bruce, St. John, Amelia Edwards, and Ruppel, to single out a few, wrote descriptions that have added to our understanding.

There is some justification for the neglect of the Nubian people by recent scholars as well as by organizations wishing only to save the monuments from the rising water behind the dam. It was presumed that the Nubians would carry a good part of their culture over into their new settlements at Kom Ombo, Egypt and Khashamangerba, Sudan: and it is true that some of it may be recovered by ethnographic research. However, there are reasons why this approach was not to be relied upon for a complete picture of Nubian life and why it was necessary to do intensive studies of Nubian culture in its original settings. Major among these reasons is the fact that the break with the old life created by the resettlement was drastic and complete. The shift was much more than simply a change of place; it also involved a break with the old styles of life.

Despite the propaganda of the press in Europe and the United States, which emphasized the tragedy of their removal and loss of country, in the early 1960s a great many of the Egyptian Nubians wanted to move. These wishes to move were mixed with much nostalgia for the past and anxiety for the future, but they came from the fact that Egyptian Nubia, as a viable place to live, had really ceased to exist some time earlier. The Nubians' conceptions of their land as a happy and blessed land of date groves and extensive fields of *durra* really derived from the nineteenth century and earlier. The destruction of Nubia was not brought about by the latest High Dam, but had been carried out in a series of stages since 1902, when the first dam was built at Aswan. At that time much of the Kenuz area, which is closest to Aswan, was innundated. This dam was raised in 1912, and again in 1933; each time the lake was extended farther south. Thus over the past thirty years most of the land of Egyptian Nubia, except for the districts closest to the Sudanese border, had been made desolate.

Each of the earlier changes of the water level necessarily wrought profound changes in Nubian life. For centuries Nubian men had migrated to the cities of Egypt to work as domestic servants. Their land had never been abundant enough to support their families well, especially since in many parts of the area during the last three centuries, the best land and crops had often been confiscated for taxes by petty governors of Turkish origin, called the *kushāf*. Another reason for the ancient migratory labor pattern had been the economic and social instability created by the back-and-forth rush of fighting armies across the Nubian landscape: the soldiers of these armies often commandeered Nubian crops, kidnapped or raped Nubian women, and pressed Nubian men into their service. Even though the migrancy pattern was a long-established one, however, the Aswan dam of 1902 and the successive raising of it made life even more precarious in Nubia. Though the people built and rebuilt their villages on higher ground, maintaining their illusions that life was still the same, their needs for remunerative work in the cities steadily increased as their productive land receded. The Old Nubia of the nineteenth century became only a memory.

In the early 1960s the only agriculture possible in North Nubia on any scale was a four-month crop of melons, plus some *durra* and *kasherengeg*. Since the growing season was not long enough to allow full ripening, grain crops could only provide fodder for a few animals during the rest of the year when the water level was up to the doorsteps of the villages. During this four-month growing season the sluice gates of the Aswan dam were opened, releasing Nile water to Egypt and making available the growing area in Nubia only for that period. In some years fluctuations of the river made it necessary to close the dam even earlier, so that even the marginal summer crop was always highly uncertain (see Scudder 1966). Thus, with successive inundations remittances from men working in the urban centers increasingly became the main sources of sustenance for the women, children, and retired men who continued to reside in the now almost completely barren Nubian villages. This situation was in sharp contrast with previous times, when at many places along the river thick groves of date palms had sheltered the houses and fields of *durra* had created fertile green strips on both banks of the Nile.

As more Nubians men spent more time in the cities, they continually absorbed more of the urban and western values that have been rapidly spreading in Egypt and the Sudan in this century. Though their love of country and their ties with their villages persisted, the Nubians also came to acquire a new set of values, and many of them came to appreciate education, medical services, access to manufactured goods, and electricity, amenities that were not available in the old Nubian villages. Though the majority of Nubian women continued to live most of their lives in the villages, during this century more and more of them traveled to Cairo or Alexandria to visit. Through their husbands and male relatives, many of whom returned home several times a year to visit, they also came in contact with urban ideas. They became increasingly dissatisfied with the conditions created by the extremely imbalanced sex ratios that characterized Nubia, which became more accentuated with each raising of the dam. In 1962, just before resettlement, a sample survey of Nubian villages showed that an average of 85 percent of the adult males were out of Nubia working in cities. It is not surprising that when we interviewed them prior to resettlement many women expressed unhappiness with the traditional life.

Thus, by the time of their total resettlement in 1963–1964, the Nubians had had sixty years of conditioning for catastrophe behind them, and were in a mood of acceptance, even if still not completely prepared for their final removal from their traditional homes. Most of them were nostalgic about leaving their country and distrustful of the government, but they looked forward to a better life after resettlement. The government was promising them new land and houses and they were anticipating opportunities for advancing economically, reuniting families and participating in the new educational and occupational opportunities of the Egyptian revolution that was being led by Gamal Abdul Nasser.[1] Only a few of the older generation viewed resettlement as a disaster (see Fernea and Kennedy 1966).

The belief of most Nubians at the time of their removal was that they were going to leave much of the old village life style behind them. Despite the fact that they regretted leaving familiar settings, with all their memories, associations, distinctive architecture, and traditional artifacts, most of these people were looking forward with enthusiasm to making some profound changes in their customs and living patterns. This attitude of preparedness for change was fostered by the Egyptian government, which desired to integrate Nubians into the national culture. For example, the schools in the new settlement, now attended by all Nubian children, have made Arabic the dominant language, teach nationalistic values, and promote an urban rationalistic point of view.

These are some of the reasons why it may be predicted without too much difficulty that much of the traditional Nubian culture, which was perpetuated without thought or effort under isolated conditions of village life, will soon be gone. Since many of the older generation have died since resettlement, by the time the predictable nativistic attempts to revive traditional customs are made, much of the ancient culture will be beyond retrieval. Even more irrevocably than is the case with the monuments remaining beneath

Lake Nasser, the distinctive experiment in living developed by the Nubian peoples will also have largely disappeared forever.

General Features and Historical Background

Earlier I alluded to the fact that Nubian religion in an amalgam of customs and beliefs from many sources. This is generally true of all religions, though they are frequently presented to us by scholars as well as by their proponents as internally consistent pristine models of unique revelation and practice. This kind of idealizing is particularly associated with the "Great Religions" which have been worked over by theologians for centuries. Islamicists, like students of the other great religions, tend to devote their exclusive attention to exegeses of the texts of great philosophers, theologians, legalists, and poets of the Middle Ages. How Islam is now lived and practiced in the village mosques of the Middle East is not generally regarded as a meaningful subject for study.

As Robert Redfield points out, however, the understanding of Great Traditions such as Christianity, Buddhism, Hinduism, and Islam, can be illuminated by the study of how these traditions are interpreted, used and adapted at the community level. He also showed that it is even more important that the student of village culture, and thus of what he called the "Little Traditions," should gain some comprehension of the Great Traditions from which the local people are selecting and modifying certain elements according to their own understanding and for their own purposes (Redfield 1960, pp. 40–50). For the Little Traditions that relate to the Islamic Great Tradition there is very little data. The goals of the present study, therefore, are to provide some insight into how Islam was practiced at the village level in Nubia as well as some understanding of how religion related to social process and of how it articulated with ceremonial practices that appear to be non-Islamic.

Islam, like other Great Tradition religions, has had much difficulty in suppressing the pagan religions upon which it imposed itself. It seems remarkable that many of the same battles against pagan customs that were waged by the first Muslims with the tribes of the Arabian peninsula during the first century A.H., such as attempts to prohibit death rituals in which women put dust on their heads, cut themselves, and wail, are still being waged among the Nubians. Though the conversion of Nubia to Islam took place some five-hundred years ago, the attempts by those who profess orthodoxy to purge *bida'* (innovations) from the Islamic practice of the Nubians seem just as vital for them as they were historically (see chapters 2 and 3).

The ceremonial system of the Nubians is full of contradictions and is still undergoing change and conflict. Nevertheless, as is usually the case with belief systems, it appears in most ways consistent to most of its adherents. Several of the chapters of this book deal with aspects of change in this system, while others describe the syncretistic combinations of non-Islamic and Islamic elements found among Nubians.[2]

Since at least the beginning of this century, the Nubians between the first and second cataracts generally have been much more oriented to Cairo and Egypt than to Khartoum and the Sudan. This is true even though they are culturally and racially closer to the people to their south than to the adjacent Egyptian peasant people on their north. The Sudanese Nubians, on the other side of the national border, have migrated primarily to Omdurman and Khartoum and have become a powerful force in the Sudan's political structure. In contrast, Egypt's Nubians have remained subordinate to the lighter-skinned Egyptians and foreign groups that dominated the country. There they have remained confined for the most part to their traditional service occupations, though recently there have been signs of change (see Geiser 1967). Egyptian Nubians have been elected representatives to the National Assembly of the Arab Socialist Union, the Egyptian legislative body set up by President Nasser in 1964. However, as a group they have still not escaped completely the ancient stigma contained in the words *barabra* (pl.) and *barbari* (sing.), terms still applied to Nubians and denoting the barbarism traditionally associated with the country beyond the cataracts in the *bilād al-sudān*, or "lands of the blacks."

The Nubians now regard themselves as strong Muslims, though they were converted to the Islamic faith relatively late in comparison with the Egyptians. It is unclear what the precise details of the ancient Nubian religion were prior to the Christianization of the region in the middle of the sixth century A.D., but judging from the many Egyptian temples which were found along this part of the Nile, their belief system must have been heavily influenced by the Pharaonic religion of ancient Egypt. One reason the character of pre-Christian, pre-Islamic Nubian religion is somewhat obscure is that there is considerable uncertainty in the archaeological record regarding the antecedents of the modern Nubians in the region known as Nubia.

Recent findings seem to indicate that lower Nubia was abandoned for a period of some nine hundred years between 1000 B.C. and 100 B.C. This period, known to some archaeologists as the "great hiatus," was probably brought about by a drop in the level of the Nile that made agriculture impossible with the then existing technology for lifting water based on the *shadouf* (Adams 1967, pp. 10–13). The *sāqia*, or cattle-driven water-wheel, was not introduced until the Roman period of Egyptian history. During this hiatus period, the great kingdom of Napata arose on the south of Nubia, followed by the kingdom of Meroe. Both kingdoms challenged the supremacy of

Egypt, and it was to the advantage of these great powers to maintain barren Nubia between them as a no-man's land.

Whatever the reasons for the long abandonment, this strip of the Nile was gradually repopulated again in the first centuries A.D., probably as the result of two major economic factors: (1) the *sāqia* was introduced, permitting much more extensive irrigation; and (2) during the same period it seems that the Nile was rising towards its previous levels, making crops possible in the old areas. In addition to the improvement of the economic situation, repopulation of Nubia was aided by the fact that Egypt was experiencing one of its periods of relative political weakness. It is still uncertain whether the people who moved into the Nubian region at this time, and who are apparently ancestral to present-day Nubians, were related to those who had been there previously.

During the period between 300 A.D. and 500 A.D. there were a series of petty kingdoms along the Nubian stretch of the Nile, the most outstanding of which was that of the Ballana kings, who left quite impressive graves (Emery 1965). Little is ascertainable concerning specific religions for this period, but it seems clear that the picture changed in the fourth century A.D., when Egypt was forcibly converted to Christianity. Nubia resisted the new religon for a few years, but eventually capitulated to the efforts of Monophysite (Jacobite) missionaries sent by the Byzantine Emperor Justinian. By 543 A.D., the Nubians were officially Christian. It seems that their Christianity was never more than a thin veneer atop their ancient native religions and that it was only maintained by a foreign elite of priests and governors. The Nubians nevertheless remained officially Christians for almost a millenium.

The region had been Christian for less than a century when the Arab armies invaded Egypt in 640 A.D. One year later these armies reached Aswan, where the Islamic tide was stemmed, and the first cataract remained the southern frontier of Islamic Egypt and the northern frontier of Christian Nubia for several centuries. During medieval times Christian Nubia flourished. It was united under the King of Makuria and enjoyed a "Classical Christian" period between 850 and 1100 A.D.

Arabs had been penetrating the area at various times for centuries, however, as peaceful settlers, as traders, and as raiders. Some came as tribal remnants of defeated Caliphates, such as the Abbassids. During the Fatimid Caliphate (969–1161 A.D.) there were many Arab trading expeditions going along the Nile, dealing particularly in slaves (Hassan 1969). Many Arab tribal leaders married into leading Nubian families and after several centuries it seems that the Nubian kinship system was gradually converted from one tracing relatives matrilineally to one tracing them patrilineally (from Ibn Khaldun, cited in Hassan 1967, p. 127). Islamic religious doctrine and legal practices also became more and more widespread through this intermarrying process.

The Muslim conversion of Nubia thus seems to have been gradual, covering several centuries, though in the late phases military victories were decisive. Salah al-Din (the famous Saladin) defeated a Nubian army that invaded Egypt in 1171, for example, and at various times unruly Arab tribes from Upper Egypt pillaged the area. Christianity held on in many parts of Nubia until the fourteenth century, however, when Islamic raiders coming from the south, in what is now the Sudan, looted the churches and finally completed the long process of conversion (Adams 1967, p. 15). Christian Nubian pilgrims were noted in the holy places of Palestine as late as the Fifteenth century (Hassan 1967, p. 125), but by the end of the fourteenth century the vast majority of the Nubians had become staunch Muslims, as they are today.

From 1517, when the Turkish Sultan Selim sent Hassan Koosy to take over governorship of the area, all through the Ottoman period, and up to the present century, much of Egyptian Nubia was ruled or dominated by descendants of this family of Turkish petty gentry. Members of the Koosy family married into local lineages and the resulting aristocracy became known as the *kushāf*. The descendants of this ruling family still regard themselves as a superior class among the Nubians.

During the Turkish period conditions of relative anarchy alternated with those of local tyranny, and military forces frequently swept devastatingly through the region. The last time battles were fought in Nubia was during the Mahdist uprising in the Sudan in the 1880s, and in the present century the succession of Aswan dams has replaced military turmoil as the principal distruptive force in the troubled history of the Nubians.

This condensed resume of some Nubian historical facts should be enough to indicate something of the background of complexity from which the syncretism that is modern Nubian religion derives. (More complete details of Nubian history can be found in Shinnie 1954; Trigger 1965; Emery 1965; Adams 1967; Hassan 1968; Fernea and Gerster 1973.)

Aspects of the Religious System

The syncretism of Nubian ceremonial practices contains three major categories of customs and beliefs: Non-Islamic, Popular Islamic, and Orthodox Islamic. These categories are not simple classifications on my part, but are recognized in practice among the Nubians themselves. One rather surprising aspect of the present religious amalgam, in view of the lengthy period of Christian dominance of Nubia, is the lack of specifically Christian elements in it. Among the few customs which the Nubians themselves regard as coming from their Coptic Christian past are some associated with childbirth. Informants stated that some of these were the practice of having the woman in labor grasp hanging palm leaves to ease the pain, the blackening of the baby's eyes with kohl, and the marking of a cross on his forehead with the same substance. A china plate or object was also struck next to the baby's ear to produce a bell-like tone and make him cry, a custom said to be a simulation of a church bell. The symbol of the cross is used as a decoration on clay storage jars and in a few other situations, but it is of minor significance.

Though there are few Christian survivals, there are many "pagan" features of the system that may be pre-Christian. There also seem to be very few survivals from the state religion of dynastic Egypt. Customs such as circumcision have survived from this period, but there is little evidence to suggest any similarity in the forms or meanings of the present rituals with ancient circumcision practices.

Orthodox Islam

Orthodox Islam refers to the doctrines and practices of the Qur'ān as interpreted by recognized legal experts (*ulamā*) who reside in urban centers. Like all Muslims in Egypt and the Sudan, the Nubians are members of the Sunnite division of Islam, and in keeping with their Sudanese affiliations, they adhere to the Malikite school of doctrinal interpretation.[3] To the Nubians, al-Azhar University in Cairo symbolizes the summit of true religious knowledge; any Nubian who has attended it or one of its schools is accorded the status of religious leader and scholar.

During this century orthodoxy has also to some degree become associated with Islamic reform ideas. In several districts of Nubia, a sect called the Anṣār al-Sunna has promulgated these ideas and has campaigned both against what its members regard as paganism and against Popular Islamic practices, which they hold to be *bīda'* (heretical "innovations"). This sect seems related to the puritanical Wahhabi movement, which fought many battles in the name of Islamic reform in the nineteenth century and is now the prevailing doctrinal force in Saudi Arabia. The chapters of this book on the Friday Prayer and on *dhikr* rituals describe some of the sorts of social and religious conflict produced by the Anṣār al-Sunna sect in Nubia.

Nubian orthodox practice includes the general Islamic elements of regular Friday prayer (see chapter 2) as well as what are called the five Pillars (*arkan*) of Islam. They are: five-times daily prayer (*ṣalāt*), testimony to the unity and singularity of Allāh (*shahāda*), pilgrimage to Mecca (*al-hajj*), the giving of alms to the needy (*zakāt*), and fasting (*ṣaum*), particularly during Ramadan. It was stated by some nineteenth-century travelers to Nubia that Nubian adherence to these Orthodox practices was not too strict (e.g., Burkhardt 1822, pp. 136–137). It is probable that until recently few Nubians made the pilgrimage to Mecca, but even allowing for the possible inaccuracy of their comments, it is curious that observant travelers in those times, such as Burkhardt and Amelia Edwards, did not mention the numerous small mosques that were evident as one traveled up river prior to the last relocation. Perhaps there were few of them before the twentieth century, though on the other hand it may be that in the period before the villages were rebuilt on higher ground (due to the previous raisings of the Aswan dam) the Nubian mosques looked more like houses. It is possible that the trend towards more strict observance of Islamic practice is fairly recent.

It seems clear, in any case, that the migration pattern which drew Nubian men to work in the city for long segments of their lives, separating them for extended periods from their wives in the villages, exacerbated the cleavage of male and female social worlds that is typical in Islamic areas. Thus men became more and more educated and more aware of doctrinal distinctions and issues in religious practice, while women remained largely illiterate and ignorant of orthodox practice. The effects of these conditions were increased by the Muslim custom of excluding females from the mosque on most occasions and by relegating women's participation in religion largely to private ritual and peripheral roles. Thus most Nubian women's religious activities remained in the non-Islamic realm, or were concerned with Popular Islamic saint cults rather than with Orthodox religion.

Popular Islam

When I speak of Popular Islam I do not want to create the impression that all the practices classified as such are distinguished in any strict way from Orthodox practices. Even many of what Nubian men call "pagan" customs are often practiced in conjunction with clearly Islamic ones with no particular feeling of incompatibility. In his valuable study of Sudanese religion, Trimingham used the term "Popular Islam" in a broader sense than I am using it here. For him the term embraces "animistic influences," which I am calling "non-Islamic," as well as the cults of saints and the activities and beliefs of the Ṣūfī brotherhoods. For the Nubians, it seems necessary to include a number of customs in the category of Popular Islam in addition to those of the saint cults and the Ṣūfis. Examples are the customs associated with the *id al-ṣaghīr* or Small Feast, which is observed throughout the Islamic World. In Nubia this joyful occasion, marking the end of fasting in Ramadan, was a folk festival with a Popular Islamic character.

In Nubia, as elsewhere, the Small Feast began with a dawn prayer in the desert near the cemetery that is behind each village. The imām (prayer leader) stood on a small dais to deliver the *khuṭba* or sermon, after which people decorated the graves with palm branches and sprinkled water upon them, since this was the time of year when the ghosts of the dead returned. An apparently uniquely Nubian part of the celebration of the *īd al-ṣaghīr* was the procession that the men made to each house in their own hamlet as well as in the adjoining ones. The women of each family waited at the door or in the *mandara* (guest room) to greet the men and offer them special foods such as dates, *sha'reya*, cookies (in recent years), and tea. At each house the Nubian greeting was *"Korig'ynal alay!"* ("Live and see holidays!") to which the other replied *"Ekon anya alay!"* ("You, too, live and see them!"). Children following the procession frolicked in their new clothes, eating sweets. After making the rounds, people gathered in groups at several houses in the village for communal meals.

The *īd al-kibīr*, or Large Feast (more properly called the *'id al-aḍha* or Feast of Sacrifice) was celebrated some forty days after the Small Feast and was more subdued in tone. All Nubian families tried to kill a sheep on that day, in commemoration of the famous event when Abraham was saved from sacrificing his son Ismail by the appearance of the substitute ram sent by God. This day also featured a prayer service and communal eating, but included no visit to the cemetery or processions. This feast is regarded as legitimately Islamic by the Anṣār al-Sunna.

Some other commonly observed Islamic holidays were also celebrated by the people of Nubia. These were the twenty-seventh day of the month of Ragab, *ras al-sana al-hijra*, the *mawlid al-nabī*, and the *laylet al-nuss*, which is simply the day that falls in the middle of the month of Sha'ban. Even if no saint's mawlid (birthday celebration) was celebrated on that day, the men of the village gathered in the mosque where they held a service in which they recited *al-du'ā*, a well known prayer of devotion to God. Women remained at home preparing a feast to be held afterwards.

The *mawlid al-nabī* is the birthday of the Prophet Muhammed, a major holiday throughout Egypt. Festivities begin the night of the eleventh of *Rabī'* I, the eve of the Prophet's birthdate, and the day is celebrated in the centers of towns and villages with a carnival-like spirit. In the mosques of Nubia, as elsewhere, long poems or *qaṣīdas* were read praising Muhammad and recounting the story of his birth, after which *dhikrs* were performed. This *mawlid* was regarded as a profanation of true religion by puritanical reformist Islamic groups such as the Anṣār al-Sunna.

The principal Popular Islamic practices condemned by the orthodox reformist sects are those relating to the veneration and worship of saints and to the *dhikr* rituals of the Ṣūfi orders (see chapters 2 and 4). The saints of the Islamic world are pious men known for miracles (*karamāt*) and revered after their deaths. They are regarded as intercessors (*wālī*) with God and their *baraka*-endowed shrines are found everywhere in the Middle East.

Veneration of saints is excluded from orthodox Islam, mainly on the grounds that the Prophet Muhammad insisted that he was only a mortal "messenger of God" (Qur'ān III:138) and ordered that no shrine be built for him. He tried to focus the attention and reverence of believers on Allāh alone, but after his death the tendency to elevate, revere and worship the spirits of holy men, along with the felt need of common people for intermediaries with the distant Allāh, combined to produce the saint cults that have proliferated throughout the area. Trimingham's statement concerning the Sudan holds for Nubia as well:

> Every Muslim believes that beside the visible order of believers there exists an in-
> visible order of saints who, under the direction of Allāh, manage the affairs of the world
> for him. So bound up are the saints with the religious life of Islam in the Sudan that
> to think of Allāh without his intermediaries is impossible (1965, p. 126).

Local saints' shrines are found throughout the Sudan and are innumerable, but it is doubtful that any area of the Muslim world can match the concentration of such shrines in some parts of lower Nubia. Saints (here called sheikhs) of any importance have *mawlids*, festival days designated as their birthdays, set aside each year. In Egypt and Nubia most of these *mawlids* fall near the middle of the month of Sha'ban, usually on the fifteenth. *Mawlids* generally feature slaughtering an animal for the feast, dancing, singing and a *dhikr*. The *Mawlid al-nabī* or Birthday of the Prophet is the most universally held festival of this type.

The chapter of this book by Messiri is an especially interesting study of the cults of sheikhs in one Kenuz district, where within a few miles more than one hundred and fifty shrines were found. I shall not anticipate her interesting account here, but below is an example from our notes, not elaborated in her paper, of a therapeutic function of this type of cult. The example illustrates the way sheikhs were regarded in Nubian popular Islam and the way the shrines fitted into daily life.

> A woman named Sa'diyya in the district of Abu Hor (Kenuz) once awoke in the
> morning to find her legs swollen and paralyzed. Since it was during winter and uncom-
> fortably cold, her family immediately recommended that she rub her legs with oil and sit
> near the fire. This did not alleviate her condition, so with the help of friends she hobbled
> to the house of Sheikh Abu Shalashil, a local curer. The sheikh questioned her at length
> about her activities on the previous days and after a while determined the cause of her
> trouble. It seems that on the day before she and her companions had been visiting the
> shrine of a saint in the neighborhood; and while inside the dome, she had begun joking
> and dancing in a sacriligious way. That night she had been visited in a dream by an old
> sheikh with a long white beard, wearing a white turban, and carrying a stick in his hand.
> The spirit asked her why she had desecrated his tomb and threatened to punish her for it.
> This being such a clear case of moral transgression, Sheikh Abu Shalashil had no dif-
> ficulty in finding the cause of Sa'diyya's illness. His prescription was that she go to the
> shrine in the morning and ask the forgiveness of Sheikh Muhammad, the spiritual

occupant of the shrine. He further recommended that she take several grains of *durra* and bury them under the tree growing next to the tomb. She was to follow this by taking seven loaves of fresh bread and throwing them one by one into the Nile at noon, all the while chanting the *Fatiha* (the "Opening" of the Qur'ān).

Although she had to be carried to the shrine by her friends, Sa'diyya followed the sheikh's orders exactly. The following night she was again visited by Shekh Muhammad in a dream. This time he told her she was forgiven, but qualified it by saying that his generosity was largely because of the elders in her family. He said he appreciated them because they were the organizers of his yearly *mawlid*. Otherwise, he stated, she would not be forgiven so easily.

That morning she awoke much refreshed and relieved. Her legs were not completely healed, but they were less swollen and painful. She continued with home remedies such as rubbing them with a mixture of sugar and the fruit of the doom palm in addition to the oil she had been using. She attributed her recovery, which occured a few days later, to supernatural forgiveness.

Though they possess an extensive pharmacopaeia, many supernatural remedies of the type exemplified in this incident are also used by the Nubians. Rituals utilizing such symbolic substances as gold, henna, and palm leaves are combined with treatments using natural herbs and various foods. The case of Sa'diyya has all the earmarks of an hysterical conversion reaction, though without more evidence we cannot be sure that some physical malfunction was not fortuitously associated with her moral transgression. What is illustrated is the attitude of the Nubians toward their saints and the ways in which local healers worked. The case also draws our attention to the fact that there is no clear boundary between the categories of Popular Islam and what we have termed Non-Islamic aspects of the Nubian religious system.

The celebration of *'Ashūra* should also be included in the category of Popular Islam here. This common Islamic holiday is the commemoration of the murder of Hussein, the grandson of the Prophet Muhammad, with a number of followers at Kerbala, Iraq, in the year 680 A.D. (61 A.H.). *'Ashūra* is now primarily a Shī'ite holiday (on the tenth of the Arabic month of Moharram) in Iran and Iraq, but it is also celebrated in Egypt and Nubia. In fact, Hussein's head is reputed to be in Cairo, brought there during the Fatimid Caliphate, which was centered there from 969 A.D. to 1161 A.D. Whether the Nubian celebrations of *'Ashūra* are survivals of Fatimid times is problematical, but they now seem quite distinctive in Nubia. For example, in one Kenuz district, Dahmit:

> The women and children burn ropes after dark and run to the river. There each puts together some stones symbolic of his or her household, the number of stones being equal to the number of members in one's household. This is to provide one's family members with the river blessing. They also take with them dishes of food from which they throw seven pieces for the river inhabitants. They all remove their clothes, jump into the river, and swim in it for blessing (al-Guind; 1967, pp. 251–2).

The burning of ropes is also reported for the Fadija districts of Diwan and

Adendan; and in the latter area tiny boats of wood bearing candles were set afloat in the Nile to be carried towards Cairo, thus assuring safe journeys for traveling relatives (Abdul Hamid Zein: personal communication). In many Fadija areas, women carried a kind of date soup (*fenti shorba*) to the Nile, where they ritually drank some and offered the remainder to the river spirits.

The *karāma* is another important part of Popular Islamic Nubian ceremonialism which is not separately treated in this book. The word *karāma* in Arabic means "generosity" and by extension has come to mean "miracle". It is used by the Nubians, for example, in this sense in referring to the miracles of saints (see chapter 4). But the Nubians also use the term in a sense closer to its original meaning to designate a kind of communal meal which is given or put on by an individual as a ritually meritorious act. Thus, *karāmas* are not regular, but depend upon individual volition and financial ability. In old Nubia, a *dhikr*, such as is described in chapter 3, was generally held after the meal, but was not always necessary, and is often omitted nowadays. In Kanuba, for example, a woman of the village once sent cinnamon tea and cookies to the men gathered in the mosque in the evening for prayers and reading. This was a *karāma* in thanks to Allāh for fulfilling a request and no *dhikr* was held. In this case the *karāma* overlapped with the concept of the vow or *nadr* (see chapter 4). On other occasions large feasts for the whole village are given as *karāmas*. These are not simply festive occasions; the giving of them confers some kind of spiritual merit in heaven to the giver. Sometimes the remembrance feast, the *attiga* (Mahas dialect) or *attaga* (Kenzi dialect) which is given by a family member one or two years after a death, is also designated as a *karāma*.

Similar to the *karāma*, but more secular in tone, are the ceremonial meals held before and after long journeys. Such arrivals and departures were particularly frequent in Nubia due to the migratory labor pattern; during certain seasons people were leaving for Cairo or Aswan or returning every month or so. Large gatherings were held before each departure. After eating food sent by several houses of the village, each person present embraced the traveler and, saying the *Fātiḥa*, wished him a good voyage. The group would then accompany him to the place where he would meet the post boat or a felucca to depart.

The person returning to the village was met by gunshots and the joy cries of the women. He embraced his closest relatives and gave or received ritualized condolences if anyone had died during his absence. As is customary at a funeral, food was again provided by someone for the group, and everyone gathered to open the gifts that the returning traveler always brought from the city. These departures and returns were so ritualized in form and expectation that they constituted a part of the ceremonial pattern of the Nubians, albeit a marginal one from the standpoint of religion.

A holiday that is difficult to assign to either Popular Islamic or Non-Islamic categories is called *Arbah Maidour*. This is the last Wednesday of the Islamic month of Safar. It is believed to be an evil and portentous day, and special ritual precautions are taken in defense against the evil spirits abroad. Kanuba is the only place in which this custom was observed, though informants claim that it was observed by all the Fadija in Old Nubia.

Non-Islamic Beliefs and Customs

The non-Islamic elements of the Nubian ritual-belief system remained largely the province of women, though men were affected by them at many points in their lives. These elements and rituals were most salient at the critical points of birth, circumcision, marriage and death, "crisis rites" that are all detailed at some length in this book. We need point out here only that the non-Islamic aspect of the Nubian belief system was primarily concerned with the spirits and beings of the Nile, variously called *melajkanijinaman* (Mahas for "river angels"), *amān nutu* (Mahas for "water people"), *essin malaikari* (Kenzi for "water angels"), *essin burui* (Kenzi for "water girls"), *nās al-bahr* (Arabic for "people of the river"), *banāt al-Ṣālehīn* (Arabic for "daughters of the virtuous") and *dogri* (both dialects).

There was also a category of pagan beliefs concerned with the jinn and *gourin* (Mahas dialect) that were more associated with desert and mountains than with the river. Belief in the Evil Eye and in sorcery was also widespread.

Another set of supernatural fears and accompanying taboos relating primarily to spirit beings of the Nile was accompanied by a concept called *mushāhara*. The *mushāhara* concept is described in detail in chapter five, but a few words may serve to indicate the types of behavior involved in the closely associated beliefs in sorcery and the Evil Eye, both of which constituted constant threats to the Nubians.

The Evil Eye was generally referred to by Arabic terms such as *ayn al-hassūd*, the "eye of the envious," or simply *hassad* (envy), and envy was the emotion most commonly associated with its being cast on an individual. People who were fortunate in some way were regarded as potential targets for envious and evil-intentioned people, whose look might cause sickness, misfortune, or death. Beautiful children, brides and grooms, or those who were lucky, wealthy, or otherwise fortunate were regarded as particularly in danger, and anyone with a persisting illness was often diagnosed as having been attacked by the Eye and precautions were taken accordingly. Any period of crisis or danger also was a time when cautionary ritual procedures were heightened.

The usual defenses against the Eye found in the general literature on the subject were also used by the Nubians, but their main means of protection was the *hejāb* (*hegāb*) or charm. These amulets were usually made of a number of ingredients recommended by a *sheikh al-hejāb*, sometimes called a *fagīr*. They might also be made by a midwife known for magical knowledge. In the Kenuz village of Abu Hor, for example, a young woman was observed wearing two *hejābs*, one for her heart trouble and one for her toothache. They each had a piece of paper with some words from the Qur'ān written by a *fagir* (holy man) sewn inside a small cloth bag. Her baby had a *hejāb* made from salt, cumin, pepper and fingernails. The baby also had a small gold band affixed to his forehead. The hand is a common symbol of defence, as are blue beads. Hands were frequently seen painted in blue, red, or white on the walls of old Nubian dwellings. Another *hejāb* which we inspected contained such magical ingredients as seven seeds of *habbit al-baraka* (a local black spice), seven cloves, seven pieces of henna, and seven needles. Nubian women also made all kinds of ritually defensive objects of beads and cloth, which they hung especially in their bedrooms. Elaborately decorated rooms were used by couples after a wedding and remained in their bedrooms, loaded with marriage symbolism, for many years. Much of the decoration, which included the typical paintings of hands, had a protective function against jinn and the Evil Eye.

Conceptions of the Evil Eye among the Nubians seem to be connected with belief in the jinn or *afarīt*, evil spirits always hovering near the habitations of man. A typical incident was described to us: A sheikh visited a sick baby boy, looked at the child, and said that the Evil Eye must have struck him when he fell over a pile of dirt while playing. The sheikh wrote a verse from the Qurān on a sheet òf paper and told the mother to soak it in a glass of water for the boy to drink. The child's recovery was attributed to the potion. The notion of being struck by the Evil Eye when falling over a pile of dirt indicates the connection of spirits with the concept in Nubian eyes, since hateful jinn are thought to inhabit such places and since there is no mention in the story of any actual person gazing at the child.

Sorcery, called *'amal* or *sehr* (Arabic), was another method by which supernatural harm could be inflicted upon a person by enemies or their paid specialists. It was also associated with the Evil Eye in people's minds. For example, a man in Diwan, who was generally believed to cast the Eye, was said to have been hired by certain people to turn his malevolent gaze on their enemies. Much more common, however, was the general type of sorcery found throughout the world in which a specialist in the spells of black magic was hired to cast them against others.

From all the information we could gather, it appears that, in comparison with many groups, sorcery was not common among Nubians; the greater supernatural dangers were those associated with *mushāhara*, the Evil Eye, and the ever present jinn. The *Fatiha* or Opening of the Qurān was a charm constantly being recited as people approached unknown areas, crossed thresholds, passed garbage dumps, and so on. The major aims of sorcery were felt to be the theft of women's husbands, a fact undoubtedly related to the long separations of marriage partners necessitated by the Nubian migration pattern. Many counterspells were used to protect brides and grooms from sorcery, since they were felt to be in special danger, especially from jealous individuals who may have wanted to marry one of them.

All of these non-Orthodox beliefs and practices are, of course, found throughout the Muslim world and many of them are mentioned in the Qur'ān. The customs of this nature that were most distinctively Nubian belonged to the set of pre-Islamic practices and beliefs associated with the river Nile. These mostly concerned the "river angels," who were regarded primarily as benefient and helpful, but who were charged with great power which could harm individuals if precautions were not taken. Beliefs concerning these creatures were by no means as distinct and systematized as descriptions may lead one to think. Often it seems that ghosts of the dead were identified with the river spirits; and sometimes they were identified with the *gourin* or jinn and the Evil Eye, as well as with the possessing spirits associated with *zār* ceremonies.

The Nubians had beliefs in a spiritual world beneath the surface of the river in which the river inhabitants occupied elaborate castles and lived a life that was very alluring to human beings. Many people in Nubia were said to have very intimate relationships with these Nile beings and those who had had experiences of possession by them were frequently considered to be in a position to intercede with them on behalf of others. Fadwa al-Guindi and Armgard Grauer, both of whom have worked in Dahmit, have brought together in chapters 5 and 6 some of the beliefs held in the Kenuz region that reveal the role of these spirits in all Nubian ceremonialism. I have added some related data in chapter 6, mostly from the Fadija area. The involvement of river spirits throughout Nubian ceremonialism will become even more apparent in the chapters dealing with the crisis rites and the *zār*. It should be stressed that relationships to the non-Islamic river spirits, particularly the Nile angels, had some role in almost every aspect of Nubian ceremonialism that took place outside the mosque. Because the Nubians have been resettled away from the Nile, and because of the consequent pressures making for the destruction of such distinctive elements of Nubian culture, these very localized spirit entities may well become extinct.

Notes

1. In recent years primary schools had been provided in all districts, and a secondary school had been established at Aneiba. Three boats with medical doctors and some facilities moved up and down the Nile in Nubia, but these services were insufficient and inferior to those elsewhere in the country. Thus they simply whetted the Nubians' desire for something better.

2. The best previously published information related to that presented here may be found in Trimingham's *Islam in the Sudan*, in Barclay's *Buurri al-Lamaab*, and in Callender and al-Guindi's *Life Crisis Rituals Among the Kenuz*. These works also are concerned with Islam as it is lived in this part of the world, rather than with theological and legal history, but neither of the first two focuses specifically upon the Nubians, though each author gives some space to them. The Callender and al-Guindi book concerns Nubians, but is restricted to life-cycle rituals in a single Kenuz community. It should be read in conjunction with the data presented here, which are much more abundant for the Fadija than for the Kenuz.

   The present book should also be read in conjunction with Trimingham's important work *Islam in the Sudan*. Many of the practices and beliefs described here for the Nubians are similar to those in the northern Sudan, as would be expected from the fact that Nubians of both Mahas and Dongolawi-speaking groups (linguistically related to the Kenuz) are important ethnic minorities there. The main differences in our treatment from that of Trimingham are that our material is restricted to Nubians of lower Nubia and that we treat fewer topics in greater depth. This statement does not apply to his description of the Ṣūfī orders, which is the most complete record of them for this part of the Islamic world. The main reason for our lesser attention to these orders in Egyptian Nubia is that they were of far less organizational significance at the time of our study than they are in the Sudan, where they have formed the basis of powerful political groups.

3. The Sunni Muslims (followers of the Sunna) are the dominant or Orthodox branch of the Islamic religion. The other great branch is the Shī'a, which is predominant in various forms in Iran, Pakistan and North Yemen. Orthodox or Sunni Islam is divided into four great legal schools of Qur'ānic interpretations: the Hanifite, founded by Abu Hanifa, 767 A.D.; the Malikite, founded by Malek Ibn Inass, 795 A.D.; the Shāfi'ite, founded by al-Shafi, 820 A.D.; and the Hanabalite, founded 855 A.D. by Ahmad Ibn Hanbal.

Chapter 2

Ritual of *Salat al-Jūm'a* in Old Nubia and in Kanuba Today

HUSSEIN M. FAHIM

There is probably considerable variance in the details of Orthodox ritual practice throughout the Muslim world, but such a conclusion must at this time be entirely impressionistic, since descriptions of actual practice in the area are almost non-existent. Therefore, this chapter by Hussein Fahim has significance beyond the local case it describes. As a Muslim himself, he is able to understand the Friday ritual from the point of view of his lifelong acquaintance with it; as an anthropologist, he has been able to see it in a detached way as well. Hussein Fahim's account is placed near the beginning of this book in order to remind the reader clearly of the central importance of Islam to the Nubians, regardless of the non-Islamic beliefs and rituals which are described later. The chapter also introduces the theme of socio-religious change and conflict in the village of Kanuba, which forms an inevitable thread throughout this work.

After the establishment of the new village of Kanuba in 1934, the Nubian migrants planned to maintain the same way of life and ceremonials, but traditional ritual has been altered, along with other aspects of culture, due to the changing conditions of life in the province of Aswan. This chapter describes and analyzes the standard Friday Islamic ritual, *salāt al-jūm'a*, both in its Old Nubian traditional form, especially in the district of Diwan, and in its new form, as it was being performed when our field study took place in Kanuba.

Ancient and present forms are described separately and then analytically, using six indices. The present form of the Friday ritual is described first since it is based upon first-hand observation and information, whereas the pre-1933 description depends upon informants' memories and is therefore less reliable.

Tabulation of Islamic dogmas and precepts does not help much in providing a comprehensive and thorough understanding of the essence of Islam in the Muslim's life. Corollary to theological studies, there is need for data on Islam that reflect observed ritual behavior within the context of social life.

19

Actual practices should be described and analyzed. Following this line of thought, this chapter is an intensive microstudy of one important ritual among Muslims of a Nubian community as it is related to their daily activities and concerns. My analysis will show that change in the form of *ṣalāt al-jūm'a* reflects in large part a trend toward conservative Islamization, in accord with orthodox teaching, rather than simply representing a unitary movement towards secularization.

Orthodox Islamic Grounds of the *Ṣalāt al-Jūm'a*

The Orthodox Islamic grounds of this ritual have been fully analyzed in many studies and an attempt to discuss them here would be repetitious. A brief statement about certain of these grounds may be necessary, however, for comprehension of the practices in this particular cultural context.

The observance of the ritual prayers is repeatedly emphasized as one of the essential duties of Islamic believers. It is the first among the four required acts of worship known as *'ebādāt*[2] and thus constitutes the second pillar of Islam. Prayers were instituted one year before the Hijra when the Prophet ascended to heaven after the night journey from Mecca to Jerusalem, as is described in the Qur'ān, Sūra 17.

"Glorified be He who carried His servant by night from the inviolable mosque to the far mosque, the neighborhood whereof we have blessed, that we might show him our signs! Lo! He, only He, is the Hearer, the one who sees."

Divine injunctions for prayers were made to the believers through the Prophet:

"Tell my servants who believe to establish prayers. And enjoin prayers upon thy people, and be constant therein."

The Prophet himself also strongly recommended the regular performance of prayers, as many of the traditions specifically state, and the final words he uttered during his last hours on this earth were, "Keep prayers! Keep prayers!" Tradition also holds that whoever deliberately omits his prayers because he does not accept them as a legal duty is considered an unbeliever, omission of prayers thus constituting the difference between belief and unbelief. A boy or a girl is therefore asked to pray at the age of seven and is punished for not doing so at ten: "Tell your children to pray when they are seven and punish them for omission (of prayers) at ten" (Ghali, p. 12).

Jūm'a (pronounced *gūm'a* in Kanuba) or Friday prayer is the weekly congregational prayer performed at noon. It was instituted in the first year of the Hijra by the Prophet in the mosque of Banu Salem Ibu Awf on the sixteenth of Rabi' I, the third Islamic month, and is considered obligatory for every believer who is neither sick nor on a journey. Friday prayer consists of two *rak'as* (see below), instead of the usual four performed on week days, and the recitation of portions of the Qur'ān aloud by the imām. A sermon must precede the prayer, and the congregation must not be less than four, including the imām (Ghali, p. 24).

The Qur'ān orders the suspension of work during Friday prayer:

"O ye who believe! When the call is heard for prayers on Friday, hasten to the remembrance of Allāh and leave your trading' (sūra LXII: 9–10).

Friday is thus the Muslims' holiday. It is said that the Prophet Muhammad favored this day more than any other day of the week and that God considers Friday the master and greatest of all other days. It is even more important than days of feast. A belief among Muslims is that Adam was created on a Friday and died on a Friday, that God fulfils believers' wishes during a certain hour on Fridays, and that the Day of Judgment will also be a Friday.

The Present Form of Ṣalāt al-Jūm'a in Kanuba

About half an hour before noon the *muādhen* (colloquial: muāzen) climbs the minaret of the village mosque and chants the following phrases aloud:

"I seek refuge with God (Allāh) from the devil, in the name of Allāh, the Merciful, the Compassionate. Hasten to the obedience of God, His generosity and munificence, and come early to pray."

This initial stage of the ritual is the *tanbīh ṣalāt al-jūm'a*, a reminder of prayer time for worshippers. The first two phrases are chanted only once, while the third is repeated several times, generally over a period of six minutes in all. The *muādhen* then waits on the minaret until noon to give the actual summons to the noon prayer, the *adhān al-dhuhr*.

The villagers start assembling at the *tanbīh* call, but before entering the auditorium of the mosque, they must perform the *wudū*, i.e., their ablutions. *Al-wuḍū* is a prerequisite for the performance of valid prayers and may be defined as purification from material or spiritual pollution. As observed in Kanuba, the worshipper washes his hands with water three times, then rinses his mouth three times, scooping the water into it with his right hand. Next, he throws a little water up his nostrils and blows it out, also three times, then washes his face three times and each hand up to the elbow three times, starting with the right hand. The head is then rubbed once with a little water, after which he washes the ears three times, then each foot three times up to the ankle. According to informants, the *wudū* is no longer valid if anything is discharged or emitted from any opening of the body thereafter.[3]

We have observed that very few people perform the *wuḍū* at the fountain provided for this purpose in the courtyard of the mosque. Informants explain that because of the lack of water in the mosque, they perform their ablutions — which only take one or two minutes — at home. Among those Kanuban worshippers who do use the fountain, several have been observed not to recite any religious phrases or words and some of them have been seen talking and laughing with each other while performing their ablutions. Since most people would rather make their *wuḍū* at home, however, the degree to which they comply with the requirements of this ritual is uncertain.

As they enter the mosque worshippers take off their shoes, leaving them near the doors where they can easily find them on the way out. After enter-, ing, they are customarily supposed to perform the *tahyet al-masjid*, a sunna[4] prayer of two *rak'as* (ritual genuflections accompanied by liturgical formulae) to greet the mosque.

Each *rak'a* consists of several physical movements with appropriate recitations. In Kanuba the worshipppers stands up facing the *qibla* niche oriented to Mecca and recites "*Allāh akbar*" with his hands open at each side of his face. Then he either folds his hands right over left against the front of the body or allows them to hang beside the thighs and recites the *Fātiḥa*,[5] followed by some verses, either one long *sūra* or two short ones, from the Qur'ān. Usually the *sūras* of *al-Nāss*[6] and *al-Ikhlās*,[7] precede each recitation with the bismillāh ("In the name of God, the Merciful, the Compassionate.") The worshipper then bows down from the hips with his hands placed on his knees, saying "*Allāh akbar!*" He repeats three times "*Subhan rabbī al-azīm*" ("Glory to my Lord, the perfect"). He then stands upright and says "*Sami'a Allāh leman hamidah*" ("God hears those who praise Him"), and "*Rabbina lak al-hamd*" ("Our Lord be praised"). The worshipper then repeats "God is greatest" while he kneels and bends forward until his nose and the palms of his hands rest on the ground. In this position he repeats three times "Glory to my Lord, the Highest". He then raises his head and sits back on his heels, with his back erect, hands resting upon his knees. Again saying "Allāh is greatest," he performs a second prostration in the same manner. From the recital of *al-Fātiḥa* to the second sitting position constitutes one *rak'a*. At the end of a second *rak'a*, the worshipper recites *al-tashahhud*, concluding by looking over his right shoulder and saying, "Peace be upon you and the mercy of God," then looking over his left shoulder and repeating the same phrase. This is called *al-salām* (the salutation) and is addressed to the two guardian angels who watch over each individual and keep record of everything he says and does until the Day of Judgment.

Worshippers entering the hall of the mosque before the arrival of the imām tend to belong to the older generation and to perform the *tahyet al-masjid*, after which they sit either alone or in small groups, while one or two may read silently from copies of the Qur'ān usually kept in the mosque. Those who go late to the mosque, however, tend to eliminate it; young informants commented that they were not obliged to pray it since it is not a *farḍ* (an act made incumbent by the Qur'ān; see note 4). The young men usually gather in the village club an hour before the *adhān* and either sit there or under a tree until a few minutes before the main prayer starts; others may come in after the imām has already started leading the prayer.

The imām's arrival at the mosque signals the beginning of the main part of the ritual. He usually wears his best *jalabeya* and turban, which worn together resemble the al-Azhar uniform. Most of the men also wear clean clothes and turbans and some of them are perfumed, in accord with a Qur'ānic verse commanding worshippers to dress well and to be clean when going to the mosque (sūra 7:32).

The imām moves in slow steady steps towards the *qibla*, in front of which he performs the sunna *taheyet al-masjid*, then turns towards the *minbar* (pulpit) and climbs to a seat facing the audience. At this moment, someone informs the *muādhen* to call for the noon prayer.

The *adhān al-dhuhr* or call to noon-prayer consists of the following statements and phrases which are recited, with a short interval after each, in two or three minutes:

> "Allāh is greatest! Allāh is greatest! Allāh is greatest! Allāh is greatest!
> I testify that there is no God but Allāh;
> I testify that there is no God but Allāh;
> I testify that Muhammad is Allāh's apostle;
> Come to the prayer! Come to the prayer!
> Come to salvation! Come to salvation!
> Allāh is greatest. Allāh is greatest;
> There is no God but Allāh."

Once the *adhān al-dhuhr* is finished, the *maudhen* leaves the minaret and joins the worshippers, and the imām starts his sermon—*al-khuṭbah*—usually read from an old copy of a book of several sermons previously compiled for various occasions. The *khuṭbahs* are written in classical Arabic, in a style that the average villager finds difficult and sometimes impossible to understand. Most preach the necessity of believing in and practicing the five pillars of Islam. The concepts of hell (*al-nār*), paradise (*al-gannah*), lawful acts (*al-hallāl*), sinful acts (*al-haram*), dependence on God and the necessity of following the Prophet are usually mentioned with special stress. At the time of this study the sermons also stressed the instructions of the Anṣār al-Sunna sect.

The sermon usually lasts from seven to ten minutes during which, as we observed, most of the worshippers show a complete lack of interest. Some men and most of the children even whispered and kept laughing and smiling at each other all the time. On several occasions, however, a Nubian political religious leader from Ballana visited the village on a Friday and delivered the sermon in the imām's place. When this respected sheikh discussed subjects like marital sexual relationships from the religious point of view, all those present listened with rapt attention.

Some informants complained that the local imām's sermons are irrelevant to their practical daily lives. One man said "*Al-khuṭbah* is useless — who would listen to it?" This attitude does not stem only from the fact that sermons are generally above the villagers' standard of Arabic; people also resent the topics selected by the imām and regard them as threats rather than as offering guidance or education. In the words of an informant: "The *khuṭbahs* always contain the injunction, 'Do not do this and that,' but they never tell people how to deal properly with their daily lives". The general feeling is that the sermons do not deal with problems resulting from change within the community of Kanuba. Among those problems, for example, is the difficult situation of some families in their new economic context. In one adaptive response to rising prices and lagging incomes, the modernist group in Kanuba decided to allow adult, relatively well-educated females to work outside the village and even succeeded in obtaining jobs for two older unmarried women. Another similar effort by the same group was the encouragement of contraception, with a view to limiting the size of families. Both these efforts towards social innovation have been opposed on religious grounds by most villagers, who believe that female professional work and interference with reproduction go against the instructions of God concerning the weakness of women and His will to give life. An informant complained that the imām of Kanuba never even tried to discuss such issues and dealt instead with petty details: "He promises that those who go early to the mosque will be given a camel in their life after death, whereas those who arrive late will only receive an egg."

The imām always starts his *khuṭbah* with the traditional salutation, "*Al-salāmu 'alaykum wa rahmat Allāh*" ("Peace be upon you and the mercy of God"), after which he recites the *shahad*, which enunciates belief in the unity of God: "*Ash-had anna lā elāha illa Allāh wa anna Muhammad rasūl Allāh*" ("I testify that there is no God but God and that Muhammad is God's Apostle"). The Prophet is praised, the phrase "*Al-ṣalāt wa al-salām alayhi*" ("Prayers and peace be upon him") always accompanying his name throughout the sermon. The *khuṭbah* ends with the imām asking God to give his blessings to all Muslims everywhere, the living and the dead. Each worshipper then holds his hands, palms facing inward, before him, and repeats "āmīn," ("amen") before reciting the *Fātiḥa*. Each asks God's help for his private problems, and then draws his palms down his face.

Having finished his *khuṭbah*, the imām descends from the *minbār*. The *muādhen* then stands up and rapidly recites the "*adhān al-qeyām*," a call to the worshippers to stand and pray, which is very similar to the "*adhān al-dhuhr*":

> "Allāh is greatest! Allāh is greatest!
> I testify that there is no God but Allāh.
> I testify that Muhammad is Allāh's Apostle.
> Get to prayer!
> Get to salvation!
> The prayer is ready to begin, is ready to begin.
> Allāh is greatest.
> There is no God but Allāh."

Then begins the *salāt al-farḍ*, the obligatory formal congregational prayer. In contrast with the usual practice in cities, the imām of Kanuba himself supervises the way worshippers stand in lines, shoulder to shoulder and foot to foot, and he usually justifies his actions aloud by referring to the Prophet's saying, "Straighten your lines; God will then have mercy on you." The imām faces the *qibla* with the worshippers behind him, who follow his movements and keep time exactly with him in the various gestures and recitations of the prayers. Old men and guests usually stand in the front line, with younger men and children behind them.

The *salāt al-farḍ* consists of two *rak'as*, which require about five minutes. Some people leave the hall of the mosque immediately after this prayer, but the majority stay on to perform the *khatm al-ṣalāt*, the closing stage of the Friday ritual, which was formerly conducted by the leader of the Popular group in the village. The imām and his conservative Anṣār al-Sunna reformers consider the *khatm al-ṣalāt* an innovation, however, and they therefore either leave the mosque at this point or keep silent.

Throughout the *khatm al-ṣalāt* the worshippers sit in circles around the floor of the mosque. During some parts of the ritual they listen to the leader in silence; at other times they repeat this recitation. The leader starts with the following phrases:

> "I beg forgiveness of God, the Great:
> God, there is no God but Him, the Living, the Self-subsistent."

He then recites the *Ayat al-Kursī* (The Throne Verse),[10] after which he adds:

> "O High! O Great! O Perfection! God,
> Eternal Glory to You,
> God the most merciful, have mercy on us;
> O God! Amen."

The worshippers then recite the following phrases in a low voice, repeating thirty-three times, counting on a rosary or on their knuckles:

> "Glory to God.
> Praise to God.
> God is greatest."

While the worshippers listen in silence the leader chants:

> "God is greatest; abundant praise to God; Glory to God the great, the First and the Last, there is no God but Allāh, Who has no partner; to Him does sovereignty belong and to Him must praise be given; God gives birth and causes death; there is no God but Allāh; Muhammad is really and truly God's Apostle; I seek refuge with God from the Devil. In the name of God, the Merciful, the Compassionate; God has said that he responds to those who appeal to Him."

All worshippers then raise their hands, palms upwards, and invoke God in silence for about a minute and the leader repeats the following:

> "O God answer our prayers, heal our sick and have mercy on us at our death; fulfill our lives, and bless the soul of our Master Muhammad, prayers and peace be upon him."

Everyone then recites al-Fatiḥa, and the leader ends the prayer, saying:

> "O God, Glory to you. May dignity and peace be upon your messengers. We praise God, the Lord of Lords, may He accept our prayer."

All worshippers then stand up, shake hands with one another, and leave the hall to sit and chat for a while in the maḍyafa of the mosque.

The men of Kanuba consider ṣalāt al-jūm'a to be their major collective religious rite and its performance obligatory. Throughout this study, the Friday ritual was performed regularly every week in the mosque, and the imām himself stressed its importance by saying, "No matter what happens, the ritual must be respected, whether it is led by me or by anyone else." The neglect of daily prayers is generally disapproved of in Kanuba, but it is not nearly so serious an offense as neglect of the ṣalāt al-jūm'a, and villagers have often been heard saying, in their Nubian dialect, "Omel salag salimini wala gomegeon salemini kefere," which means "He who never prays on a Friday is not a believer." Whoever misses this service usually gives a reason to justify his absence, such as having been ill or away from the village. Irregular attendance is matter for gossip and censure and in fact, one of the main reasons for regular attendance is the fear of public opinion. An informant once told the writer, expressing a common attitude: "Like most of the people here I go to pray so as to avoid criticism."

Most of our informants agreed that the Friday noon prayer is not only an important religious rite, but also an important social occasion, which often serves political and economic purposes. There is a weekly opportunity after the service for old and young males to hold a village-wide gathering in the *maḍyafa*, where they sit together for as long as half an hour or more. This meeting is considered very important, especially by the "week-end" group, who find it a good chance to meet each other and to keep in touch with those who live in the village permanently. Five young men who were interviewed actually said that their regular appearance at Friday prayer was not due to their sense of a religious obligation, but to their desire to meet and talk with the "weekend" group, and that occasionally it happened that they met before the prayer had started and did not enter the mosque at all, but sat either in the club or the *maḍyafa* and talked.

Apart from gossip, this social gathering usually leads to a serious discussion of village problems and politics. During our field work some of the main problems discussed in these meetings were related to the reclamation and irrigation of desert land owned by the people, the registration of women to vote, and a plan to provide the village with a railway station. The political leaders of the village thus get a chance to consider different points of view and to promote their own ideas concerning specific problems. Meetings also offer a good chance to collect dues or signatures for petitions to government officials. General announcements of importance to the whole village are often made then.

The Friday reunion is also an occasion to carry out small business transactions or customary social obligations. People congratulate each other over births and weddings and give their condolences to the relatives of the dead. Some of them even take this chance to offer syrup, food, or candy if they have just had a marriage in the family, a success in examinations, or a recovery from an illness. After about half an hour or an hour's time, the crowd generally breaks up into groups of friends, who sometimes move over to one of their houses for lunch.

The Traditional Form of Ṣalāt al-Jūm'a in Diwan Nubia

The traditional ritual of *ṣalāt al-jūm'a* in old Nubia started an hour before noon as the *muādhen* began the *tanbîh wa ṭabrik*, which consists of the *tanbîh* formula already described with an addition of a set of phrases praising the Prophet:

> "Prayer and peace be upon you, the Apostle of God.
> Prayer and peace upon you, the beloved by God.
> Prayers and peace upon you, the most honorable of
> God's creatures, upon you and all your companions."

This part of the ritual took about ten minutes. The *tanbîh* in its present form has replaced this longer form because of the Orthodox group's rejection of praise for anyone but God.

Before entering the halls of the pre-resettlement Diwan mosques the worshippers were said to have performed *al-wuḍū* in the same manner as at the present time, but informants claim that people were then more serious while performing it than they are now. In Old Nubia, there was never any doubt about ritual washing since it was always done publicly. It was usually accompanied by the utterance of some phrases such as "God forgive me," and "I testify that there is no God but Allāh."

After this introductory part of the ritual, *al-tilāwa*, which is a recital of specific parts of the Qur'ān, was begun. The sūra of *al-Ḳaht* (The Cave) was first recited by the *moqrī*.[11] Recitation of this sūra, in particular, was recommended by the Prophet, who said that whoever recites it would be forgiven by God on the Day of Judgement. During recent years, should the *moqrī* have been absent for one reasón or another, a radio was tuned to a Qur'ānic broadcast from Cairo. In Old Diwan, it was said, almost all the worshippers went as early as possible to the mosque to listen to *al-tilāwa*, which took about half an hour.

Informants unanimously report that the percentage of population who went regularly to worship was very high in old Diwan. Men delayed their business to a later time of the day or postponed it to another day altogether so as not to miss the Friday prayer. This was also true of the early, mid-1930s days in Kanuba. Anyone who was away made every effort to be back in the village before noon. Up to the late 1930's and early 1940's women also attended the Friday ritual in the mosque. They formed lines behind the men, from whom they were separated by a curtain. Non-Nubians from the surrounding Daraw area were also welcome to pray with the Nubians of Kanuba and some of them did so at times.

In old Nubia, after the recitation of the Qur'ān, the *muādhen* chanted the *adhāñ al-dhuhr*, using a formula identical to that presently used in Kanuba. Informants claim that since almost all the worshippers prayed the sunna *tahyet al-masjid* either at this point or during *al-tilāwa*, a second *adhān* was chanted after a short interval, that is, the *adhān al-khuṭbah*, a repetition of the *adhān al-dhuhr*, to give people more time.

This *adhān* was followed by the sermon, *al-khuṭbah*, given by the official Imam. In the first decade of Kanuba's existence the popular religious leader of the village generally preached instead of the appointed imām. Informants reported that this Ṣūfī sheikh's sermons were very long, that is, equal in length to those given in Old Diwan, which usually lasted fifteen to twenty minutes. Almost all adult men, younger men, and children were present in the mosque before the *khuṭbah* and according to old informants, no one wished to miss it. Without being essentially different from the present sermon, the *khuṭbah* usually centered around daily problems and attempted to relate them to Islamic teachings. Consequently, people considered *al-khuṭbah* an enjoyable way to learn more about their religion.

In old Diwan the *adhān al-qeyām*, which followed *al-khuṭbah* and preceded the *ṣalāt al-farḍ*, was similar to the *adhān al-khuṭbah*, except for the statement, "The prayer has been set up," which was repeated twice after "Come to salvation."

The traditional form of the *ṣalāt al-farḍ* was exactly the same in the number of *rak'as* in the way each *rak'a* was prayed, and in the time it took. Informants say that in the *khatm al-ṣalāt* following the *ṣalāt al-farḍ*, a verse from the Qur'ān was recited, followed by praise of God and some phrases asking God's blessing of the Prophet Muhammad, a form that is still respected at the present time.

The *khatm al-ṣalāt* covered seven to ten minutes; almost all the worshippers performed it and it was followed by a *dhikr*, which was held in the mosque. The *dhikr* was an essential part of the Nubian Friday prayer and, like the *tilāwa*, was favored by the people (see chapter 3 for the description of a *dhikr*). A majority of the men, youths and even children were keen either to take part in it or at least to watch it. Between 1934 and 1944 almost all the Kenuz men of Kanuba shared in the *dhikr* with the Fadija group from Diwan, which points to a much stronger social integration in the village at that time than at the time of our study in 1963–64. The main feature that distinguished the *dhikr* ritual of the *ṣalāt al-jūm'a* from an independent *dhikr* was the initial recitation from the *Burdah* of al-Būṣīrī.[12] The leader chanted sections from this Ṣūfistic poem of praise and the crowd repeated his words, after which they stood up either in a circle or facing each other in two lines. The leader of the *dhikr* would then chant certain formulas, such as *Allāh hayy* (God lives), which the participants repeated in the same tone, rhythmically swaying their bodies. From time to time the chanted formula was changed, as was the tone of voice. The *dhikr* lasted about half an hour, incense was burned and sometimes cinnamon tea was offered afterwards. Worshippers usually then went home immediately.

In old Diwan and in early Kanuba the performance of the Friday noon ritual was extremely regular. The absence of any individual was severely censured by the group and fathers were questioned and publicly blamed about the absence of their children if they went irregularly. The regular practice of Friday prayer was socially favored because public demonstration of faith was a prerequisite to membership status in the community; irregular attendance provoked blame, which was directed not only at the individual, but at his family and his tribe as well. Consistent attendance was a sign of piety, a quality very highly valued by the people of Nubia and, in fact, the main qualification for leading roles and positions in the village of Diwan and in Kanuba. Each family strove to have the most pious members of the village and to gain power and leadership in consequence.

A Comparison Between Friday Prayer in Old Diwan and in Kanuba, with an Analysis of the Changes

Each performance of the *ṣalāt al-jūm'a* is, in practice, a unified whole. For the purpose of analysis and comparison, however, it can be divided into parts.

ṢALAT AL-JUM'A

Old Diwan: the Traditional Form	Kanuba: the Present Form
1. *ṭanbîh wa tebrîk*	1. *ṭanbīh*
2. *al-wuḍū*	2. *al-wuḍū*
3. *al-tilawa*	3. *taheyet al-masjid*
4. *taheyet al-masjid*	4. *adhān al-dhuhr*
5. *adhān al-dhuhr*	5. *al-khuṭbah*
6. *adhān al-khuṭbah*	6. *adhān al-qiyam*
7. *adhān al-qiyam*	7. *ṣalāt al-farḍ*
8. *al-khuṭbah*	8. *khatm al-ṣalāt*
9. *ṣalāt al-farḍ*	
10. *khatm al-ṣalāt*	
11. *al-dhikr*	

A comparison of the two forms of the ritual will clearly indicate the major structural changes that have taken place. It is quite obvious that the present form is shorter; the ritual now consists of eight parts instead of eleven. Three phases, *al-tilāwa*, *adhan al-khuṭbah* and *al-dhikr*, are no longer performed. Two of these, however, *al-tilāwa* and *adhān al-khuṭbah*, are still preserved in the *ṣalāt al-jūm'a* as performed in the nearby mosque of the Kenuz Nubians in the town of Daraw and in many mosques in Cairo.

In addition to the elimination of ritual components, other parts of the Kanuba Friday prayer have been altered and — especially in the case of *al-khuṭbah* and *khatm al-ṣalāt* — shortened. Some weeks after the death of a popular leader who championed the old customs, the present reformist imām attempted to stop the performance of the *khatm al-ṣalāt*, but the group upholding popular Islam and traditional practice opposed him. The whole ritual, which now ends in less than one hour, traditionally lasted two hours. Thus, the elimination of some parts and the shortening of others has led to simplification.

During his long sojourn in Cairo as a youth, the official imām joined the Ansār al-Sunna and was a practicing member for several years. When he returned to Kanuba in 1934 he began advocating the sect's teachings and gradually obtained some support. At the time of our study he was continuing to promote the ideas and practices of the sect and consequent divergences of opinion over doctrine and practice had divided the villagers into two opposing groups, which still exist. One group favors the maintenance of "traditional" Nubian practice, including the *dhikr*, and reveres famous local sheikhs, particularly the ones who had tombs built for them in old Nubia. The opposing Anṣār al-Sunna, on the other hand, are intent on stamping out practices which they regard as *bīda'* (novelties, heretical innovations that have seeped into the true teaching). These reformers consider all Ṣūfism heretical because it centers around various leaders and holy men, instead of focussing entirely on God. They specifically oppose visits to cemeteries while their pamphlets and periodicals attack *mawlids*, cults of the saints, and most other practices of Popular Islam, all of which are considered *bīda'*.

Because of the similarity of their ideas to those of the puritannical Wahabbi movement of Arabia, the followers of the Anṣār al-Sunna doctrines are called Wahabbis by those villagers of Kanuba who do not belong to that sect. The Kanuban members of the Anṣār al-Sunna reject this appellation, however, claiming that they only follow the Qur'ān and the Sunna, without being members of any movement. Members of the traditional or Popular Islamic group, who find their puritannical approach to religion negativistic and unnecessary, refer to themselves as *al-Ṣūfiyya* or the Ṣūfīs, and they are sometimes called *al-mishwahābiyyîn* or the non-Wahabbis.

Informants attribute changes in the present Friday ritual in Kanuba to the *wahābiyyīn* of the village, who claim that in the Prophet's day only a minimal form of the ritual was performed and that worshippers read the Qur'ān individually and in silence. According to them, the reading of the Qur'ān aloud disturbs worshippers, who sit in silent awe of God. In the words of the imām, their leader, "It disturbs their meditation. In Mohammad's days, moreover, there was only one *adhān*. Therefore the *adhān al-khuṭbah* is a *bīda'*." The Orthodox reformative group has thus succeeded in bringing about changes in ritual that conform with the brevity and simplicity thought to have been characteristic of the early period of Islam.

Such changes in the ritual pattern have not been accepted, however, by the entire village. Strong opposition to the imām's alterations of the traditional Nubian form is directed by the *mishwahabiyyîn* and this divisive issue represents a conflict between the two groups that has been manifested not only in religious disagreements, but also in other aspects of Kanuban life. Members of each group tend to gather separately, for example, for entertainment and other social activities. The *wahābiyyīn* spend their spare time at a shop belonging to the imām, while the *mish-wahābiyyīn* sit on the *mastaba* outside the other shop in Kanuba, at the house of the leader of the popular Islamic group. When the *wahābiyyîn* go each afternoon to the mosque to pray and to listen to the imām's daily religious lesson, the *mish-wahābiyyîn* spread mats in front of their leader's shop, where they pray, chat, and listen to the radio. Members of each group buy their goods from their own leader's shop and each leader provides loans for needy members of his own group. In time of need, however, the two groups cooperate and they participate together in community-wide ceremonies such as those that take place during Ramadan or the Small Feast.

The response of the Kenuz minority in Kanuba to changes in the form of ritual has been particularly antagonistic. The Kenuz in general favor traditional Nubian Popular Islam and see the Fadija majority as using the introduction of unacceptable religious practices to exclude them from community affairs. Of the twenty adult Kenuz men in the village, only five or six go regularly on Fridays to the Kanuba mosque and only one or two linger after prayers to talk. Religious practices, however, are only one of the reasons for disagreement and conflict between the Kenuz and the other villagers. Still more basic are the monopolization of village power and influence by the Fadija from Diwan and their feeling of superiority to the Kenuz, most of whom attend the *ṣalāt al-jūm'a* in the mosque of the Kenuz in Daraw, three kilometers from Kanuba, where a large number of other Kenuz people are settled. Some Kenuz women pray at that distant mosque as well.

The following incident is an illustration of the villagers' response to the changes brought to the ritual by the imām's group: At about noon on Friday August 2, 1973, the writer joined some young men sitting under a tree, who had a transistor radio tuned to a program of light Arabic songs. Vehement arguments and vociferous discussions were going on concerning the celebration of the *mawlid al-nabī* (the Prophet's Birthday), which the *wahābiyyīn* in the village had criticized as a non-Islamic tradition that must be strictly condemned and abolished. The men were discussing the most effective way to hold this celebration, most of them being opposed to the attempts of the imām's Anṣār al-Sunna group to stop them from observing it as they always had at the appropriate time of the year. One of the men loudly and provocatively suggested taking the radio inside the mosque and listening to the Qur'ānic recitation broadcast from Cairo, so as to spite the *wahābiyyīn*. The whole group accepted his suggestion and belligerently went over to the mosque, where the radio was put near the *minbar* and tuned in at high volume to a reading of the Qur'ān. The men split into two antagonistic circles: The *mish-wahābiyyīn*, sitting around the radio, defiantly displayed their resistance to the imām by loudly intoning "*Allāh! Allāh!*" at various pauses in the recitation, while the *wahābiyyîn* in response turned their backs to the radio and stared intently at copies of the Qur'ān. But nothing unusual happened until the end of the recitation, when the radio was turned off and the people moved to the *maḍyafa* of the mosque. There a heated argument took place between the two groups and the imām threatened to destroy the radio if such an incident ever happened again. Bitter arguments, accusations and debates went for several days.

Comparison of the present and the traditional forms of the *ṣalāt al-jūm'a* shows the main differences in structure and content, differences related to the changing social process of the village of Kanuba. The two forms of the ritual are better compared by means of six indices, a mode of analysis that may help in further determining the degrees and types of change introduced in the Kanuban pattern of the Friday prayer.

1. REGULARITY OF THE PERFORMANCE OF THE RITUAL AND DEGREE OF PARTICIPATION

Data indicate that the *ṣalāt al-jūm'a* ritual was always held regularly in both old Diwan, where all eligible villagers used to attend, and in Kanuba. Observation during the whole period of our field work in Kanuba corroborated informants' reports of its continuing complete regularity. If Kanuba has never in its history missed a performance of this ritual, however, the degree of participation has declined, for although the number of men presently in the village exceeds their number before 1960, the proportion of males performing the ritual is smaller than before and the number of participants on the whole has actually decreased. For example, out of twenty intensively interviewed adult male informants, only fifteen perform the Friday ritual regularly, every week unless they are ill or away. Old men are more regular in performance than young ones, but children, whose attendance in the mosque and performance of the prayer were compulsory parts of their religious education, as well as a major responsibility for their parents, are now less controlled during performance and their attendance is quite irregular.

This change in the degree of chilren's participation parallels the movement from the old system of the Qur'anic *kuttab* schools, with their emphasis on religious education, to the system of compulsory education for children in government schools where the education is primarily secular. Though parents still depend to some extent upon the school for instructing the children in religious matters, a shift of emphasis has occurred and the time devoted to religious instruction is now a minor part of the curriculum.

During my visits to the Kanuba school, I observed the activities of a special group the pupils had formed to study Islamic doctrine and practice under the supervision of a teacher. Pupils were also observed performing the daily noon prayer in the courtyard of the school. A system of reward and punishment had been established and boys known as "religious police" were responsible for compelling the pupils to pray before they could escape to play. This control, however, which was not fully effective, was restricted to only one daily prayer in school and no particular enforcement of prayer was observed on the children at home. Thus, the children's religious indoctrination follows a much less intense, less meaningful, and less complete process than in old Nubia.

Women were also in the habit of attending Friday prayer in the mosque, but they no longer do so, partly due to the fact that they are now occupied with cleaning the house and cooking. They stay home for their husbands, many of whom return from their work in nearby towns only on Fridays, when special dishes are usually prepared for them. They sometimes invite two or three friends home for lunch and if a man is invited elsewhere, his wife sends a tray of her cooking with him. (One particular group of men frequently gather in the village club to eat together after the post-service ritual; other smaller groups get together less often to eat at each other's houses. These groups are formed on friendly and neighborly bases rather than on kinship.)

The frequency of the individual's performance of the ṣalāt al-jūm'a has been affected by the community's changing social and economic life. In Kanuba, due to social and economic change, Friday noon is no longer thought of as a holy period devoted to sacred activities alone, as it was in old Nubia, but has become rather like any other time of the week. The "week-end" Kanubans, especially, take advantage of the Friday holiday to undertake business, such as marketing, and to fulfill social obligations. Most informants do not hesitate to confess, in fact, that business transactions and social duties matter more to them than the performance of a ritual. The improvement of bus transportation in the region of Aswan meanwhile encourages villagers to use this free time going to markets at a distance of several kilometers and carrying out social obligations in the surrounding area.

While the absence of an individual from the mosque is still looked upon as reprehensible, irregular attendance is not nearly the matter of vital concern and the breach to family honor that it was in the past. It is now largely a matter of individual responsibility, though gossip continues to exert some pressure towards conformism. Piety, as manifested in regular performance of the religious rituals, is still theoretically required to reach high status and village leadership, but this criterion has been weakened in practice. In fact, teachers, technicians and government employees constitute about 90 percent of the leading figures in the community of Kanuba. Other criteria, such as education and professional status, are now more important than religion in determining prestige among the people of this community. These factors became clear in answers to questions about children's aspirations,[13] About 90 percent of the interviewed informants expressed the desire to see their children complete a higher education, particularly in technological and medical studies. Only one individual in the community wanted his son to have a religious education at al-Azhar, the Islamic university.

Since religiosity and the regular performance of rituals in Kanuba is associated with old age, de-emphasis on religion has resulted in weakening the relationship of age to status in determining leadership. As a consequence, neither piety nor old age are any longer viewed as primary conditions for the accession to power and authority in Kanuba.

2. ORGANIZATION AND MANAGEMENT OF THE FRIDAY RITUAL

The Kanuban weekly mosque ritual is congregational in both its traditional and present forms. Unlike daily prayers the Friday rite is neither private nor individual. It must be performed in the mosque with many members of the congregation and has a fixed time of performance, differing from daily prayers which, although they have prescribed times throughout the day, can be delayed for a limited time if necessary.

The ritual, which is led by the imām — a villager appointed by the government for the job — or, in the imām's absence, by another man renowned for his knowledge of religion, is characterized by high organization and specialization. Each part of the ritual follows a strictly organized pattern and a number of people cooperate in performing the ritual acts, each undertaking a different role according to his abilities and qualifications. For example, the custodian cleans the mosque and prepares it for the ceremony, the muādhen gives the call to prayer, the moqrī repeats incantations at various points, and the imām gives his sermon and leads the worshippers in performing the two rak'as prayers and so on.

The performance of the Friday ritual concerns the whole village. It is not like other rituals such as karāmas, which concern certain families or tribes at particular times, and its attendance is not limited to those who are invited. Furthermore, all eligible males are still expected to go to the mosque and perform.

3. LENGTH OF THE RITUAL

In Kanuba the weekly prayer has become shorter and less complex due to the elimination of some of its traditional components and to the simplification of others, so that it now takes less than one hour instead of the two hours it traditionally required. The time devoted by the average worshipper to religious activities is further limited because he goes late to the mosque and leaves it early; most people, particularly the young men, enter the hall of worship a few minutes before *al-khuṭbah* and leave immediately after *ṣalat al-farḍ*.

The shortening of the rite has been rationalized by the *wahābiyyīn*, who are a majority in the village, but it also generally satisfies the working men and the "week-end" group, who can thus devote more time to business and to their secular activities, such as sports, on Friday afternoon, or to recreational parties in the evening. The shortening of the ritual is in fact an adjustment related to social changes and new demands.

4. SECULAR ACTIVITIES ASSOCIATED WITH THE RITUAL

While the traditional Friday ritual centered on religious functions, it has now become an occasion for both sacred and secular activities. According to our observation, the time devoted to secular activities after prayer actually exceeds that devoted to the religious service. It must not be assumed that the *ṣalāt al-jūm'a* has been transformed into a party, however, though secular activities have become an essential part of the Friday mosque gathering. I venture to suggest that the post-service secular gathering has become an integral part of religious and social community life because of the role it plays in encouraging people to go to the mosque, as well as because of its other social functions.

5. EXTENT OF AWARENESS OF THE MEANING OF THE RITUAL

Twenty informants were intensively interviewed by the writer concerning religion. Their answers betrayed a general lack of knowledge and understanding of the meaning and substance of the ritual. For example, only five men — including the *muādhen* and the imam — knew the phrases of the *adhān* and were able to tell the difference between its traditional and its present forms. Only two men knew the content of the *khatm al-ṣalāt*, despite the fact that they heard it every week. Although informants said that the *ṣalāt al-jūm'a* is the main act of Islamic devotion, and that its performance in groups and in the mosque is a sunna, it has clearly become a convention for them and has lost much of its intended meaning. Only three informants could quote some Qur'ānic verses and *hadīth* (traditions of the Prophet) indicating the general significance of prayer, only one informant being able to remember, for example, the Qur'ānic verse saying "Prayer preserveth from loudness and iniquity" (sūra 9:45).

Nevertheless, all informants stressed the significance of the ritual as regards the solidarity of the community and the preservation of equality among the people. The only Qur'ānic injunction that most of them are familiar with is this tradition of the Prophet: "Keep prayers! Keep prayers! You will ever preserve your solidarity as long as you all pray! Keep prayers! Keep prayers!"

6. DEGREE OF COMMUNITY INTEGRATION

Description of the traditional rite has shown how members of different ethnic groups in the village, and some outsiders as well, used to perform the rite together. At the present time, however, as previously noted, very few Kenuz villagers go to pray with the Fadijas and they rarely attend the social reunion after the prayer. At the time of this study, no outsiders from nearby villages ever came to Kanuba, and none of the surrounding non-Nubians (i.e., ethnic groups of Sa'īdîs, and Qa'afra, 'Ababda, etc.) joined the Kanubans for Friday prayer despite the fact that the mosque is closer to them than any other. The only non-Kanubans were two or three men who worked at the construction of new houses in the village and who left the mosque immediately at the end of the prayer.

Although the ritual of ṣalāt al-jūm'a still plays a part in maintaining the Kanuban social structure, it is also a source of conflict between different groups in the community. Regular attendance, the organization and management of the ritual, and the intense communal spirit shown in post-service activities demonstrate the positive role of the ritual in the life of the people of Kanuba, but the modification of the ceremony has increased the social rift between Fadija and Kenuz Nubians, which had begun to widen after the departure of the Popular Islamic leader in 1960. During his stay in the village, this leader had succeeded in bringing Fadijas and Kenuz together in an integrated and cooperative communal life. Due to his championing of popular Islamic tradition, his dynamic personality, and his tolerance for group differences, he was respected and esteemed by the Kenuz people, even though he was a Fadija. The particular alterations of the Friday prayer ritual and the general changes brought to the whole religious system by the imām and his group, however, have exacerbated a natural split deriving from ethnic contrasts and have further divided the villagers into opposing factions. Because they continue to favor traditional Popular Islamic beliefs and practices and do not accept the reforms of the Anṣār al-Sunna, most Kenuz now go to pray outside the village in other mosques of the area, while those who occasionally go to the Kanuba mosque generally leave immediately after the ritual and almost never join the Friday community gatherings. Meanwhile the pattern of interpersonal relationships among Fadijas themselves has come to reflect this Kenuz-Fadija split in the community, so that Fadija *wahābiyyīn* tend to mix and deal with the imām, who owns a variety store, while Fadija *mishwahābiyyîn* lean on their leader, who owns the only other store in the village. Even the fact that the Fadija *mish-wahābiyyīn* have the same traditional religious convictions as the Kenuz has not led to an alliance between the two, however, suggesting that linguistic and cultural differences override fundamental religious agreement.

Summary

Within the past fifteen to twenty years the traditional form of the *ṣalāt al-jum'a* ritual in Kanuba has undergone considerable change. The tendency of this change has been towards both Islamization and secularization of the ritual. Initiated by the religious reform of the Wahabbi-like group in the village, changes in ritual have proceeded hand in hand with a general attitudinal secularization. But if the present form of the ritual as performed in Kanuba is shorter and less complex than in old Nubia or in the earlier days of Kanuba itself, it is of particular theoretical interest that such ritual streamlining is not simply a product of secularizing influences, but is even more closely related to forces of religious conservatism, for in this case, the usually antithetical forces of the sacred and the secular have reinforced one another.

Though the degree of participation of the eligible people of the community in Friday prayer is not as high as in the past, it is still regular, and it remains an important concern of the whole community. Secularization, as manifested in the mundane services and activities accompanying the ritual, is one of the reasons for its conserved importance. The traditional service was wholly sacred, but the people of Kanuba now tend to regard both the sacred and secular purposes and activities as equally integral parts of a whole and in spite of their statements concerning the religious importance of the Friday prayer, their motivations to attend are now more heavily influenced by secular interests than by religious ones. Thus, although there are socially destructive elements suggested in the rivalry of the *wahābiyyīn* and the *mish-wahābiyyīn*, and in the disaffiliation of the Kenuz, the ritual is still an integral part of the social structure of the community, which it helps to a certain degree to maintain.

Changes in the *ṣalāt al-jūm'a* are parallel with and related to the economic and social changes that have taken place and are still evolving in Kanuba. This chapter has shown, for example, how alterations in the occupational system of the community have affected the regularity of the working men's performance of rituals and have introduced the secular post-service gathering instead of the traditional *dhikr*. This is an indication, once more, that many of the changes which have produced the present form of the *ṣalāt al-jūm'a* are attributable not only to the reformative religious movement led by the imām, but also to the fact that these changes fit the social and economic conditions of the community of Kanuba.

Notes

1. This chapter is a revised portion of my M.A. thesis entitled "Change in Rituals in Kanuba: *Ṣalāt al-jūm'a* and *al-Dhikr*," which was submitted to the Department of Sociology and Anthropology, at the American University in Cairo, September 1966.

2. The Five Pillars of Islam consist of *al-tashahhud* (bearing witness) and *al-'ebādāt* (services, observances). *Al-tashahhud*, without which one cannot become a Muslim or be accepted as Muslim by God, consists of the belief in and the utterance of this statement: "I testify that there is no God but God and that Muhammad is God's apostle." *Al-'ebādāt* are prayer, fasting, almsgiving, and pilgrimage.

3. The relevant Qur'ānic verse says "O ye believers! As ye rise up for prayers, wash your faces and your hands (up to the elbows), and lightly rub your heads and (wash) your feet up to the ankles." (sūra 5: 6).

4. *Sunna* is a term used by Muslim in referring to customary practices based upon utterances and deeds attributed to the Prophet by tradition. The word *farḍ*, on the other hand, applies to practices sanctioned directly by the Qur'ān and therefore not merely customary, but incumbent upon believers.

5. *Al-Fātiha* is the opening sūra of the Qur'ān and it runs as follows: "Praise be to Allah, Lord of the Worlds, the Beneficent, the Merciful, Master of the Day of Judgement. Thee (alone) we worship and Thee (alone) we ask for help. Show us the straight path, the path of those whom Thou hast favored, not (the path of) those who earn Thine anger nor of those who go astray."

6. The sūra of *al-Nass* (Mankind, Qur'ān XXIV) reads as follows: "Say, 'I seek refuge in the Lord of mankind, the King of mankind, the God of mankind, from the evil of the sneaking whisperer, who whispereth in the hearts of mankind, of the jinn and of mankind.'"

7. The sūra of *al-Ikhlās* (Sincerity, Qur'ān CXXII) reads as follows: "Say: 'He is Allāh, the One! Allāh, the eternally Besought of all! He begetteth not nor was begotten; and there is none comparable unto Him.'" The translation of these surās and other Qur'ānic verses is taken from Mohammad Pickthall, *The Meaning of the Glorious Koran* (Mentor Books, 1963).

8. The *tashahhud* (bearing witness) formula includes the following phrases: "Peace be on thee, O Prophet, and the mercy of Allāh and His blessings. Peace be on us and the righteous servants of Allāh. I bear witness that there is no God except Allāh. And I bear witness that Muhammad is His servant and messenger; O Allāh, succor Muhammad and the followers of Muhammad, as Thou didst

succour Ibrahim and the followers of Ibrahim. And bless Muhammad and the followers of Ibrahim in the worlds. Surely Thou art the Praised, the Glorious." (See M. Ghali, "Prayer," *Essentials of Islam Series*, 4, Cairo, 1964, pp. 22–23.)

9. The imām is supposed to enter after all are congregated.

10. The *Ayat al-Kursi* (The Throne Verse, Qur'ān II: 255), asserts the following: "Allah! There is no God save He, the Alive, the Eternal. Neither slumber nor sleep overtaketh Him. Unto Him belongeth whatsoever is in the heavens and whatsoever is in the earth. Who is he that intercedeth with Him save by His leave? He knoweth that which is in front of them and that which is behind them, while they encompass nothing of His knowledge save what He will. His throne includeth the heavens and the earth, and He is never weary of preserving them. He is the Sublime, the Tremendous."

11. The *moqrī* is a religious official whose role is to recite the Qur'ān in the mosque. In Cairo, he usually gets paid.

12. *Al-Burdah* (*The Mantle*) is the familiar title of *Burdat al-Madīh al-Mubarak*, a panegyric by Sheikh Muhammad al-Būṣīrī (1211–1294 A.D.). Written more or less in the form of a *qaṣīda* (ode), *al-burdah* is divided into ten parts of between ten and thirty two verses each, as follows: *al-gharām wal-hayām* (Love and Fondness), *madīh al-nabī* (Praise of the Prophet), *mawlid al-nabī* (The Prophet's Birth), *al-mo'gezāt* (Miracles), *Sharaf al-qur'ān wa madihe* (The Nobility of the Qur'ān and its Praise), *al-barāh wal-mihrāg* (The Night Journey and Ascension), *jihād al-nabī* (The Prophet's Struggle), *al-ṭawaṣul* (The Entreaty), and *al-monagāh* (The Soliloquy). There is a complete English translation of a popular Cairene edition of al-Būsīrī's *Mantle* in Arthur Jeffery, ed., *A Reader on Islam: Passages from Standard Arabic Writings Illustrative of the Beliefs and Practices of Muslims* (The Hague; Mouton, 1962, pp. 605–620).

13. The questions were prepared by Kennedy and were administered by the writer to 50 percent of the adult men of Kanuba.

Chapter 3

Dhikr Rituals and Culture Change

JOHN G. KENNEDY AND HUSSEIN M. FAHIM

As pointed out in the first chapter, Nubian ceremonialism comprises three distinguishable categories: Orthodox Islam, Popular Islam, and Non-Islamic or "pagan" beliefs and practices. Fahim's presentation in chapter 2 has outlined the principal Orthodox ritual as practiced by some Nubians, and the present chapter and the one following detail the two major aspects of Popular Islam among this group, continuing discussion and description of Nubian cultural and religious change as exemplified in the village microcosm of Kanuba.

As in most parts of the Islamic culture area, an important feature of the religious life of Egypt and Sudan is the *dhikr* (or *zikr*), the most important ritual of the Ṣūfī brotherhoods. Despite the wide geographic extent and historical depth of Ṣūfism in this part of the world, it is rare to find in the literature any but the briefest accounts of the *dhikr*. In essence, the *dhikr* is a ritual means of attaining an ecstatic state of spiritual union with God by verbally or mentally chanting certain litanies in concert with repetitive body movements. This chapter describes two actual *dhikr* performances as observed among the Nubians of Egypt, one in Old Nubia and another in Kanuba. The comparison is intended to show how differences between these performances are indicative of social processes and cultural changes among Nubians.

One of the *dhikr* rituals described here was witnessed in Diwan, Old Nubia, in 1963, before the relocation. All informants agreed that this performance adhered closely to the traditional Nubian pattern. It thus represents as close an approximation as it is possible to reconstruct of one aspect of the relatively stable integration of Nubian ceremonialism that was characteristic of Nubia during the late nineteenth and early twentieth centuries. The second *dhikr* was observed in Kanuba and reflects important changes which have taken place in the culture of these Nubian villagers, who have now been resettled outside Old Nubia proper for thirty-odd years. It may well indicate the directions of change which will go on in the religious practices and beliefs of the Nubians who have recently been resettled at Kom Ombo.

Ṣūfism

Ṣūfism arose out of *zuhd*, the asceticism which flourished during the first century A.H. (seventh century A.D.). In all parts of the Islamic world of that period there were wandering ascetics who came to be known as Ṣūfīs, possibly because of their wearing *ṣūf* (wool). The foundation of the early Ṣūfī belief system was a severe asceticism based mainly on the fear of God (Gibb 1958, p. 102). The first organization of this movement appeared in the second century after Muhammad, when small groups of ascetics met to recite the Qur'ān and other religious poems aloud (Trimingham 1965, p. 212).

These recitations gradually took on a liturgical character centered around the classical Arabic term *dhikr* (*zikr*), "remembrance." In the Qur'ān this word refers to worshipping God, but among Ṣūfīs it came to mean a particular method of worship, justified in the Qur'ānic injunction: "Remember God with frequent recalling" (3:41). Constant repetition of the name of God enabled the Ṣūfī to attain the goal of spiritual ectasy or *wajd*. The ascetic emphasis in Ṣūfism had changed to one on mysticism by the third century after the Hijra, and the general basis of the movement had shifted from the fear of God to the mystical attitude of love and adoration of Him. To the Ṣūfīs, Allāh was the only real being, and the method of finding one's true being was by losing individual consciousness through abandoning the self in the divine Oneness (Trimingham 1965, p. 189).[1] Within mysticism religious leadership meanwhile shifted from the *'ulamā* (orthodox religious scholars) to the lower middle or artisan classes, a shift resulting in conflict between orthodox Islam and the Ṣūfī orders (Gibb 1958, p. 104).

During the fourth and fifth centuries A.H. (tenth and eleventh A.D.) Ṣūfism grew in strength, though still frowned upon by the *'ulamā*. It was during this time that the *dhikr*, from being simple congregational recitations of the Qur'ān and meditation over it, began to develop a more liturgical quality. Especially emphasized was the recitation of chants. The great popularity of this form of worship increased the hostility of the *'ulamā* towards the Ṣūfīs because they feared that the *dhikr* might come to take the place of the mosque as the center of religious life (Gibb 1958, p. 105).

In many ways Ṣūfism was a reaction against the rigid scholasticism, intellectualism, and legalism which had grown to dominate Orthodox Islam in the centuries after Muhammad's death. Since it represents a kind of rebellion against traditional practice it has been throughout its history repeatedly attacked by orthodox leaders. From the second century after Muhammad onwards, nevertheless, the Ṣūfistic attitude of personalistic involvement became increasingly the dominant alternate religious force in the Middle East. Gibb even attributes the remarkable spread of Islam to the fact that through Ṣūfism the religion was able to introduce a method of worship which was more attractive to the common people than the somber ritualism of Orthodoxy (Ibid. 53, p. 2).[2]

Thus by the thirteenth century A.D., the movement had begun to develop large organized orders that spread over the whole Islamic world. These orders are not sects, since they are all recognized as equally legitimate; members of different orders pray in the same mosque and attend the religious rituals and ceremonies of the other orders. Their differences are in their degree of organization and in their *dhikr* rituals.

The Ṣūfistic movement permitted charismatic leaders to develop individual "ways" or *turuq*, and these leaders attracted groups of followers who often gathered around them in *zāwiyas* or schools *zāwiyas* where they could practice together their ritual exercises and contemplations. Leadership of Ṣūfī orders was based upon personal qualities: "Pious men of outstanding personality, reputedly blessed with a gift of miraculous powers — found disciples crowding to them" (Ibid. p. 151). The Ṣūfistic "seeker" tried to pursue a series of steps on a path leading to purity or perfection, the ultimate state of which was known as *wajd* or *bāqa*. Theoretically, he might pass through stages of *murīdi* (discipleship), *tonquat* (potentiality), *'arīf* (knowledge), *fanā* ("passing away"), or *tawhīd* (union, the summit reached by perfect concentration and meditation), and *bāqa* (saintship). When the stage of *bāqa* was reached the attainer theoretically returned to the world as a teacher and guide.

Unlike the generally egalitarian structure of Muslim communities, the Ṣūfī orders were hierarchical, with levels based on degrees of "holiness," believed to be acquired from God through the Prophet Muhammad. Membership was generally of two kinds: A higher class of initiates and the disciples (sheikhs, *khalīfa* or *naqīb*)[3] engaged in religious duties and a large body of lay-members (the *murridīn*, or aspirants). The two groups met on stated occasions for the *dhikr*, but otherwise carried on secular occupations in village or town. In addition to these initiates and disciples, another type of Ṣūfī was the dervish or *darawīsh* who, though belonging to a particular *tarīqa*, devoted his life entirely to religion, wandering from place to place, reciting the Qur'ān, chanting religious hymns, and begging for his livelihood (Barclay 1964, p. 176).

The most important ritual activities of the Ṣūfī orders have been their individual forms of the *dhikr* ritual, the major distinction being between silent contemplative styles and more violent physical forms. As Trimingham notes: "Each order has its particular method of recitation, and devotional manuals, which are so common, give their various methods of practicing the *dhikr*. The vocal method has always been regarded by true Ṣūfīs as vulgar and more fitted for 'laymen'" (1966, p. 212). It appears that "laymen" have always outnumbered the "true" Ṣūfīs, however, so that combined body movement and recitation of repetitive phrases have characterized the *dhikrs* of most orders. This certainly is the case with the Nubian forms of the ritual.

In the perdiod from the Middle Ages through the nineteenth century various *ṭuruq* became powerful political forces throughout the Muslim world. In Egypt these Ṣūfī orders were long in the religious ascendancy and played a major role in the political and social life of the country (Heyworth-Dunne 1938 p. 10). This situation persisted in nineteenth-century Egypt and Lane's account of Cairo in the 1830s frequently mentions activities of the Ṣūfī orders. He also gives some partial descriptions of their *dhikr* rituals, and it is evident from his account that, along with the large processions of the orders, *dhikrs* were integral to all the large festivals of the time (Lane 1963, pp. 450–61). Even today, despite a considerable decline in membership and power, the Ṣūfī religious fraternities have large memberships in Egypt. They are all now legally under one head, who is elected by the leaders of all the *ṭuruq*, but who must be approved by the government.

The branch of Ṣūfīsm that became dominant among Nubians in the nineteenth century and which still claims most of them is called the *tarīqa al-Mirghānnîyya*. Its founder, Muhammed Uthman al-Mirghanni (1763–1853), grew up in Mecca and was a pupil of the famous Ṣūfī Sheikh Sayyid Ahmad Ibn Idrīs, who sent him first as a missionary to the Eastern Sudan. In his travels through the country he established a reputation for the performance of miracles. In 1817 he made a journey to Egypt with the purpose of converting the Egyptians to his *tarīqa*. He had very little success in the cities and villages of that country, but "once he got among the Nubians his passage from Aswan to Dongola was a triumphal procession, and the Nubians, impressed by the splendor of his equipage, flocked to offer him allegiance" (Trimingham 1965, p. 232).

Although the Mirghanni Way became the dominant and almost exclusive one in Nubia, more recently several other "ways" have been accepted in some districts. One of these orders, known as the *Khalwatīyya*, was founded by Omar al-Khalwati around the year 1397 A.H., and apparently came to Nubia by way of the Sudan after it had expanded in East Africa in the early eighteenth century. One of the main variants of the *Khalwatīyya* is called the *Ṭarīqa al-Dayfîyya*, founded by Ismail Dayf. Many Nubians from Diwan espouse this *tarīqa* as well as that of the *Mirghānniyya*.

In addition to its performance in the regular *hadra*[4] twice a week, the *dhikr* ritual became integrated into almost all aspects of Nubian ceremonial life. It was a part of the weekly mosque prayer and of all ceremonies relating to birth, circumcision, excision, marriage, and death. *Dhikrs* were also performed at sheikh's *mawlids* (see chapter 4), as well as during the four days of the Small Feast (*'īd al-ṣaghīr*) and the Big Feast (*'id al-kibīr*), while the twenty-seventh of the Islamic month of Ragab was a time of special *dhikr* ceremonies which all men over the age of puberty were expected to attend in addition to the *hadras* regularly held on Monday and Thursday evenings. It is evident that the *dhikr* was an extremely important component of traditional Nubian religious life.

The performers of the Nubian *dhikr* ritual were commonly called *dhakīra* and when they performed it together they constituted the *maglis al-dhikr*, the term *maglis* (gathering, concourse) referring both to the ritual actions (*dhikr*) and to the actors (*dhakīra*). The *maglis* usually took place inside the mosque but on occasion it would be held in any other place, as long as it was clean. Only men were permitted to participate formally, but male children about twelve were allowed to sit nearby to watch. Since all healthy adult men were expected to attend, absence was usually noted and absentees were later reprimanded. As for Muslim prayer, *dhikr* performers were expected to be in a state of complete purity which included not only bodily cleanliness achieved by ritual ablution but also serenity of the soul. Cleanliness was regarded as difficult to assure in women and children, who also deemed incapable of meditation, and they were therefore excluded from the *maglis*.

During the performance of the *dhikr* the atmosphere of awe and respect for God was enhanced by burning incense around the *maglis*. Informants say that the perfume of the burning incense is said to give an agreeable scent to the area that encourages the performers to continue when they tire. Sometimes a state of trance is attained, and passing the burning brazier under the nostrils is believed to be efficacious in aiding the enraptured one to return to consciousness.

A *Dhikr* Ritual in Diwan (Old Nubia)

The occasion prompting this particular *dhikr* was the Prophet's Birthday (*mawlid al-nabī*), but the timing of the performance was somewhat out of the ordinary: Having been ill at the regular time of the Prophet's *mawlid*, the twelfth day of the Islamic month of Rabī' I, a certain wealthy man of Diwan had not been able to celebrate it and had made a vow to perform this *mawlid* when he recovered.

On the afternoon before the *mawlid*, many women and girls from the village had arrived at the house to assist in baking bread and in preparing enough food for the large number of expected guests. On the following day, the day of the *mawlid* itself, the house buzzed with the chatter of the women of the neighborhood working until about five o'clock in the afternoon, when guests from more distant areas began to arrive. They came from a much larger area than the village itself, since invitations had been sent to all the hamlets (*naja's*) of Diwan and to important people and friends in the adjacent districts of Abu Handl and Derr. Each group of guests was met at the door by the host, who seated the men on large mats spread in the outer courtyard of the house. Women were sent into the inner courtyard, where they immediately sat down and began to help with the preparation of the ceremonial meal.

The mats in the larger outer courtyard were arranged in such a way that those seated upon them would be able to observe the *dhikr*, which was to be held in an open, porch-like part of the house. The men in the courtyard chatted, while in the area where the women were preparing food a few male cooks began to cook vegetables and meat in large pots over open fires. These men were members of former slave families, which had traditionally belonged to the household of the host and although they were no longer slaves, they continued to perform such traditional tasks for their former masters.[5] Two sheep had been slaughtered and the meat was boiled in chunks, while traditional Nubian *shaddi* bread (made from *durra*), onions, tomatoes, rice, and a green spinach-like vegetable called *ittir* were prepared in large quantities by the women.

The entire front courtyard was eventually filled with people, including the women, who had come in from the back region of the house; eighty-five men, forty-one women, and thirty children in all. As people settled into their seats and continued discussing the topics of the day, several of the former slaves passed among them, serving small cups of cinnamon tea. At about seven o'clock, several adolescent boys, assisted by four older men of slave origin, served *fatta* (the traditional Nubian ceremonial meal — bread with boiled soup poured over it and then covered by rice and meat chunks) on large trays covered with colorful Nubian baskets, accompanied by dishes of vegetables served with flat pieces of *shaddi* bread. People were not served individually; the trays were distributed on the mats so that groups of five or six men could dip with their bread into the bowls of *fatta* at once. As darkness fell over the white-turbaned crowd, several kerosene pressure lanterns were lit. The house was now joyously humming with conversation and the food was quickly consumed. Boys cleared away the empty trays while others simultaneously served more tiny cups of cinnamon tea.

As the dishes were carried out we became aware of several small clay pots of incense whose fragrant smoke now wafted over the semi-darkened courtyard. The sheikhs who were to perform the *dhikr* ceremony began rising from their seats in different parts of the crowd and moved into the lighted porch area, seating themselves in two long rows facing each other. Most of the twenty-five sheikhs forming the *maglis* were older men, the religious leaders of the community. In the center at one end sat the *naqīb*, whose role it was to lead the chanting and to maintain order. At the end of the two rows of sheikhs sat a group of about ten adolescent boys, who at the urging of their elders formed a small circle. Meanwhile the women were gathering at the rear of the crowd and some of the younger girls peered through the door of the adjacent inner courtyard, the mass of black dresses of the huddled women contrasting with the light-colored expanse of the men's gowns.

The *naqīb* was a thin, ascetic-looking sheikh in a black overcloak, white turban, and thin-rimmed glasses. At his signal, an older man in the center of one of the lines of the *maglis* began chanting certain passages from the Qur'ān. This initial part of the ceremony was termed the *tilāwa* (recitation) by our informants, and the man who chanted it was called the *moqrī*.

After a moment or two, another chanter (*munshid*) took up the chant (*inshād*), and was followed by another, and another. When the fifth *munshid* had chanted, the entire *maglis* began singing in unison, repeating each phrase many times. This second segment of the ceremony was called the *istighfār* (supplication), in which such phrases were recited as: "God help us to forget our sins," "Help us to overcome the evil ones," and "God is true." Each phrase was intoned about one hundred times by the *maglis*. A gesture from the *naqīb* signalled the conclusion of this portion of the ceremony and, in a loud voice, he recited *al-Fātiḥa*, the opening verse of the Qur'ān, after which the group repeated what is known as *estiftāh al-dhikr* (the opening of the *dhikr*). This consists of a theme of one hundred words requesting God to bless all other prophets, the angels, and other favorites of the Prophet.

The performers were quiet for a moment, then the *naqīb* started the *tahlīl*, repeating *la-illāha-illa-Allāh* ("There is no god but God") a hundred times, while the men began to sway rhythmically from side to side with the words, gradually increasing the tempo until the end of the section, approximately ten minutes later.

After this, the *naqīb* began in a chanting voice to read a long narration of the history of the earth before the birth of the Prophet Muhammad from the Mirghanni text, *Mawlid al-Nabī*,[6] while two women rose from the audience and advanced near the performers, beating a rhythm on their drums (*ṭars*).[7] The *munshids* took turns reading each passage, with the group chanting a short, answering refrain as they swayed more vehemently back and forth to the rhythm of the drums. The speed of the performers gradually increased. At points where the name of the Prophet was mentioned the audience chanted in unison, *"Allāh humma salli wa sallem 'alēh"* ("prayers and peace on him"), and the women standing at the rear of the crowd emitted a chorus of joyful ululations (*zagharīt*). Many people clapped with the rhythm of the drums and the swelling and diminishing of male voices, intermittently penetrated by the pulsating joy-cries of the women, kept the crowd enthralled. Two more older women, overcome with emotion, pressed through the crowd until they reached the chanting sheikhs, where they stood quivering ecstatically; at first, several men from the audience tried gently to restrain them, but since they were obviously in trance, no real attempt was made to exert authority over them. It was recognized that they were possessed by spirits. After about fifteen minutes, the chanting came to a conclusion, the drumming and swaying stopped, and another old man of the *dhikr* circle again read the opening verse of the Qur'ān.

This quiet interlude was soon followed by a second reading from the Mirghanni book, with the drumming and chanting as before.[8] This time, the crescendo rose to an even more fervent pitch, and the audience participated with great enthusiasm. One of the refrains repeated by the *maglis* was: "Oh God! Prayers and peace be upon the Prophet." Occasionally, two of the *maglis* sheikhs assumed the role of *munshids*, and in a duet sang the leading part of the *qasīda*.

Incense in a clay container was passed periodically among the chanters by a young boy, so that inhalation of fragrant smoke could bring each performer in closer contact with the divine, while at the same time chasing away dangerous jinns. Several times as a finale of movement was reached and one of the sheikhs dropped out of the performance in a trance-like state, people in the audience could be heard whispering *"magzūb."* At various points a *munshid* called out *"Maddād! Maddād! ya rasūl-Allāh,"*[9] expressing the sentiment that the ritual was going well. There was some flexibility in the performance and at intervals some of the older singers departed from the Mirghanni text and chanted parts of the Qur'ān they had memorized. Finally, the book was once more passed to one of the *munshids* so that he could begin reading the chant describing and glorifying the Prophet's birth.

At this point the members of the *maglis* rose to their feet and began repeating verses in unison, bending their bodies to right and left as the drumming increased in intensity. Soon many people in the crowd began swaying rapidly, right and left, to the rhythm of the movements of the *maglis*, while a group of women in the rear moved ecstatically to the beat of the *tars*. Occasionally, a man brought around a pitcher of water and with a dipper served people in the audience who wished to refresh themselves. The drumming and swaying went on for about fifteen minutes, with growing intensity. Then it stopped, to be followed by a momentary lull. The drums did not again take up their rhythm. This time the Prophet was praised with such phrases as "He is beauty," "He is light," repeated at intervals, while several men took turns reading verses from the Qur'ān.

At this point, one of the older sheikhs stopped the antiphonal praising by reading a *Fātiḥa* for the dead. He asked God's forgiveness for all the faults of which the people present might be guilty. This aspect of the ceremony was identical to that which traditionally terminated the Friday prayer in Nubia (see chapter 2). As each phrase was read, the audience intoned *"amīn,"* and finally, in a loud voice, one of the sheikhs repeated *"la illāha illa Allāh Muhammad rasūl Allāh."* (There is no Gòd but Allāh. Muhammad is the apostle of Allāh.) Again, a *Fātiḥa* was silently recited by all the performers, and the *dhikr* was officially finished. This terminating part of the Nubian *dhikr* ceremony is called *khatm al-dhikr*.

The boys and servants once more passed among the crowd with cinnamon tea and incense. Informants say that cinnamon tea gives strength and energy in case the performers should decide to make another *dhikr* immediately. In the present instance it was after midnight, and the people began quickly filing out of the house and moving towards their homes.

Other Forms of Dhikr Rituals in Diwan

On other kinds of occasions the Nubian *dhikr* ritual frequently was abbreviated from the type described. Those held at weekly *hadras* differed in the fact that, though most adult males attended, they did not involve the whole community. *Hadras* usually took place in the mosque following the evening prayer, though sometimes they were held in the courtyard of the *ṭarīqa* leader's house. Thus, the *hadra* had neither the excitement provided by the women with their joy cries, nor the social atmosphere resulting from the communal meal. The *manzuma* (verse recitation) part of the *dhikr* was often much abbreviated in the *hadras*, and readings might be selected from various poems other than the Mirghanni book. Those held regularly after the congregational Friday noon prayer service also were shortened versions in comparison with the one described and were not nearly as enthusiastic. In most ordinary *dhikr* ceremonies drums were not used.

Dhikrs accompanying life-cycle ceremonies, such as circumcisions or weddings, featured communal processions to saints' shrines as well as feasts like the one described. In the Diwan area the entire village made a long procession to and from a saint's shrine several kilometers distant, where a large feast was cooked and eaten, and the men performed a *dhikr* before making the long dancing procession back home. Circumcision and marriage rituals varied between fifteen and forty days in length, and *dhikrs* were often held every evening of the ceremonial period (see chapter 6). In addition, individual Nubians often went to a shrine in the vicinity and made a vow to a saint, promising that they would give him a *karama* in return for certain favors. *Karamas* frequently involved a *dhikr* following a communal feast, and these, too, were shorter versions of the one described. They usually omitted parts of the Mirghanni poem praising the Prophet or substituted verses from al-Būṣīrī's *Burdah* (see below and chapter 2).

The frequency and intensity of *dhikr* rituals in various districts of Nubia differed according to the degree of enthusiasm and leadership qualities of individual local religious leaders. In some villages two consecutive *dhikrs* were held on each Monday and Friday evening, while in other areas one such ritual held every week or two was viewed as sufficient.

Sūfism and *Dhikr* Rituals in Kanuba

Since the founding of Kanuba in 1933, Popular Islam has declined in the village, while at the same time Orthodox Islam has been strengthened almost in proportion. Complicating these developments is the fact that life has been progressively secularized, a situation reflecting the Nubians' experience as migrant laborers in the urban centers. One result of these changes has been the loss or repudiation of many traditional Nubian rituals and beliefs. Nevertheless, as will be shown in ensuing chapters, a good many non-Islamic customs were perpetuated among the women, who, remaining for the most part in the villages, did not have as much exposure as the men to either Orthodox Islam or to secularizing urban influences.

When Kanuba migrants from Diwan established their new community in 1934, they planned to maintain the traditional Nubian religious system, but many Popular Islamic features declined or were dropped during the early years. Since their own saints' tombs were covered with water or left in Old Nubia, rituals associated with saints declined and *dhikrs* became rare. During the late 1940s and 1950s, however, the community witnessed a revitalization of Popular Islamic features. In particular, there was a resurgence of *dhikr* rituals.

This interest in Popular Islam was especially stimulated by one dynamic village religious leader who was an adherent of the Ṣūfī order of Dayfiyya. He held high status among the people of Kanuba because of his al-Azhar education[10] and his government position as headmaster of the preparatory school in the nearby town of Daraw. Charismatic qualities additionally made him a popular and dominant figure in Kanuba life and politics. Thus, during the period of his residency, this leader, by community consensus, acted as the informal imām in the mosque services, even though another man had been appointed imām by the official religious hierarchy of the country. He was also the formal organizer and leader of Popular Islamic activities such as saints' *mawlids* and nightly *dhikrs*.

As described in the previous chapter, in this period of dominance by Popular Islam the village was simultaneously the scene of an opposing religious movement whose members were called the *Ansār al-Sunna al-Muhammadīyya*, This group attempted to purify Nubian religion of all beliefs or rituals which it believed were not Islamic in character or origin. We have already alluded to the basic differences between these two groups in matters of religious doctrine and practice and to the ways they have become demarcated along the lines of factional conflict in secular matters as well. At one time the doctrinal conflict became so bitter that local dispute-settling mechanisms failed and officials high up in the Egyptian Islamic hierarchy sent a religious mediator to settle the argument.[11] After hearing the case, this mediator ruled in favor of the traditional Popular Islamic group (*al-Ṣūfiyya*), and thus gave official approval to their continuance of Sūfistic practices. However, the *Ansār al-Sunna* refused to accept the verdict, and one informant reported that "Every day there were more quarrels and disputes, not only among men, but also among the women. The village was about to split apart in disorder and confusion."

In the years from 1940 to 1961, the dynamic leader who had headed the opposition to the *Anṣār al-Sunna*, the charismatic Ṣūfī sheikh mentioned above, and in chapter 2, led daily *dhikrs* during the summer evenings and was an enthusiastic proponent of all Popular Islamic practices. When this sheikh moved from the village in 1960, the official imām, with the help of an increasing number of supporters of the *Ansār al-Sunna*, was able to bring about significant reformative change in the religious practices of Kanuba. From that date to the time of our study in 1964, a gradual shift had taken place in favor of the conservative Orthodox approach, even though, as will become apparent, resistance to it continued.

A *Dhikr* Ritual in the Resettled Village of Kanuba

A family residing in Kenuz Bahari, one section of Kanuba village, sent a messenger to announce a *karāma* celebration to be given in thanks for fullfillment of vow previously made to God. The safe arrival of a son who had been away for more than a year had been requested in prayer.

On the appointed evening, accompanied by members of several village families, we were welcomed into the large courtyard of the host's house, and with three of the village leaders we were ushered into the open veranda, which looked out on the courtyard. There we were seated at a table while about fifty guests found comfortable places on benches or mats around the courtyard. A few moments after we entered, adolescent boys related to the host family began bringing in trays of *fatta*, which they served to the guests in the traditional way. The sheep's head was ostentatiously presented in a large bowl to the two religious leaders, the conservative imām, and the present Sūfi sheikh, who sat facing each other across the same mat.

This ceremonial meal was finished in about half an hour and mats were spread in the center of the courtyard to prepare for the *dhikr*. Each of the two religious leaders situated himself on one side of the long mat with his followers near him and several men soon began chanting and reading various passages from the Mirghanni *mawlid* books which lay open on the mat. At several points individuals turned to the Popular religious leader, requesting him to recite certain memorized praises of the Prophet for which he was well known. He complied and then sent his son to bring copies of another song book from his home, the *Burdah* of al-Būṣīrī, a book of panegyrics written by a Berber sheikh who lived in Alexandria. Though no music was written for these verses, everyone knew the appropriate melodies.

The groups earnestly sang these holy praises for about twenty minutes, but the entire performance began to take on an air of levity very quickly. The participants looked as if they were enjoying it tremendously, and some of them lurched back and forth so vigorously that they almost rolled over, provoking laughter from the group. Many of the younger men did not know the words, so they gathered around the books in groups of three or four to read.

The older men, who were mostly lined up on one side of the mat and leaning against the wall, attempted from time to time to inject a note of seriousness into the occasion, and the young men, concealing smiles, responded by temporarily acting as if they were going to take the ritual seriously. As the singing continued, however, one of them signaled to some boys nearby and drums were brought out of a back room, which were placed ostentatiously in front of the Popular religious leader. This was an action that was a direct challenge and affront to the imām, since it was known that he regarded all singing and body movements in the *dhikr* as innovative non-Islamic impurities.

The imām reacted as expected; he made a stern gesture to remove the drums. The young boys did not move and averted their smiling faces. Others were giggling and laughing in the background and no one made any motion to obey the elderly leader's order. Several young men further affronted the imām by obstreperously encouraging the Popular Islamic leader to start drumming, but still nobody made a move. It seemed to be an impasse. After a few moments of tense silence, the imām haughtily set an ultimatum: if anyone began to drum he would leave. This momentarily seemed to stop the impetus towards a more uninhibited kind of performance and the men again gathered around the song books for several more religious songs, led in a serious manner by both the Popular leader and the imām.

One of the men was requested by the others to chant some of the Qur'ān, which he did, imitating the famous chanters of Cairo who are often heard on the village radio. The chanter worked himself into a deep trance, and finally became so excited by his efforts that several men standing nearby forcibly stopped him, shaking him back to consciousness. One of them shouted, "*Bas*! *Bas*!" (Enough! Enough!) evoking laughter from the group by using the same tone mothers employ with children. Several jokes were heard in the background. At this point two boys entered the courtyard with censers and passed the incense to everyone, allowing each person to inhale the smoke for a few seconds. The incense was followed by cinnamon tea in small cups.

After this brief interlude, which relaxed the tension, one of the young leaders picked up a drum. Looking straight at the imām he tapped it twice in direct opposition to the leader's orders. Seeing that his wishes were going to be countermanded, the latter arose in anger and calling two of his followers, stalked out of the courtyard.

No sooner had the opposition departed when the Popular leader hit the drum with several swift beats and clapped his hands, signaling for the *dhikr* to proceed. Most of the men then formed two lines facing one another, simulating the *maglis* form of the traditional Nubian *dhikr*. Meanwhile, the women, who were grouped around the doorway to the courtyard, began to shake their arms violently in rhythm with the loud beating of tambourines. "*Allāh hayy! Allāh hayy!*" ("God lives!") the crowd shouted again and again.

Now the feigned seriousness was gone, and the affair took on the air of an uninhibited leaping dance. At one point the *dhikr* lines broke up and one man began imitating the movements of a traditional Nubian female dancer, running into the middle of the circle with a shuffling effeminate step. The dancing, shouting men made a wide circle around him, first closing in and then opening out again in time with the drumming. It was a humorous caricature of a Nubian wedding dance. The dancer became so excited that he grabbed a long pointed metal rod, and as he danced, brandished it half-menacingly at various members of the taunting crowd.

The huddled women and children still were watching through the door of the other courtyard, at times unleashing penetrating joy-cries. These *zagharīt* did not seem to have any particular order or timing, as they had in Diwan, but were rather more like enthusiastic impulsive shouts. Some boys of around twelve and thirteen years of age then joined the dancing and added their antics to those of the young men.

Several older men who were not participating in this informal *dhikr* sat around the fringe of the courtyard and seemed to be enjoying the entertainment. At one side we saw a man asleep on a bench and noted that he was one of the troublemakers of the village, a self-appointed unwanted "leader" who often expressed boredom with any kind of community celebration or ritual activity. Another man, who had recently returned from Cairo and who had traveled abroad as a cook for a wealthy official for many years, did not seem to know even the basic pattern of the *dhikr*. He could not follow what the rest of them were doing, and, though trying hard, always seemed out of step with the entire proceeding. Twice during this performance one of the young leaders of the village came over to us and whispered that people were simply enjoying themselves and therefore their profanations of sacred ritual should not be held against them.

After about two hours of "dhikring" in this way, people began to leave the courtyard to return to their own sections of the village. Part of the group was not ready to go home, however, and they gathered outside in the street to continue to dance. One man held the lantern high as several boys took the roles of female dancers, again imitating the steps used in wedding dances. They became more vigorous than ever and began to clap and to beat the drums again, but after about half an hour their enthusiasm waned, and people dispersed to their houses.

Discussion

The *dhikr* as performed in the resettled village of Kanuba in 1963 clearly illustrates many features differing from those of the traditional form described earlier. The spirit of religious dedication noted in Diwan was absent, as were the Ṣūfī ideals of purity of soul, meditation, and union with the divine. The traditional pattern of the *dhikr* was not followed, nor even known. For example, there were no *naqīb*, *moqrī*, or *munshids*. The *istighfār* was not recited and the excerpts from the Qur'ān repeated at various points were not taken seriously. Many of those present did not even listen to them and some were laughing in other parts of the courtyard. The *estiftāh al-dhikr* was not changed, but the recitation of a *qaṣīda* was fragmentary, with verses taken from several different books. These were remnants of the traditional form, and the overall performance was characterized by spontaneity, disorganization, and secularism at variance with the formal pattern and sacred quality of the traditional *dhikr*.

Rather than beginning quietly and then gradually and systematically building to a climax of rhythmic action, the men began moving excitedly and somewhat randomly at the outset, laughing and joking. The whole atmosphere was recreational. Sacred words were chanted, but the spirit of religious dedication, which had so impressed us in Diwan, was absent. Another difference was the individuality of participation, such as was shown, for example, when one of the young leaders initiated a step of his own, a kind of irregular jumping different from what most of the others were doing. During the most excited part of the *dhikr* men were bending low and boisterously leaping high in the air with loud shouts at any time they felt moved to do so.

The changes that are occurring in Nubian religious behavior in this village are particularly well-illustrated by the conflict between the two religious groups during the performance of the *dhikr* ceremony. The forced departure of one of the foremost religious leaders in the community (who was, in fact, the imām of the village mosque), and the domination of the performance by the young irreligious elements of the community, are dramatic indications of the inroads of secularism into Nubian ritual behavior. Not only was the authority and teaching of the puritanically orthodox *Ansār al-sunna* denied, but the traditional elements of Nubian Popular Islam were also overridden. When the Popular Islamic leader, who is a deeply religious man, sanctioned the *dhikr* at Kanuba, he had little notion that it would lead to the wild performance described, and the next day he humbly apologized to us for it.

The kinds of changes we have described in the structure and meaning of *dhikr* rituals in Kanuba are reflected in many aspects of village ceremonialism. Principal Orthodox rituals such as the Friday congregational prayer, the Ramadan night prayers, the *'id al-ṣaghīr*, and the *'id al-kibīr*, for example, now exclude the Ṣūfī *dhikrs* which were traditionally part of these rituals in Nubia. Likewise modified to conform with the reductive and reformative trends typical here have been rituals of the twenty-seventh of Ragab eve and the first of Moharram the first day of the Muslim calendar.

Ceremonial activities related to popular and pagan aspects of religion have also undergone change. The *dhikr*, which was an integral part of almost all rituals, has been eliminated from most of them, or has become secularized in the manner described. As an *independent* ritualistic activity, the *dhikr* has also lost its integrity in the religious system of Kanuba, and during our stay in the village, a *hadra* was never held. As we have seen, the present form of the *dhikr* is characterized by infrequency, irregularity, and lack of traditional religious feeling. It has become, primarily, a form of secular entertainment rather than the powerfully sacred matter it once was.

Lacking strong leadership, those Kanuba villagers favoring Popular Islamic practices such as the *dhikr*, have largely given them up, though some women continue surreptitiously to visit graves to propitiate the dead, to visit sheikh's tombs and to attend *zar* ceremonies in neighboring towns. The Ansār al-Sunna doctrinal position has been additionally strengthened by the fact that some villagers who have recently returned from urban centers seem generally apathetic toward certain religious matters that were formerly of great importance; they have picked up some of the secular urban attitudes. Such matters as medicine and education have meanwhile been taken over by governmental agencies, which have representatives in the village; and this has further weakened Popular Islam, which through its saints' shrines and Qur'ānic *kuttāb* schools, formerly provided the basis of both curing and teaching. Secularization, apathy, and loss of leadership should not be overemphasized, however, since religious matters are still of great importance to the villagers of Kanuba. Debates in the mosque still take place frequently, especially during Ramadan. Throughout the year, in the evenings on the village *mastaba*, arguments are constantly heard about the proper interpretation of the Qur'ān and the *hadīth*, as well as about questions regarding both Popular Islamic and pagan beliefs.

It is not simply that the Popular and pagan beliefs are considered wrong or irreligious in comparison with orthodox ones. There is also an attitude of derision towards many of these beliefs, which is derived from a growing general knowledge of science and medicine and a wider awareness of conditions in the outer world. Most of the young men thus regard such activities as visiting graves and shrines and belief in river spirits as old-fashioned and silly. A few of them even scoff at Orthodox Islamic belief, although, if pressed, they generally declare that they believe in such central features as the five pillars of Islam (prayer, fasting, alms-giving, pilgrimage, and belief in God). With the exception of one or two of the young men who could almost qualify as agnostics, regular attendance at the Friday mosque is still nearly universal in Kanuba. Religion is still important in determining social ranking in the community, but is much less so than it was in the past. Occupation is now the principal criterion, though the total social ranking of an individual is based upon economic status, relationships to high-ranking tribes in Old Nubia, and personal qualities. All these attributes now supercede the formerly dominant criterion of piety.

A major reason given by people in the village for the drastic change and reduction in general ceremonial since their move from Old Nubia in 1933 is that they are now poor in comparison with previous times. There is some justification for this economic rationale because in Old Nubia there was far more familial support for the long and expensive ceremonials that occupied much of their time. Also important was the fact that in Old Nubia most of the material used in communal religious ceremonies (food, palm trees, etc.) was locally produced. Actually, however, economics are only part of the story. The resettled villagers of Kanuba have been quite successful in making an economic niche for themselves in an area of southern Aswan province. Most of the men work in clerical positions or jobs of a similar type in which their income is relatively high in comparison with the majority of surrounding Upper Egyptian farmers. The economic argument is at least a partially simplified explanation for changes that are deep and widespread.

Conclusion

In Kanuba, the *dhikr* ritual has lost most of its religous meaning and function. Its perpetuation at all seems to be due to the fact that the younger adult generation of the village needs to express its revolt against tradition through a religious vehicle. In such profoundly conservative regions as Upper Egypt, moves to effect significant social change, attempts to exert leadership, or efforts to rebel against authority must all be cloaked in religious garb if they are to attain success. Only with some sanction from Islam can the young men of Kanuba resist the puritanical restrictions insisted upon by the Anṣār al-Sunna group. If at the same time their somewhat intemperate behavior and their secular attitude toward religion in general has alienated those members of the older generation who are supporters of traditional *Ṣūfistic* practice, this group of leaders is nevertheless also in opposition to the reforming group and is thus frequently the ally of the young in political endeavors. It remains to be seen whether the young men will be successful in their revolt, or whether the powerful undercurrents of tradionalism can reassert themselves once again.

Recent data from the Kom Ombo Nubian resettlement area indicate a parallel decline of *dhikr* rituals there as well, though general religious change is still not so pronounced as in Kanuba. In many districts of New Nubia the *dhikr* that was usually held after the Friday noon prayer has been eliminated, and the number of *dhikrs* performed throughout the year has also been drastically reduced. For example, recent information from New Diwan indicates that only four *dhikrs* were held there during the first two years after resettlement.

Of course we cannot make definitive predictions in this regard for New Nubia. Beliefs have incredibly strong roots and it is common in situations of drastic culture change that "culture revivals" occur at a later time. This happened in Kanuba in the 1940s and 1950s as we have described.[12] As in Kanuba, however, the trend towards secularism may well prevail in the longer run in New Nubia as well.

The decline of *dhikr* performances in both Kanuba and in the New Nubian settlement at Kom Ombo corresponds to a general decline of Ṣūfistic practice in Egypt (Gilsenen 1967; p. 11). This loss of political importance and religious ascendance in the country by the Ṣūfī orders is undoubtedly the result of many factors, including the secularization resulting from the

nationalistic modernization programs of the revolutionary regime, particularly since the government has in general discouraged the *turuq* (Barclay
1966; p. 205).

However, internal matters of organization have also contributed to the
decline. In a recent study of Ṣūfism in the country, Gilsenen argues that
Egyptian Ṣufi orders have been unable to maintain their political and
social positions because "they are internally ill-fitted to withstand the
challenge which the social and economic development of the late nineteenth
and early twentieth century Egypt presented" (1967; p. 15). He argues that
internal structural weaknesses, such as reliance on charismatic leadership, lack of development of any types of organization more complex than
leader-followership, local authority, and multiple membership were factors
that made the orders vulnerable to attacks by Orthodox movements as
well as to challenging social and economic changes (*Ibid.*, pp. 14, 15, 16).
These challenges came not only from the reactionary orthodox elements, but
also from Ṣūfi groups themselves, who felt that many of the movements had
degenerated into emotionalism with no pure spiritual content. Concerning
the *dhikr* ceremony itself Gilsenen notes:

> Despite the fact that Koranic [sic] justification for the *dhikr* is plentiful, it has been
> particularly the subject of attack by the *ulamā*, by members of other religious organiza-
> tions such as the *Ansār al-Sunna*, and by many who do not belong to the orders. The
> *turruq* are accused of using a ritual designed to free an individual from the sensual self
> to indulge the senses: of degrading the *dhikr* to the point that it becomes little more
> than an excuse for uninhibited emotionalism at the lowest level, pampering to the
> basest instincts of the uneducated (1967; p. 16).

The social, economic, and religious forces that have been influential in
bringing about the general decline of Ṣūfism in the cities of Egypt have also
affected the Nubians. In Kanuba the effects of such changes can be clearly
seen at the village level and the move of all the Egyptian Nubians to their new
homeland at Kom Ombo has brought them out of their relative isolation and
carried them into the mainstream of national religious developments. The
increased pace of living, new economic hardships, and the emergence of
an individualistic spirit resulting from a sudden shift in ways of life brought
about by resettlement have all accelerated the decline of Nubian ritualism in
general and of the *dhikr* performance in particular. The pattern of change
which the newly resettled people are now following has already been traced
in the previously resettled community of Kanuba.

Nevertheless, despite the trend towards the eclipse of traditional Ṣūfi
ritualism, religion remains of great significance to Nubian life. Under the
stress of present changes, the superficially incompatible forces of conservative revivalistic reform and Western scientific secularism compete for
domination of the Nubian world view. Both these trends emphasize the

rational, intellectual side of Man. Though dormant at the moment, however, the great power of such movements as Ṣūfism to stir peoples' emotional energy and to awaken their desires for transcendance of life's problems should not be overlooked. An historically justified ideology, a framework of organization, and the powerful ritual form of the *dhikr* stand available to charismatic leaders of the future in Nubia, as they do also in the rest of Egypt.

Notes

1. "The whole of Ṣūfism rests on the belief that when the individual self is lost, the Universal Self is found, or in religious language that ecstasy affords the only means by which the soul can directly communicate and become united with God. Asceticism, purification, love, gnosis, saintship — all the leading ideas of Ṣūfism — are developed from this cardinal principle" (Nicholson 1963; p. 59).
2. "Despite the views of some advanced leaders, despite a tendency toward the neglect of the ritual prescriptions of Islam, despite even the outside influences which ran counter to the traditional outlook of Islam, its strength lay in the satisfaction it gave to the religious instincts of the people, instincts which were to some extent chilled and starved by the abstract and impersonal teaching of the Orthodox, and found relief in the more directly personal approach of the Ṣūfists" (Gibb 1949; p. 135).
3. The sheikh is the head of a particular *ṭarīqa*, and the *khalīfa* or *naqīb* is his successor. The *naqīb* is the guardian of the *dhikr*. Initiation or "taking the *ṭarīqa*" varies among orders only in the details, but the basic element of initiation includes the performance of certain prescribed *awrad* (daily prayers) and the *dhikr*.
4. *Hadra*, which literally means "presence," refers to the close presence of God to his worshippers when remembering Him. *Hadra* rituals, which were sometimes referred to as *al-rateb* (something regular), were always practiced on the blessing nights of Monday and Thursday, when, according to the Prophet, the affairs of His creation are submitted to God (Fahim 1966; p. 125).
5. "The slave trade of the eighteenth and nineteenth centuries left its mark of Nubia. Some of the people living in Nubia today trace their lineage to slaves who where carried to the Middle East from the heart of Africa by way of the Nile Valley" (Geiser 1967; p. 165).
6. *Mawlid al-Nabī (Birthday of the Prophet)* is a book written by Muhammad Uthman al-Mirghanni, the founder of the Ṭarīqa al-Mirghannīyya, who asserted that the Prophet, whom he saw in a dream, ordered him to write a *qaṣīda* to glorify his birth. It has a subtitle. "The divine secrets about the birth of the most honorable human creature," and includes two parts. The first part describes in prose the Prophet's descent, his birth, growing up, his message, his *Hijra* (flight) and sacrifices. The second contains *"Madīh al-*

Nabī" ("Praise of the Prophet"), a *qaṣīda* (ode) of fifteen verses, and "*Al-Manga-hega*" ("Glorification of the Prophet's Birth"), a poem of thirty-four verses. Uthman Mirghanni, *Mawlid al-Nabī* (in Arabic, Cairo, 1947).

7. *Ṭars* are tambourine drums usually about a foot and a half to two feet in diameter, three or four inches deep, and open on one side. Trimingham points out that the Mirghanni *ṭarīqa* in the Sudan does not ordinarily use the drum (1965; p. 236). Though we observed drumming several times in Nubian *dhikrs*, it was by no means considered a universal or necessary component.

8. These verses contain mystical references to Muhammad which idealize him as a mysterious quasi-deity:

When God wished to project the higher and lower worlds, He took a fistful of His light and it was Muhammad b. Adnan. He (the Prophet) said to Jabir, "The first thing God created was the light of your Prophet as an answer to His problem and I was a prophet when Adam was yet water and clay." The Prophet said to Gabriel, "How old are you, O Gabriel?" He said, "I do not know, except that a planet appears in the Fourth Heaven once every seventy-thousand years (these are the concealed signs) and I have seen it seventy-two thousand times exactly." The Prophet said, in order to make known his rank and the secret of his light, "By the glory of my Lord, I am that planet which you have seen, O Gabriel, in the sky of the Benefactor, and other things which pens cannot put to paper and even the two writers of good and evil cannot preserve."

(From the *Mawlid al-Mirghanni*, chapter 2. Translated by J. S. Trimingham 1965; p. 210).

9. In this case, *magzūb* (*magdhūb*) which means "possessed" "magnetized," refers to ecstacy due to God's direct communication and love, the state of oneness with divinity sought in the *dhikr*. *Maddād* refers to supernatural help, and may be uttered either out of joy or to encourage the performers. *Rasūl Allāh* means "God's apostle."

10. Al-Azhar is the famous Islamic university in Cairo, founded in 969 A.D.

11. Conflict is traditionally resolved within the community. Taking a case outside the community is regarded as an admission of the failure of the local political system.

12. A cautionary comment by T. Thayer Scudder is appropriate here:

"At Kariba [where people were also resettled as a result of a large dam] Colson and I noticed a definite cutback in religious activities during the transition period. About six years after relocation, however, there was a resurgence of family, lineage, and neighborhood ritual, analogous perhaps to the situation in Kanuba in the 1940s." (Personal communication).

Chapter 4

The Sheikh Cult of Dahmit

NOWAL MESSIRI

It has often been remarked by those of us studying the Nubians that the Kenuz are in many ways a paradoxical group. They pose an historical riddle: How and when did they get separated from the linguistically close Dongolawi, who are South of the Mahas speakers? Why and how have they retained so many more of the older Nubian customs than other ethnic groups, despite their much greater proximity to Aswan and thus to Cairo and Alexandria?

We offer no answer to these questions here. I mention them to make the point that al-Messiri's chapter on a Kenuz district depicts a situation which was undoubtedly widespread in Old Nubia in the last century; and has gradually eroded in many areas since the advent of the first Aswan Dam in 1902. The same kind of difference between the subgroups of Nubians applies to the tribal organization, which is much more attenuated in the Fadija area. It is also certainly the case with regard to saints' shrines and cults, which were common earlier south of the Kenuz, and which, during crisis rites, we revisited by processions and *mawlids* (see chapters 8 and 9). At the time of resettlement, however, there were far fewer active shrines and cults among the Fadija and Arab-speaking Nubians than among the Kenuz. Nowal al-Messiri's chapter describes a significant part of the Popular Islamic religious culture that was typical of all of Nubia until the last few decades.

During a year's work on a project in Cairo and Alexandria interviewing Kenuz Nubians from the community of Dahmit, Old Nubia, it became apparent to me that the cult of sheikhs (or saints) was important even to migrants from that community who were working in the cities. These migrants were anxious to visit Nubia during the time of its religious festivals, and most of them sent annual contributions to Nubia for the ceremonies of the cult. A short time later, when my chance came to work in Dahmit, I noticed that shrines of sheikhs were numerous and distributed all over the district, and that cult ceremonies consumed a great deal of the people's time and energy. It was clear that the sheikh cult was intertwined with many other aspects of the culture and social organization. Since these people were to be resettled

61

shortly, it seemed important to describe the shrines, rituals, and beliefs related to this cult and to analyze its meaning and importance in the lives of the Dahmit Nubians.

Dahmit and Its Religious System

Dahmit was one of the twelve Kenuz *'omodiyyas* in Nubia. Before resettlement it lay on both banks of the Nile between the *'omodiyyas* of Dabout to the North and Amberkab to the South and was composed of twenty-four villages or *naja's*, of which fourteen were on the Eastern bank and ten on the Western bank of the river. In the census of 1960, which was taken prior to resettlement, the smallest of Dahmit's 24 *naja's* had only 9 residents, the largest 281. The total population was 1221 persons, 846 females and 347 males. The percentage of adult males of working age in the total male population was very low. Of the total population of the main tribe in Dahmit (the Mehannab) for example, only 10 percent were adult males; their average age was sixty-eight and there were no males in the age range of twelve to thirty-nine (Callender 1966). This severe sex imbalance, characteristic of Old Nubia and particularly marked in the Kenuz area, was due to the continuous labor migration of adult males to the urban centers.

Dahmit was comprised of three main social units, the tribe, the *naja'*, and the *'omodiyya*. The tribe was the most important of these and is the only one that still successfully survives among migrants in the city (Ibid.; p. 6). There are twelve patrilineal tribes, and though there is some variation, members of each tend to be concentrated in one *naja'* or in adjacent ones. In Dahmit, identification with one's tribe is more important to an individual than identification with the residential group. Each tribe is divided into several lineages and lineages are divided into families. This tribal structure was of great significance to the organizational and ceremonial aspects of the sheikh cult in Old Dahmit.

Though women outnumbered men in Dahmit, political authority rested in the hands of men, e.g., the official positions of *'omda*, *ghafir*, *sheikh al-balad*, and sheikh of a tribe. No woman made a decision on a major issue, such as marriage of a daughter, or moving to the city, without consultation with the male representative of the tribe in the village or with male relatives in the city. In addition, women were considered the responsibility of the male members of the tribe, irrespective of the degree of kin relationship.

The principal Muslim rituals, the prayer and mosque service, were separate from the cult of sheikhs, and confined to the male members of the community. In one of the larger villages, Naja' al-Jami', only three elderly women prayed, and of these only one performed the prayer properly. Lack

of knowledge of the Arabic language among most of the women seems to
have been one barrier which prevented them from being introduced to the
formal teaching of Islam, thus probably contributing to the importance of
the non-Orthodox sheikh cult in the village.

1. THE SHRINES

One outstanding feature of the cult in Old Dahmit was the high number
of sheikhs' shrines, approximately 150, found in the district. Historically,
these structures fell into three main types: (1) those built by adults to commemorate a particular sheikh; (2) those that had not been built as shrines,
but had had the names of sheikhs bestowed upon them; and (3) those built
by children, sometimes with the help of older persons.

Of those built specifically in commemoration of particular sheikhs only
four shrines still existed at the time of the study; the others had been
covered by water after the last raising of the Aswan Dam in 1933, and had
never been rebuilt. These four shrines were named after their spiritual
guardians: Al-Barassi, Hassan and Hussein, Hamad, and Muhammad.

This type of shrine was a rectangular or square whitewashed building.
With the exception of that of Sheikh Hamad, which had four entrances,
each of them had one entrance and a dome (*qubba*). The shrine of Hassan
and Hussein had twin domes annexed to each other, each representing one
of the twins. Only the two shrines of Hassan and Hussein and Muhammad
had symbolic coffins in their interiors, but inside all of them there were
candle-sticks and incense pots.

The second type, those structures or places that were not originally
intended as shrines included various kinds of buildings or ruins that had
been designated in dreams to individuals as habitations of sheikhs. For
example, the shrine of Shelshel was an ancient Greco-Roman altar, while
the shrine of Omar was composed of two slabs of granite with Kūfic inscrip-
tions on them; a military fortress constructed during the reign of Muhammad Ali had been appropriated for use as the shrine of Yakoub. In many
other cases shrines were nothing more than rings of stones that were difficult
to distinguish as being of either ancient or recent construction.

Shrines of the third type, those built by children, were structurally very
similar to the adults' shrines except for their miniature size. Naja'al-Shema
was the only village in the district that had no shrines of this kind or of any
other kind. Wess'ya, on the other hand, had more than twenty children's
shrines.

The location of any shrine and the initial development of the belief in a
particular sheikh are determined by the *ishāra*, or signal. The *ishāra*
principle is a very important and basic concept in the cult. Cult sheikhs are

intangible supernatural beings, spirits revealed through their deeds, and the principal means by which they communicate with believers is through dreams. The *ishāra* given for building a particular shrine comes initially in the form of a dream. Usually, a respectable, pious, and married person[1] dreams that a particular sheikh commands him or her to build a shrine in a certain place or to commemorate some particular spot as his shrine. The following morning the dreamer looks in the designated spot for some grains of *ghalla*,[2] a stick, or some similar mark. If he finds it he shows the "signal" to the people to substantiate his claims to the miraculous dream. The *ishāra* thus has two necessary parts, the dream and the validation of the dream.

There was no general pattern to the placement and distribution of the shrines. They might be found far away in the mountains or inside the courtyard of a particular house, depending on the *ishāra*. Since the founding of a shrine depended on the supernatural experience of individuals, there was theoretically no limit to the potential proliferation of shrines and ceremonies, although under some conditions such a system actually permits some limitation of its expansive qualities. After 1933, for example, as a result of the raising of the water level, some shrines were under the water during winter, while others totally disappeared. No attempts were made to rebuild most of them, for no dreams or *ishāra* appeared to validate a new location.

The children's shrine was an exception to this pattern of constructing the shrine after an *ishāra*. It was built by children with the help of their adult relatives in imitation of the shrines built by adults. Frequently, however, after the child had built his shrine, an *ishāra* was given to an adult person that validated its transformation into a full-fledged adult shrine.

In Egypt, Morocco, and other Muslim countries most saints' shrines are built around the relics or actual bodies of holy men or women. Cairo, for example, owes a good deal of its reputation as an important Islamic religious center to the fact that a number of its *mawlids* center around the relics or actual remains of members of the immediate family of the Prophet Muhammad (McPherson 1940, p. 31). In other parts of the Middle East such shrines may also be associated with places where a holy man had sat or prayed while alive. Neither of these features was typical of the sheikh cult of Dahmit. Only four of the shrines in this area represented the original burial place of holy men who had lived in Dahmit; the rest were cenotaphs.

It is interesting to note that all of the four shrines of "real" sheikhs had been covered by the high water resulting from the 1933 raising of the Aswan dam and had not been reconstructed during the period between then and the resettlement of 1963. The shrines of Sheikh Saleh and Sheikha Farahat, ancestral sheikhs honored by their tribes, and the shrine of Sitt'Aisha, con-

sidered by believers to be a martyr who died in Nubia during the Arab invasion in the seventh century A.D., were not rebuilt because no *ishāra* had
been given after they were inundated. The fourth original tomb was that of
Abu Hamad, at Naja' Betikol, considered to be the ancestor of the Fagarab
tribe. Before this shrine was inundated an *ishāra* had been given for a new
place, but it was still not rebuilt, the explanation offered being that the
ishāra to rebuild the shrine designated a place far away in the mountains.
The members of the tribe did not like this location and decided to move
the shrine to some other more convenient spot. When they attempted to
open the old tomb to move the corpse, however, they were faced by hund-
reds of scorpions, which prevented them from fulfilling their task. They
attributed this horrifying phenomenon to the sheikh's disapproval of the
new spot of their choice. Therefore the shrine itself was never moved,
though a *mawlid* is annually celebrated at the place designated in the
ishāra dream.

All the rest of the more than 200 shrines in Dahmit were dedicated to well
known sheikhs whose bodies rest in Sudan, Egypt, or some other Islamic
country.

2. SYSTEMS OF BELIEF AND RITUAL

The belief system clustered around the sheikh cult of Dahmit was relatively simple and similar to that in other parts of the Middle East, but the
ritual system was more complex and more localized in its development. A
practical concept of mutual reciprocity between the supernatural being
and the people was fundamental to a sheikh cult. In Dahmit, sheikhs were
expected to render to believers certain services, for as saints they possessed
baraka (grace, power to bless) and were capable of performing miracles
(*karāmas*). In return, adherents of the cult were expected to express their
gratitude and recognition for such services in the form of *nadr* (vows), *ziāra*
(visits) and *mawlids*, in addition to building the shrine and caring for it.

Baraka

Most of the sheikhs had specific kinds of *baraka*, benevolent supernatural
power, which they were expected to exercise on behalf of the needy and sick
and for the protection of those working in the city. It is of interest to note that
the kinds of services that the sheikhs were expected to render reflected
anxieties attributable to the relative isolation of the community. Medical
doctors, for example, were lacking in this part of Old Nubia. When in pain
some believers called upon a sheikh for help, and all the sheikhs of Dahmit
were thought to have therapeutic powers, especially Hassan and Hussein
al-Barassi (the twins), who are said to have given seventy-seven *ishāras*

designating spots distributed all over Egypt and the Sudan. To the people of Dahmit such abundant signals were considered to be manifestations of the power of a sheikh, indicating his fame and a widespread belief in him.

A good example of the direct relation of the *baraka* concept to the relief of anxieties inherent in the external environment of Old Nubia is that of Sheikh 'Arif. This saint, whose original tomb is in the Sudan, was believed to hold a supernatural power over scorpions. Though he had no adult shrine in Dahmit, people passing through a part of the district that was known to harbor many scorpions called on Sheikh 'Arif to protect them from the feared sting of these arachnids.

Other sheikhs were also famous for specialized *baraka*. The special *baraka* of Sheikh Hamad was manifested through his power to protect the people from foreign invasion. It was said that his shrine was located high in the mountains especially for that reason and that when invaders saw it at a distance they thought it was a guarded fortress. This sheikh was therefore often called "Abu Nabout," a nickname appropriate to a *ghafir* or watchman. Sheikh Shelshel had the specialized *baraka* of protecting the crops from being stolen. His shrine was located in the fields, and among miracles attributed to him were the paralysis of several thieves and the deaths of their offspring. Sheikh Yacoub was famous for helping women bear children.

Karāmas *or Miracles: Examples of Myths*

> Hazim Zild Mahmoud, one of the sheikhs of the Arab tribe among the Nubians of Dahmit, was known as a pious sheikh who was never properly able to perform the Muslim prayer in the Arabic language. A humble Nubian shepherd, he knew only two words in Arabic, those meaning "stick" and "goat." Therefore, as the story goes, whenever he wanted to pray he would say, "My goat and stick. Please God, make my prayer longer." Once an al-Azhar graduate passing in a boat heard him praying that way; he called him over, and told him the proper words of the prayer. As the al-Azhar graduate left with his boat, Hazim wanted to pray, but forgot the words, so he called out to his new friend. The man did not hear him so Hazim followed him by walking right across the surface of the water. Catching up with the boat he asked to be reminded of the proper words once more. The Azharite was so startled to see Hazim walking on the water that he told him, "The *baraka* you have is enough. Pray in any fashion you like." Many of the Nubians of Dahmit repeat this incident whenever they are criticized for praying improperly.

Hassan and Hussein, the twin Sheikhs (al-Barassi) of the Mehannab tribe, were the Prophet's grandsons. Their numerous miracles tended to appear whenever inexplicable events took place or whenever there was some disturbance in the cultural pattern. The following story is one of the myths supporting the cult of these Sheikhs:

> Though the dancing of men and women on public occasions is a traditional custom

of the Nubians of Dahmit, a certain member of the Mehannab tribe, after visiting the city, accepted the Orthodox Islamic strictures regarding the immorality of dancing and decided to prevent his girls from dancing in the annual *mawlid* of Hassan and Hussein. As soon as he made this decision, however, he became paralyzed. Members of the tribe attributed this condition to the fact that he had angered the tribal sheikhs. Therefore, on the day of the *mawlid* he was carried to the shrine, where he apologized to the spirits, allowed his daughters to dance, and was immediately cured.

Regardless of the truth of such accounts (and many of them do seem to contain at least a kernel of fact), they provided the validation of the beliefs and rituals of the sheikh cult. In the Hassan-Hussein myth recounted above it is interesting to note the element of social control, and the way in which the story symbolizes Nubian cultural identity.

Nadr, Ziāra, and Mawlid

The *nadr*, *ziāra*, and *mawlid* constituted the main features of the ritual system of the sheikh cult. Literally, the Arabic term *nadr* means vow. In the present context, a *nadr* is a conditional request to the spirit sheikh. In effect, an individual makes a bargain, asking for a certain favor with the promise that if it is given, the sheikh will be ceremonially rewarded. The reward itself was also called *nadr*, as is the whole vow-reward process. Dahmit men who were sophisticated in Muslim religious theology stated that the request was actually asked from God and that the reward was given through the sheikh as an intermediary. This belief was not current among the majority of the villagers, however, and popular usage of *nadr* in Dahmit referred to a practical and direct relationship between sheikhs and individuals.

Ziāra is an Arabic term meaning a visit, but here it denotes a special visit to the sheikh's shrine. Visitors to the shrine often take with them donations which are also called *ziāra*. While the *nadr* is made to the sheikh, the *ziāra* is made to the shrine. The donations given at the time of the *ziāra* and the material reward of the *nadr* are distributed in a special way that will be discussed later.

A sheikh's *mawlid* is a special festival held in commemoration of him by his adherents. The essential elements of the sheikh's *mawlid* in Dahmit are the following:

(1) Slaughtering of a sacrificial animal given by the group celebrating the *mawlid*.
(2) *Ziara* to the shrine.
(3) Dancing and singing.
(4) Making and giving *nadr*.
(5) Contributions of bread and money by members of the *mawlid*.
(6) Participation of members of other tribes, *najas* and *nahias*.

(7) Selling of sweets and toys.
(8) A communal feast of *fatta* and meat.

3. ORGANIZATIONAL ELEMENTS

The Hierarchy of Sheikhs: Their Relationship to Social Structure
The sheikh shrines in Dahmit formed a hierarchy of importance which
was related to different levels and aspects of social structure. The types of
sheikhs recognized by the people and their rank were associated with the
following features of social structure: the tribe, the lineage, the family, the
individual, and children collectively.

Tribal Sheikhs
Sometimes a sheikh was recognized by members of the tribe (*qabīla*) as
their own esteemed spiritual guardian. These sheikhs were usually revered
by members of other tribes as well, but they had come to be identified with a
particular tribe, which has assumed responsibility for their shrine and
rituals. Some of these tribal sheikhs were mythical ancestors of the members
of the tribe. The Mehannab tribe, for example, traces its ancestry to al-
Hassan, the grandson of the Prophet Muhammad. Since Hassan was one of a
pair of twins, both he and his brother, al-Hussein, were revered together and
they had a double shrine.[3] Another example is Abu Hamad who is the fore-
father, nineteen generations removed, of the members of the Fagarab tribe
and was buried at Naja' Betikol in Dahmit. Sheikh 'Omar, however, the
tribal sheikh of the Ghalmab tribe, is not considered an ancestor, nor are
the tribal sheikhs of the Gerbab or the Hawateen.
    Not all Dahmit tribes have their own spiritual guardians; and at cere-
monies tribes without sheikhs of their own joined with tribes who had a
shrine in the locality. The Hindiab and Albakab tribes of the villages of Max
and Karmdol, for instance, were allied with the Fagarab tribe and participated in its *mawlids*. The Khalsab tribe of Naja' al-Shema was originally from
the nearby '*ǝmodiyya* of Dabout, and at the time of the study, in addition to
participating in *mawlids* of the Fagarab, some members of the tribe still
traveled to participate in the ceremonies of the sheikh of the Khalsab tribe at
Dabout. The "Arab" tribe[4] of Dahmit, in the village of Boga'a Gibli, was
associated with the Ghalmab tribe. Tribes that had affiliated themselves with
other tribes for ceremonial purposes were minor tribes in terms of number
and political authority in the *'omodiyya* of Dahmit (Table I).

Lineage Sheikhs
While the Gerbab tribe as a whole honored the twin Sheikhs al-Barassi,
whose shrine was located at Naja' al-Khor, members of the Mousab lineage

TABLE I   Location of Tribal Sheikhs and Distribution of their Adherents by Naja'

Sheikh	Naja' of Sheikh	Tribes	Distribution of tribe members by naja'	Annexed tribes	Distribution of annexed tribes by naja'
Hassan and Hussein	Jamà'a	Mehannab	Main construction at al. Jama'a and Almanya. Members of this tribe were found in every other naja' of Dahmit	—	—
Sitt 'Aisha	Mot Ghalab	Merioweki	Meter 'Ali, Diptakogi Beni bekol, Fadin nishi Mot Ghalab, Boga'a Gibli	Awnalab	Boga'a Gharb, Meta 'Ali, Mehana
Al-Barassi	Al-Khor	Gerbab	al-Khar, Kogi, Sherushi, Betli-Kol, Kolodo Koliseg		
Abu Hamad	Max	Fagarab	Garbouk, Max, Karmdol	Khalsab Salmab Albakab	al-Shema Kamdol
Omar	Bega	Ghalmab	Boga'a Gibli, Kolisey	Arabs	Boga'a Gibli

Tribes are listed in order of numbers of members, proceeding from most to least.

of this tribe also honored Sheikh Shelshel, whose shrine was located in the *naja'*. The expenses for the *mawlids* of this sheikh were contributed by members of the lineage in the village and by donations from members of the lineage associations in Cairo and Alexandria.

Another more complex example is presented by Sheikh Saleh and Sitt 'Aisha, both of whom were sheikhs of the Merioweki tribe. Around ten years earlier both these sheikhs were reported to have been supported jointly by all lineages of the tribe. By the time of the study, however, their cults had become separate from one another. The shrine of Sheikh Saleh on the Eastern bank of the river was supported by one lineage of the Merioweki, while the shrine of Sitt 'Aisha, located on the Western bank, was supported by the other four lineages of the tribe, and she was also considered the sheikha for the tribe as a whole (Table II).

Family Sheikhs

Families[5] sometimes had special relationships with sheikhs due to a dream

TABLE II   Tribes, Lineages and Lineage Sheikhs*

	Tribe	Lineage	Lineage Sheikh
1	Mehannab	Fargounab	
		Mokladab	
		Mowadab	
		Sheklab	
		Berrydi	
2	Hawatten	Hammalab	
		Moridab	
		Sakiab	
		Ghatasab	
3	Merioweki	Ahmadab	
		Khatibab	
		Moh. Soliman	
		Dahinab	
		Hamadab	Sheikh Saleh
4	Gerbab	Fartousab	
		Mousab	Shelshel
5	Fagarab	Malkab	
		Asmanab	
		Habanab	
6	Ghalmab		
7	Arab	Hamadab	
		Gama'ab	
		Eidab	
		Didanab	
		Albekab	
8	Awnalab	Abshihab	
		Kontab	
		Makinab	
9	Hindiab	Hassinab	
		Gebrab	'Amr and Omran
		Shargawi	
10**	Ghalsab		
11	Salman		
12	Albakab		

*Tribes are arranged according to their size with the largest tribe the Mehanab having the figure No. 1. According to Callender the Mehannabs at Dahmit number 220.

**These last three tribes are originally from Dabout and Amberkab, thus their lineages in Dahmit are fragmented. All together they number about 50–70 individuals.

contact between spirits and family members. Sometimes this family then became the link between the sheikh and other members of the community. A sheikh might appear in a dream to a member of the family, giving him certain commands to transmit to other members of the group, to use a particular formula, for example, or to perform a certain action in order to help the recovery of a sick member of the community.

Personal Sheikhs

Sheikhs thought to be exclusively related to individuals, usually women, were numerous in Old Dahmit. These individual relationships were recognized by the rest of the community, who spoke of "the sheikh of so and so." In dreams the women received commands from the sheikh and felt it imperative to obey them. The commands ranged from such easily implemented acts as lighting candles on a special day of the week to demands for slaughtering a sheep or goat as a sacrifice (Table III).

Children's Shrines

Children's shrines constituted a slightly different category from those described above, since they were not necessarily associated with a spirit being. When I speak of children's shrines I mean those that were built and maintained by children. Many of them had no names, though children who were named after sheikhs sometimes built shrines and gave them their names. This kind of shrine constituted the majority of the shrines in the area. Children's sheikhs have been placed at the end of our discussion because they were built in imitation of the adult shrines and at the time of construction did not have important religious significance. They are interesting, however, in that they often assumed such significance through becoming venerated by adults and validated by a sheikh's dream-visit to someone.

Children's shrines were respected by the adult members of the community and the idea of destroying any of them for practical purposes (e.g., building a wall on the spot) never came to their minds. When such decisions arose,

TABLE III   Range of Dream Commands

Moderate	Less Moderate	Demanding
Lighting Candles	Preparing Tea	Slaughtering Sheep
Lighting Oil	Preparing *Sharbāt* (beverage syrup)	Slaughtering Goat
Burning Incense	Preparing Cooked Lentils Preparing Cooked Rice	

the builder either made a curve in the wall, leaving the shrine outside intact, or incorporated it inside the building. Children were also encouraged by adults and given all the aid necessary for constructing their shrines.

Discussion

Radcliffe-Brown's statement that "the form of religion and the form of social structure correspond one with another" (Radcliffe-Brown, 1952, p. 161), generally applies to the cult of sheikhs in Dahmit. The structural hierarchy of the sheikhs corresponds to a large extent with the makeup of the social structure of the community. The tribe was the most important social unit, and social relations were much more often determined by kinship affiliations than by residence (Callender 1966, p. 6). The welfare of the tribe had a higher social value than that of the lineage, which in turn was more important than the family and the individual. This ranking is correspondingly reflected in the attributed supernatural power and the social importance of the associated sheikhs and in the relative size of their ceremonies.

The tribe and tribal unity played an important role in the lives of the people of Dahmit. For example, such things as the distribution of agricultural land, access to *sāqia* water, the associations in the urban centers, and government aid were all organized on tribal bases. The sheikh cults were clearly another manifestation of this tribal organization and identification. They also symbolized the tribal unit as well as the rivalry among different tribes. This interpretation is born out by the fact that the cults were invariably associated with kinship units rather than with the village and district residential units.

Members of the tribe were always anxious to have more successful ceremonies for their tribal sheikhs than the other tribes and most members of the tribe cooperated voluntarily to accomplish this aim. From Table II we note that there is not perfect correspondence among all tribes in relation to the various types of sheikhs, e.g., all lineages and families did not have sheikhs. To what are these variations due? What do they indicate? To what extent did the sheikh cults contribute to the tribal unity or disunity? These variations are not simply random; there were certain aspects of the social structure of the tribe and changes occurring in it that may help explain these differences. For example, under some circumstances a tribal sheikh became a lineage sheikh, and vice versa.

The Merioweki tribe presents an interesting example. One lineage of this tribe inhabited Naja'al-Boga'a on the Eastern bank of the Nile, while the other four lineages of the tribe resided on the Western bank. At one time in the past, as we have noted, the Merioweki had been represented by two sheikhs, one in each area, and all members of the tribe had cooperated in supporting both of them. About two years before resettlement a conflict in the tribe had led to limiting the responsibility of the Hamadab lineage on the Eastern bank of the Nile to Sheikh Saleh, while the four lineages who lived on the Western bank were held responsible for Sitt 'Aisha. The immediate reason given for the split was that members of the lineages of the west suspected the honesty of the eastern lineage regarding the expenses of the ceremony of Sheikh Saleh.

A number of other social conditions might also help explain this split, such as the double expenses that some members of the Merioweki tribe had to bear. The reason why the split took this form, leaving one lineage, composed of only about one fifth of the tribe, with the whole burden of supporting a formerly tribal ceremony, probably has to do with the river's bisecting the tribe and minimizing social interaction between the two segments. The Nile could be crossed only in one of the few feluccas in the area and seems to have been a serious barrier to the unity of all the tribes living in Dahmit. The Merioweki tribe felt this most strongly, since it was the only one with a whole lineage settled on the opposite side of the river from the main body. This tribal split with regard to responsibility for the two sheikhs thus reflects a geographical situation and may indicate the development of a new tribe. At the stage in which the process was observed, the emergence of a lineage sheikh in competition with a tribal sheikh at least indicated fragmentation and disunity among members of the tribe.

This example might also shed some light on the question of why all tribes did not have lineage sheikhs. When tribal unity was strong and the size of the tribe not too great, there seems to have been no necessity for the extra expense and energy that each sheikh required. When necessity, population pressure, or conflict reached a certain level, the *ishāra* appears to have sanctioned the incipient need for fission. The case of the Merioweki indicates that changes in the hierarchy of sheikhs reflected changing social conditions and thus testifies to the close functional relationship between the sheikh cult and the social structures of Dahmit.

The Gerbab tribe was another tribe in which one of its subsegments had a lineage sheikh. This tribe was composed of only two lineages, and while the ceremony of al-Barassi was a responsibility of all members of the tribe, the Mousab lineage, who lived in a village by themselves, financed and organized another ceremony for Sheikh Shelshel as well. Thus again geographical separation played a role in the segmental autonomy symbolized by sheikh shrines, for the members of the other lineage of the Gerbab tribe were scattered in several adjacent villages. A difference from the case of the Merioweki is that, within informants' memories, Sheikh Shelshel was always known to be a lineage sheikh, and had never acquired the status of a tribal sheikh and that members of the Mousab lineage were also responsible for the tribal Sheikhs al-Barassi. This example thus shows a lesser degree of disunity among the lineages of the tribe than was the case among the Merioweki, but it might indicate a prior step in a similar process of tribal segmentation.

Another case that shows the close relationship between changes in the hierarchy of sheikhs and changes in social conditions is that of Sheikh Muhammad, who also belongs to the Merioweki tribe. He began as a family sheikh and had remained one until the shrine of Sitt'Aisha, the tribal sheikh, sank beneath the rising water of the Aswan Dam in 1933. After that time, members of the Merioweki tribe had turned their interest to Sheikh Muhammad and the tribe as a whole had began celebrating a *mawlid* for him in addition to the traditional one for Sitt'Aisha. With the increased reduction in the number of male members due to the migration necessitated by the dam, however, the tribe had found it impossible to support the additional ceremonies for Sheikh Muhammad and he had descended to his former position as family sheikh for the Hamedi family, in spite of the fact that no new shrine was built for Sitt 'Aisha.

Theoretically, if members of one lineage decrease to the extent that they compose only one family a lineage sheikh may be demoted to a family sheikh. However, no adult shrine can be demoted to the status of those for children, which are always imitations of adult structures.

Movement upward in the sheikh hierarchy also occurs. In fact, family sheikhs are in most cases elevated personal sheikhs. When the rights to the sheikh of an individual woman are inherited or shared by other members of the family, the spirit and his shrine become associated with the family unity.[6] Usually the belief in such a family sheikh continues because members of the family in the new generation experience new miracles that revalidate the association.

A brief history of the development of Ambab Amir will illustrate the process of change from a children's shrine into a family sheikh shrine. A boy by the name of Said Hassan Muhammad built a shrine next to his home but did not name it. Later, the boy's grandmother, Fatma Shattey, saw a sheikh in a dream who told her that he was Ambab Amir, a sheikh in Amberkab, and asked her to recognize the boy's shrine as his palace. He also requested that Fatma burn *bakhūr gawli* (a type of incense) inside Said's shrine every Thursday and Sunday night. This Fatma did, and after she died some years later, her daughter Beha also began seeing visions and took charge of the shrine. Thus the continued association of this sheikh with the family was supernaturally reaffirmed.

When, fifteen years after the children's shrine was built Beha went to Aswan for a visit during my stay in the village, a mischievous boy by the name of Fadl broke off the top point of the structure, then fell sick. No one knew the cause of his sickness. Sheikh Amir appeared to Beha in the dream and told her, "As the shrine was broken, it should be repaired." The sheikh was wearing a green jalabaya and a green turban, "just like the people of Hejaz" (Mecca), Beha said. After the dream she asked Fadl's family to rebuild the shrine so that the boy might recover, which they did and the boy became well again. Subsequently the people of the village often made offerings of lentils, tea or rice to this sheikh when they asked him for favors, and distributed them at his shrine when he answered their requests.

Another example of upward mobility is that of Abdul A'al, a children's sheikh who was in the process of becoming a tribal sheikh. In 1949 a group of eleven children from eleven families of the Hawateen tribe spent fifteen days building a shrine at Naja' al-Wesseya. They thought of naming it "Sheikh Abdul A'al," using the nickname of one of their friends; the father of this boy reportedly became furious and asked them to change the name. The 'omda's son was one of the builders, however, and the 'omda insisted that the shrine keep the name Abdul A'al.

Each of the eleven families became interested in the Sheikh Abdul A'al and helped the children organize and celebrate a full-scale mawlid. Mothers baked cakes and the boys as a group bought two pigeons to serve as sacrifices. The following year the children collected enough money to buy half a sheep, which was cooked by their mothers, and the year after that they were able to serve a whole sheep. For the feast of this third year they asked the assistance of their fathers in slaughtering the sheep, thus actively involving adult men in their ritual activity for the first time.

The final phase of the shrine's movement from one level to another came five years after its original construction. At this time one of the children's mothers saw in a dream a sheikh who called himself Abdul A'al. Thus, the shrine was legitimized, and the dreamer became the official naqiba, or keeper, of what had become, in part, an adult shrine. Favors now began to be asked from the sheikh. For example, whenever a woman of the village wanted to accompany her husband to the city she would throw a piece of his jalabeya inside the shrine and make a nadr.

Children's mawlids do not usually have a fixed date, but the date for this one became fixed. Though the shrine came to be of ritual interest to the adult members of the Hawateen tribe, at the time of the study the children were not yet excluded from supervising its ritual.

Other Criteria for the Hierarchy of Sheikhs

The positions of particular shrines in the sheikh hierarchy of Dahmit are further revealed by the nadrs or vows made by individuals. These are indicative of the relative strength of belief in sheikhs at various social levels. Table IV shows that 36.6 percent of all nadrs were made to sheikhs of

TABLE IV Hierarchy of Sheikhs in Terms of *Nadrs*

TYPES OF SHEIKHS

Type of *Nadr*	Tribal			Lineage	Family	Individual	Children's	Total
	of one's tribe	of other tribes in Dahmit	outside Dahmit					
1. Sugar	20	9	2	6				37
2. Money	10	12	8	4				34
3. Visit the shrine		13	19					32
4. Sharbat	11	3		5	1	2	1	23
5. Candles	1			2	3	6		12
6. Goat	10		1					11
7. Rice					2	5	1	8
8. Dance in *mawlid*	8							8
9. Lentils					3	1		4
10. Sheep	2							2
11. White-wash the shrine	1							1
Total	63	37	30	17	9	14	2	172

the individual's tribe, and that 75.5 percent of all *nadrs* were made to tribal sheikhs, suggesting that people believe that tribal sheikhs were more capable of rendering favors than any other type, a measure of the higher status of their shrines. On the other hand, more *nadrs* were made to personal sheikhs than to those associated with families, which may be due, in part, simply to the fact that there were more personal sheikhs than there were family sheikhs.

Children's shrines ranked lowest in the hierarchy of shrines because they were imitations of adult shrines rather than being dream-validated, and because they were, initially at least, of more concern to children than to adults. In my observation, children rarely made a vow. In all the *mawlids* I witnessed, not a single child fulfilled a *nadr*. The two *nadrs* made to children's sheikhs reported in Table IV were made by adult women.

Personnel

Although most of the sheikhs of Dahmit were identified with shrines, not every sheikh who was recognized by the people had an organized staff or an elaborate set of joint rituals associated with him. The number and roles of the personnel who actively participated in the rituals relating to a particular sheikh were determined, to a large extent, by the social type of the shrine and the number and complexity of rituals associated with it. Thus the personnel of the cult of a personal sheikh (where one individual was involved) was quite different from the personnel of the shrines that were of great importance to all members of a tribe.

Role of the Naqīb (Naqība, f.)

The *naqīb* was the most important member of the staff of any sheikh cult, and was found at each of the levels I have described. It was the only role which was absolutely necessary. In Arabic, the term *naqīb* means, literally, "a representative of a certain group." As it was used in the cult, *naqīb* refers to a human representative of a particular sheikh in a certain locality. The role was a specialized one that necessitated certain responsibilities, involved certain expectations, and had conventional criteria for its assumption.

Qualifications and means of assumption of the role of Naqīb

As I have described, the post of the *naqīb* of the cult was initially bestowed on an individual by the other members as a result of the person's claim of a dream visitation or a vision of the spirit. The *ishāra* signal, however, only occurred to persons who were respectable, pious, and married or once married. The first person in this category to dream of the *ishāra* and to find the validating signs of a particular sheikh was accepted as the *naqīb* of that sheikh. These requirements applied to all forms of sheikhs with the exception of some of those shrines built by children. A child who consciously decided to build a particular shrine was called the *naqīb* regardless of whether he claimed to have had a dream. Once a belief in a particular sheikh became of concern to more than one individual, the role of the *naqīb* became hereditary, irrespective of whether the inheriting *naqīb* or *naqība* had had a validating dream or not.

Succession in the role of the *naqīb* of all family sheikhs observed in this study was through the female line from mother to daughter, probably due to the fact that most family sheikhs had evolved from personal ones that were mainly of interest to women. Among tribal and lineage sheikhs the post of the *naqīb* was hereditary, but did not necessarily follow a female line nor even a unilateral pattern, for succession to these *naqīb*ships could be through the father, grand-father, aunt, husband, or mother. For instance, the previous *naqīb* of the shrine of Hassan and Hussein had assumed the role after his mother died, and had been followed by his younger son, since the older son was working in the city. The first *naqīb* of another shrine, Sheikh Omar, had been Ghandour, followed by Kalam, Hassaballah, Hassan, and finally Ghanim, who was the *naqīb* at the time of resettlement, the post passing from father to son until Ghanim, who was the son-in-law of Hassan rather than an offspring. The position had gone to Ghanim because all the sons of Hassan, Hassaballah and Kalam were in the city and Ghanim admitted that when he died the post would go back to the sons of Hassan, unless they decided otherwise.

Age was also a factor, and there was preference for the *naqīb* to be of the older generation. According to informants, if the son were a young man, succession could go from the father to a brother or uncle. Members of the Mehannab tribe consider the role of the *naqīb* of Hassan and Hussein to be an honor inherited in a particular family of the tribe. Among all the shrines that had a hereditary succession of *naqībs*, members of the community still remembered the first caretakers of their sheikhs, as well as the successions of *naqībs* for at least five generations back.

There were five male *naqībs* from the five tribes of Dahmit who celebrated annual *mawlids* for their tribal sheikhs. All these men were between the ages of sixty-five and one hundred and their average age was eighty years. The celebration of a tribal *mawlid* required not only a male *naqīb* but one who was at the same time a responsible elder. This requirement seems due mainly to the great organizational effort necessary for such occasions and further indicates the great social and religious importance of these cults in the district.

In all cases where shrines were under the care of an adult male *naqīb* there was also a female *naqība* to assist him. Though in many cases the role of the *naqīb* was among the important and honorable leadership roles in the community, the positions of the *naqības*, were customarily given to needy women. Frequently a *naqība* was blind, aged, or had no male relatives to assist her. Although there were only five tribal sheikhs for whom a *mawlid* was celebrated, there were six *naqības*: Sheikh Hamed, who in the not-too-distant past had had a tribal *mawlid* held for him annually, still had a *naqība* but not a *naqīb*. All the six *naqības* of a major shrines were widowed, two were blind, and all were above seventy years of age. The male *naqīb* was the one who made the final decision as to his assistant's appointment, though the *naqība* role might be passed down in a family if, for example, the *naqīb* had a needy widowed daughter.

Role of the naqīb
   The jobs of neither the *naqīb* nor the *naqīa* of the tribal shrines were fulltime occupations; in fact, the *naqīb* performed only once a year during the time of the *mawlid*. In theory he was responsible for the shrine at all times, for collection and distribution of *nadr*, and for supervision of the general organization of the annual *mawlid*, but the only actual responsibilities taken by the *naqīb* were for the celebration of sheikh's *mawlids*. The *naqība* generally responsible for the other ongoing duties, and honesty was considered a virtue important to her role.
   Before the *mawlid* the *naqīb* called a meeting with male leaders of the tribe in which they jointly decided the day of the celebration, the kind and number of sacrificial animals, and the appointment of the persons to buy them. Decisions were also made regarding the amount of money each member of the tribe should pay and who was to collect it. As a payment for his responsibilities the *naqīb* collected one fourth of the animal *nadrs* slaughtered on the day of the *mawlid*; the *naqīb* of al-Barassi was unique in that he additionally took one fourth of the animal *nadrs* made at times other than the *mawlid*.
   Male caretakers were rare below the level of the tribal shrine, as all lineage, family, and individual sheikhs were ordinarily under the exclusive care of females. The responsibilities of the tribal and the lineage *naqības* were similar. In addition to lighting candles and burning incense in the shrines at various times, they were responsible for filling the water-jars placed around the shrines. It was said that the jars should be kept full so that the sheikhs might drink. If a death occurred in the community the candles were not lighted, but the jars were always filled with water. During the *mawlid* the *naqība* was responsible for setting the fire for the cooking and for guarding the cooked meat from dogs or children who might take from it; and if she was blind, she was assisted by a relative in these tasks.
   Sometimes, women went to the *naqība* to obtain special favors from the

sheikh and it was her responsibility to pray for them so that their wishes might come true. In compensation she received the *ziara* money and *ghala* contributed by individuals who visited the shrine. In most cases, the *naqība* lived near the shrine, so most individuals wishing to visit the sheikh would go to her first to notify her of their intentions, though sometimes petitioners would go directly to the shrine to speak to the spirit.

On the day of the *mawlid* the *naqīb* divided the great amount of *nadr* received on that day with the *naqība*. She might be given a cone or two of the sugar *nadr*, the legs of the sacrificial animal, or occasionally the head. Most of the income of the *naqības* depended on *nadrs*, for they were usually incapable of performing any other job and generally did not get enough remittences from relatives in the city. Thus, the job was really a form of charity. Very often, aside from these recognized payments, members of the community sent cooked food for these women to supplement their meager existence. The male *naqīb* and the assistant *naqības* of tribal shrines were the only personnel of the sheikh cult who received any remuneration for their ritual services.

The minimal responsibilities of the *naqības* of personal and family sheikhs were likewise the weekly lighting of candles, burning of incense in the shrine, and keeping the water pots filled. *Naqības* of family and personal sheikhs also sometimes made *nadr* and *karāmas* for them, either to thank them for certain favors or to ask for their benedictions.

In addition to the *naqīb* and the *naqība*, who were the major functionaries, the sheikh cults in Dahmit had other staff members who operated mostly during the annual *mawlid*.

The Drummer

Any person was eligible to be a drummer as long as he had acquired the appropriate skill. Not every tribe or sheikh had its special drummer and in all of Dahmit there were only two men well known for this ability. They provided the drumming at all *mawlids* and were paid symbolically with a cone of sugar from the tribe putting on the *mawlid*.

The drum used at Dahmit was called the *noggar*. It was made from two large Sudanese war drums, one a little longer than the other, which were joined together. Two small sticks about twenty-five inches long were used, and the drummer sat on the ground keeping a simple three-beat rhythm pattern of two strokes on the large drum and one on the smaller.

The Butcher

Though the person who slaughtered for the *mawlid* ceremony was usually simply the village butcher, in one of the tribes the role had become hereditary. Usually the butcher of the *mawlid* received the neck of the animal as his reward. He was responsible not only for killing, shearing, and cutting the animal into pieces, but also for putting it on the fire and, with the assistance of the *naqība*, cooking it. After slaughtering the animal he used a wooden tube to inflate the skin, enabling him to remove it easily with a knife. The animal was then hung on a piece of wood held between two persons, and butchered, the whole process being carried out in the open air next to the shrine.

The Dance Master
   During the day of the *mawlid* the role of directing the dancing was a very important one. The dance master usually held a palm reed in one hand as his symbol of authority for keeping the dancing circle in order. He decided when a fresh dancer should enter the dancing circle and it was he who determined the order in which the different tribes would dance. He also had the responsibility for collecting the *nadr* gifts carried by each of the dancers and putting them into a sack. The role of dance master required great physical effort, but it was done voluntarily and was not a paid position.

Hosts
   For the *mawlid* of Sheikh Saleh of the Ghalmab tribe there was a group of specialists who acted as hosts. They wore special belts to distinguish them from the rest of the participants. These belts were the property of the shrine and were kept at the *naqīb*'s house. The hosts were responsible for serving tea and water to the guests. Anyone wearing the host belt was expected to wear it until the *mawlid* was over; he was not to go home nor chat with anyone during the time of his duties and was required always to be ready to serve the guests. This host role did not exist for any other tribal *mawlid* of Dahmit; generally any member of the tribe was expected to serve.[7]

Summary
   The main components of the sheikh cult of Dahmit were the shrine, the belief and ritual systems, and the organizational elements. In this section I have discussed two main organizational elements of the cult system: First, the fact that sheikhs did not have identical status, but formed a hierarchy, with the tribal sheikhs ranking highest and children's shrines having the lowest position; and second, the fact that the organization of ritual was accomplished through cooperation of the members and designated personnel of the cult.
   The sheikh cult as a social system with its components and organization provides a partial picture of the community structure of Dahmit, for tribal organization, with its divisions and subdivisions, frictions and rivalries,

strengths and weaknesses, is well represented in the tribal and lineage sheikhs and their upward and downward mobility. The individual and family sheikhs reflect similar processes as well as the demographic condition of sex imbalance in the area.

Children's shrines are indicative of certain patterns of socialization. Encouraging the children to build their own shrines and celebrate their own *mawlids* were means of arousing the children's interest in the general sheikh cult as well as in learning and practicing some of its rituals. The amount of aid given to children in these creative efforts towards autonomy seems quite unusual in comparison with many societies.

4. RITUALS

The rituals associated with the cult of sheikhs can be conveniently divided into two major categories: individual rituals, which were performed at times of critical events of major concern to persons as individuals, and joint rituals, which were the concern of most members of groups such as the tribe, the district, the village, and the family.

Individual Rituals

In addition to the individual rituals practiced by the *naqībs* and *naqības* of the cult, explained earlier, there were individual rituals, mainly in the forms of *nadr* and *ziāra*.

Nadr. A *nadr* was simply a vow made to the sheikh but there were various reasons and rules for making and fulfilling such vows. An individual made a request to a sheikh with the promise that if it were granted, the sheikh would be rewarded and the reward varied according to the type of request and the individual making the *nadr*.

In order to determine the social significance of this ritual, seventy women from all villages of Dahmit district were asked about the types of *nadr* they made and the reasons for making such vows. Only six women of the seventy interviewed stated that they had never made a *nadr* in their lifetimes, while the average number reported was 2.7 per individual. Reasons given for making a *nadr* are shown in Table V.

Table V indicates the intense concern of the people regarding marriage and children, since they were the motivation for more than half of the *nadrs* made. Due to malnutrition and the inefficiency of medical services in the area, infant mortality was high and because of the labor migration of males, Nubian women did not have as frequent opportunity of becoming pregnant as most women in rural Egypt. Coupled with these demographic facts was the extremely high value placed on children by the Nubians, which

TABLE V

Reason for making a *nadr*	No. of *nadr* for each reason
1. To get a child	50
2. Marriage for oneself or a member of the family	40
3. Recovery from sickness	39
4. Return of a relative from the city for a visit	21
5. Success in school examinations for a member of the family	9
6. Finding a job for a member of the family	8
7. Well-being of one's animals	5
Total No. of *nadrs*	172
Total No. of women interviewed	70

gave a special status to married women in Dahmit. Traditionally a bride was even expected not to leave the village unless she had borne a child, while a man having a barren wife was given all encouragement to divorce and remarry or to take a second wife. With such a combination of circumstances, it is not unusual to find that the highest frequency of *nadrs* to sheikhs were related to fertility and marriage.

Due to the sex imbalance of Dahmit, there was a constant fear that girls would not have a chance to get married. A girl was called *beneta*, but once she had passed the age of somewhere between twenty-five and thirty years she was called *fatāh*. The immediate reaction to a person referred to as *fatāh* was pity and sympathy and the expression of hope that a *fatāh* might get married was the most frequent verbal reward she received for any service she did.

It is clear that the other kinds of favors asked of the sheikhs also corresponded to the needs and anxieties of the members of the community. For example, the scarcity of medical facilities in the area made it reasonable that the sheikhs were expected to help in recovering from illnesses. There was also high anxiety relating to the migrancy pattern. Relatives in the city were a major source of income and when they returned to the village, they were expected to bring presents for many of their relatives. Visits of the migrant men to the village were looked forward to with considerable emotion, since mothers usually sent their young sons to the city when they became teenagers, hoping that they might be successful. Years might pass before they were able to return. For such a mother, the expectation of seeing her child again was more important than anything else.

To the lonely wife in the village, the visit of her husband was regarded as the main indication of his love and interest in her. During such a visit, the wife generally wore her best attire and gold jewelry, kept just for such an occasion. The wife whose husband was in the village was thus easily detected by her dress, and when she went out one often could hear the term *khanta* directed to her by other women. The term meant that she was "feeling like a woman," i.e., having sexual intercourse, and might indicate either joy at her good fortune or jealousy. Thus, a wife whose husband returned for a visit to the village gained both psychological satisfaction and social prestige. Table V, then, directly reflects the practical nature of the sheikh cults and their relationship to the particular anxieties of this Nubian community.

The kinds of *nadr* given as rewards to particular sheikhs for fulfillment of requests were numerous and varied. For the sample of women interviewed the types of *nadrs* noted are presented in Table VI.

Because of their cost, the most esteemed *nadrs* were sacrificial sheep and goats. Those who made such a sacrifice were relatively few. At the time of the study the average cost of a sheep was approximately two pounds, and that of a goat was about ninety piasters. Since such amounts might equal the total of a month's remittance from the city, the more common *nadrs* were donations of a cone of sugar, a bottle of *sharbāt*, or a small amount of cash.

A common type of *nadr* was simply a visit to the shrine. For example, visiting a distant shrine such as that of Sheikh Bahr in Amberkab was

TABLE VI

Types of *Nadrs* (arranged according to frequency)	No. of *Nadrs* per each type
1. Sugar cones	37
2. Money donations	34
3. Visit to the shrine	32
4. *Sharbāt* (syrup)	23
5. Candles	12
6. Goat	11
7. Rice	8
8. Dance in *mawlid*	8
9. Lentils	4
10. Sheep	2
11. Whitewash the shrine	1
Total	172

The cone of sugar cost about twenty piasters, while the bottle of *sharbāt* was approximately fifteen piasters. A cash payment never exceeded five piasters.

regarded as an especially effective *nadr*. As indicated in the chart, the *nadr* might also take the form of performing certain ritual services, such as dancing in the *mawlid* or white-washing the sheikh's shrine.

Generally, women resorted to *nadr* more frequently than men, and men did not prevent women from making *nadrs*. One of them slaughtered a sheep after recovery from sickness, while the other had slaughtered a cow fifty years before when a son was born to him after a request to a sheikh. The higher frequency of *nadrs* among women might be due to the fact that they had more needs and anxieties than men and to the fact that they were not educated and knew less of the outside world and of scientific causes and effects than did men.

Once the sheikh had been appealed to and the vow fulfilled it was expected that the request should be granted, but there was no fixed time between making a vow and fulfilling the vow. It was not necessary to wait until the sheikh had complied with the request. Sometimes the *nadr* obligation was completed on the same day as the vow was made, and sometimes, as can be seen in Table VII, there were considerable delays in living up to *nadr* promises. The principal reason for this time interval was economic. *Nadr* makers tended to postpone the fulfillment of a *nadr* until they were financially capable. Members of the cult were always anxious to fulfill a *nadr* as soon as possible, however, and if, in the meantime, they stumbled while walking or saw nightmares, they sometimes considered these as reminders by the sheikhs of unfulfilled *nadrs*.

Ziāra.   Whenever anyone casually passed by an adult shrine he said "Sellah!" or "Destor!" or recited the *Fatiha* without necessarily entering the shrine, but the *ziāra*, or visit to the shrine was an actual sheikh cult ritual practiced either privately or collectively. Individuals visited the shrines at critical periods of their lives to get the *baraka* of the sheikh, at

TABLE VII   Time Between Making Nadrs and Fulfilling the Vows

Period of Time	No. of nadrs
Less than one month	27
One month to six months	40
Six months to one year	60
One year to five years	32
Five years to ten years	10
Ten years and over	3
Total	172

marriage, for example, or after giving birth, or before leaving for the city. Before marriage, in particular, the bride had to visit a sheikh's shrine. Usually she was accompanied by a group of friends and relatives and in many cases she visited more than one shrine. At each she left a few piasters for the *naqība*. Table VIII shows the type of sheikh shrines that the seventy women of the sample visited when they married.

In Dahmit a visit to a sheikh's shrine was also one of the major rituals of the wedding ceremony. It was considered that the *zeffa* (marriage procession of the groom) should pass by a shrine before going to the bride's house. There the procession stopped and the groom read the *Fātiha* and hung up a flag that had been dipped in the same henna[10] that had been used for dyeing his feet in the ceremony of the previous night. Before departing from the shrine the groom left a few piasters for the *naqība*. It was believed that if an unmarried girl circled the shrine seven times when the groom's *zeffa* was visiting the shrine, she would get married within the same year. It was preferred that the groom visit the shrine of his own tribal sheikh, but after many tribal shrines were covered by the water in 1933, the closest adult shrine was visited.

The Sheikh's Mawlid

In Dahmit the tribal *mawlid* was the most important joint ritual of the sheikh cult. Sometimes it took place on what was held to be the sheikh's birthday, but often it occurred on his presumptive death day or on another day of particular significance to the participants. The Kenuz Nubians use the term *mawlid* interchangeably with the Arabic term *al-nuss* meaning "half of the month." They do not have a special word in their language for *mawlid*.

Though it is perhaps impossible to ascertain the exact date when the tradition of *mawlids* began in Dahmit, there is some evidence indicating that it is a recent development. The first *mawlid* celebrated in Dahmit is said to have been that of Sitt'Aisha at Mot Ghalab and is reported to have been an imitation of the *mawlid* of Sheikh Bahr in the district of Amberkab, south of Dahmit. Informants believed that about two hundred years ago

TABLE VIII   Type of Sheikh Visited at Marriage

Bride's tribal sheikh shrine	30
Tribal sheikh shrine of another tribe	27
Bride's tribal sheikh shrine and other tribal sheikh shrines	8
Did not visit a sheikh's shrine	2
Total	67
Total No. of women interviewed	70[11]

Dahmit had had no *mawlids* of its own. Inhabitants of Mot Ghalab (the closest Dahmit *naja'* to the border of Amberkab) used to go annually, it was said, to the *mawlid* of Sheikh Bahr, on the fifteenth of Sha'ban, until one year they quarreled with the people of Amberkab when the latter refused to give them their turn in dancing. The next year the people of Mot Ghalab began celebrating a *mawlid* for their own local sheikha Sitt'Aisha, on the same date.[12]

Another indication of the recent origin of sheikh's *mawlids* in Dahmit came from the recounted histories of cult practitioners. Although members of the tribes were adept at reckoning their relationships both vertically and horizontally, the hereditary succession of the post of the *naqīb* was in no case traced back more than four generations and people had an accurate memory of the first *naqīb* of each sheikh.

In addition, tradition said that the *noggar* of Sitt'Aisha (the double war drum used for keeping the rhythm of dancing in the *mawlid*) had been brought to Dahmit 187 years before. This *noggar* was considered to be an innovation in the Kenuz area and members of the Merioweki tribe still boasted about it. Thus, in comparison with the *mawlids* of lower Egypt, those of Nubia were apparently relatively recent.[13]

The Month of Mawlids

For each *mawlid* there was both an ideal, officially recognized date, and an actual date. In Dahmit, Amberkab and some other Kenuz districts, there was a concentration of many *mawlids* during the Arabic lunar month of Sha'ban, particularly in mid-Sha'bān. The ideal date for all *mawlids* is the fifteenth of Sha'bān, though for various reasons only two *mawlids* were actually held on that day. Each of the other tribes recognized another specific day for their *mawlid*, but as Table IX shows, these recognized dates did not always coincide with the actual date on which the *mawlid* took place.

This table illustrates the concentration of *mawlids* during the month of Sha'bān. The only exceptions were the *mawlids* of Hamad and al-Barassi held by the Gerbab and Mehannab tribes, a divergence that could be partially explained by the fact that these two tribes each used to hold two *mawlids* annually: The Gerbab tribe still celebrated the *mawlid* of Shelshel in addition to that of al-Barassi, and to hold both these expensive celebrations during one month was not practical, an explanation concurred in by the Mehannabs, who had formerly held a *mawlid* for Sheikh Hamad in addition to that of Hassan and Hussein.

According to informants, about forty years before, all of the *mawlids* of Dahmit had been celebrated on the fifteenth of Sha'bān. As a result of migration and the sex imbalance after 1933, however, the number of men in each tribe had decreased to the extent that no one *mawlid* could be totally

TABLE IX *Mawlids* of Dahmit

| *Mawlids* | | Officially recognized | Actual date |
Sheikh	Tribe	date	1963
Shelshel	Gerbab	10 Sha'bān	25 Sha'bān
Al-Barassi	Gerbab	15 Ragab	18 Ragab
Omar	Ghalmab	25 Sha'bān	cancelled
Hassan and Hussein	Mehannab	15 Sha'bān	15 Sha'bān
Hamad	Mehannab	Any time in summer	no longer held
Muhammad	Merioweki	15 Sha'bān	no longer held
Abu Hamad	Fagarab	17 Sha'bān	17 Sha'bān
Saleh	Merioweki	22 Sha'bān	cancelled
Sitt'Aisha	Merioweki	15 Sha'bān	27 Shawal

successful without the simultaneous cooperation and help of male members of other tribes. Informants pointed to the example of the dancing circle, which was vital to the *mawlid*. For this there had ideally to be at least six men physically capable of dancing, a requisite that in the recent period was rarely met among the resident members of any one tribe at any one time. Thus, though the ideal pattern could not be identical with actual practice, people believed that the fifteenth of Sha'bān was the proper date for a *mawlid*; and this is the reason why, whether a *mawlid* took place in the middle of that month or not, it was still called *al-nuss*, "half (of the month)."

Explanation for the choice of Sha'bān as the month of *mawlid* ceremonies could be sought in Islamic custom. The month has a special significance for Muslims generally and informants believed that in this month, in particular on the fifteenth day, the final age of each individual was determined. They also stated that there was a tree on which each lead represented an individual's life and that when an individual's leaf fell on the fifteenth of Sha'bān it indicated the end of his life during the coming year. Sha'bān is also a suitable month for *mawlids* since it is the one preceding Ramadan, a month in which, for practical reasons, no *mawlids* can be held. These explanations were not directly connected with the sheikh cult or with the *mawlids* in general but at any rate it was clearly practical to have many *mawlids* during one month, since it gave migrants living outside the village a better chance to attend a larger number of ceremonies.

A number of factors operated that might bring about adjustments in the recognized dates of the *mawlid* ceremonies. A death in the tribe could cause the postponement of the *mawlid* for some days or its cancellation for the year, as happened in the case of the *mawlids* of Sheikh Omar and Sheikh Saleh, as indicated in the table. While these two *mawlids* were cancelled for the year, the *mawlid* of Sitt'Aisha was postponed only till after Ramadan and the Small Feast. The change of the date might also be influenced by the illness of an important member of the tribe or by a dispute among its members.

Members of the Mehannab tribe point to the superiority of their *mawlid*, since its date (fifteenth of Sha'bān) never changes, no matter what the circumstances. The story goes that this attitude stems from the time when a *naqīb*'s mother died on the day of the *mawlid* and the *naqīb* insisted that the body be buried and that the ceremony continue.

It was considered preferable to have each *mawlid* separately and there were even supernatural sanctions supporting this preference. The fifteenth of Sha'bān was the recognized date for both Sitt'Aisha among the Merioweki on the West bank of the Nile and Hassan and Hussein among the Mehannab on the East bank and it is reported that often members of each tribe wanted to attend the other's *mawlid* at the expense of missing part of their own tribal *mawlid*. Several mishaps took place, however, such as the sinking of a boatful of people crossing to the other *mawlid* and such events confirmed the common belief that a sheikh gets angry when members of the tribe leave his *mawlid* for another one. Sitt'Aisha's date was therefore changed so as not to coincide.

Preparations for the *mawlid* usually started one or two weeks before the big night — *al-Nuss*. The first action was a meeting of the *naqīb* of the sheikh with the male leaders of the tribe. This meeting was open to any male tribal member, but usually the representatives of the different lineages were the only ones who came. Generally, such a meeting was held after the Friday prayer when the men were already assembled. At this meeting the actual day of the *mawlid* was set and the decision confirmed by reading the *Fatiha*. During this meeting the number of those coming to the *mawlid* was estimated according to the social conditions of the area. For example, a death in another tribe meant that expected guests from that tribe would be few. The number of returning migrants was also calculated.

Depending upon the projected number of participants, resolution was made as to the kind and number of *dabīha* (sacrificial animals) to be bought. In previous times a cow had been slaughtered for *mawlids* but at the time of the study sheep and goats were the common sacrificial animals. A representative of each tribal lineage, generally a butcher or an animal merchant, was chosen for purchasing the *dabīha*.

Since the *mawlid* was a chance for everyone to wear his best attire, for weeks beforehand the dressmakers were busy sewing new clothes for men, women, and children. One week before *al-nuss*, the regular evening gathering place of tribal men and women was moved to the square of the *mawlid*. On this evening people danced, sang, and beat the drums, with relatives and friends from nearly villages often joining them. Two days before the *mawlid* the women of the tribe, with the help of neighbors, relatives, or friends, baked special bread for the occasion called *raghīf.* Each house was expected to contribute *raghīf.*

On the eve of the *mawlid* everyone readied himself by taking a bath. This, like all Muslim religious ablutions, purified the individual, as no one should enter the shrine unless he had been ritually cleansed. Women applied henna to their faces, hands, legs, and feet, and kohl to their eyes. It was very important to look attractive on the day of the *mawlid,* especially for unmarried girls, as this was the best opportunity to find a suitor among urban migrants visiting the village for the occasion.

The Day of the Mawlid

Early in the morning of the day of the Mehannab *mawlid* of Hassan and Hussein, the children sang in Kenzi, with some Arabic words: *"Al-'Ada, al-'Ada, Habib Allāh,/kol sana daima"* ("Lover of God keep up your custom/ May we have this feast annually"). As they sang they filed through the village visiting each house and collecting dates or bread, which they ate or distributed among themselves.

It would have been humiliating for the hosts of the *mawlid* if their guests did not find enough drinking water, so early in the morning girls and young married women voluntarily filled the water jars of the shrine. It was considered a pleasure to do services on the day of the *mawlid,* and one might receive the *baraka* of the Sheikh if she helped a thirsty person find water.

Men decorated the shrine and the nearby dancing square with flags called *beyrag.* These *beyrags* represented several Ṣufī orders, but in Dahmit participants of the *mawlid* could seldom identify them. The flags were sent by members of the Cairo and Alexandria Nubian associations, and the designs on them had no religious significance for the villagers.

A flag pole called the *sari* was always put up near the shrine, and this area, marked by other flags at each corner, was where the dancing took place. In cases where the Sheikh had no present shrine, as in the case of Sitt'Aisha and Abu Hamad, the *sari* pole symbolized the shrine. In the district of Dabout the *sari* served as more than a gathering place; visitors went around it and kissed it for *baraka.*

Vendors from nearby villages or districts arrived during the day of the *mawlid* to display their wares along with the local merchants. These were mainly sweets, peanuts, lupines, and toys for children. The visiting merchants displayed a variety of goods, while women specialized in one product such as home-cooked lupines or *taamiya* (fried cakes made of beans, parsely, and spices). Mothers and relatives were expected to be generous, for the day was a special one for children, and children took advantage of the situation to buy whatever they desired. A child sometimes spent as much as ten piasters on that day.

Some shrines had a special place similar to a Christian altar where the animals for the feast were slaughtered in the morning. This altar was generally formed by a piece of rock placed at the entrance of the shrine. The cooked meat was supposed to be ready by 11:00 a.m. because a breakfast composed of *fatta* with meat was offered to the male guests at that time.

The animals donated by the tribe were slaughtered first, followed by those given as *nadr* to fulfill vows. Sheep were more valued than goats and tribes boasted about the kinds and numbers of *dabīha* they provided at their *mawlids*. The Mehannab tribe was subject to ridicule in the year of the study because they had celebrated their *mawlid* with only two goats, while the smaller Gerbab tribe slaughtered three sheep.

The women of the tribe came to the *mawlid* wearing their best clothes, nearly all of them carrying a basketful of bread. The amount and the mode of donating bread differed from one tribe to the other, but in general each woman in the tribe provided a customary amount of bread for each male member of her nuclear family, whether they were actually present or in the city, three *raghīfs* per male relative in some tribes, and two or two and a half in others. Some tribes required that the bread be offered broken in a special bowl (*zebdia*); others asked for the whole loaves, which were cut at the *mawlid* area by some of the men of the tribe and put in *zebdias*. It was obligatory that each woman of the tribe provide her share, but extra bread might be given in fulfillment of a *nadr*. When all the bread was cut in large slices, hot soup was poured over it, with chunks of cooked meat. The *fatta* constituted the only dish of the ceremonial meals.

The success of the *mawlid* was judged by the number of outside participants. A constant eager look could be discerned in the eyes of the members of the host tribe as they scanned the river to the north and the south in hopes of sighting boats from other villages and districts. By noon all guests were expected to be present. When a group of guests arrived either by boat or along a path, cries of joy and gun shots saluted them.

The men gathered together irrespective of their village or district, but the women of each *naja'* tended to cluster separately, beating their *tars* and singing:

Singer tode oyrboori erton jelma
(Beautiful one you are very pretty)
Hajibiged emma gabrel tomma
(Your eyebrows are killing)
O yirbon ringa meka dolli
(Because I know I love you)
Yo delli eshme'na raygo dolli manna
(Why don't you love me as I love you)

This song went on to describe the beauty of the beloved one and ask for his love. One woman usually sang, with the rest answering in chorus, and they continued singing until the men were ready to begin dancing.

Dancing in the *mawlid* was a group activity that occupied a central role in the *mawlid* ceremony. It was of interest to both sexes, and once it started most of the people moved to the *sari* area, where they either participated in dancing or showed their interest by commenting, criticizing, and encouraging the dancers.

The dancing most characteristic of the *mawlid* of Dahmit was called the *kaff* dance and is the same type of dancing as generally practised at Nubian weddings and on other joyful occasions. The *kaff* dance was a group circle-dance accompanied by drums and the vigorous clapping of the men. Two or three ṭars were used but the principal beat was set by the tribal *noggar*, played by a special drummer seated at one side of the *sari* area.

Singly or in twos or threes, their faces covered by their shawls, women entered the circle. Some carried bottles of syrup, cones of sugar, or plates of cakes as offerings in fulfillment of *nadr*, and some even danced holding the baby for whom a *nadr* was made.

The dance master, carrying his stick, attempted to keep the size of the circle uniform. He was also responsible for ending the turns or cycles of the dance.

Young, unmarried girls were encouraged to dance, and elderly women were not prevented from taking part. However, the dancing of young married women, aside from those making a *nadr* was forbidden in the villages on the East side of the Nile, though it was allowed on the West bank. All men were entitled to dance, irrespective of their age or marital status, but as mentioned earlier, there were a number of them who were known to have mastered the art of dancing and who were usually expected to provide much of the entertainment at any *mawlid*.

In the period just prior to the study the dancing of women in the *mawlid* had been subject to a great deal of criticism because of a growing belief that it was anti-Islamic and immodest. In recent years the Mehannab tribe had allowed only young girls to dance in *mawlids* and the leader of the Gerbab tribe had gone so far as to forbid completely the dancing of women in the *mawlid* of al-Barrassi. Thus in 1963 some men entered the dancing circle and imitated the movements of the women.

Outside participants in the *mawlids* of Dahmit were mainly from the two adjacent districts of Dabout and Amberkab, and means of welcoming these guests was to give them a turn in the dance. This was another job of the dance master, who would announce, "This is the turn of Amberkab," for example, whereupon the men from Amberkab could join the circle and participate in the *kaff* dance. The order of turns for different groups was determined by lot; the dance master collected four head caps, one each from a person of Amberkab, Dabout, Dahmit, and the fourth from a member of the host tribe of the *mawlid*. Mixing the caps together in his lap, he selected one by chance for each turn.

At noon the part of the *mawlid* called the *keswa* procession was held. The procession may have been modeled on the traditional Egyptian *keswa* procession. Here the *keswa* was a cloth cover for the coffin of the sheikh. In times past, the Cairo Association of the tribe would annually send a new *keswa* for the *mawlid*, but after plans were announced to resettle the Nubians, the Association had ceased the practice. Traditionally, one special *keswa* was always kept for use during the *mawlid* ceremonies, while another covered the simulated coffin during the year. The symbolism of the *keswa* was closely related to the shrine as a symbol of the sheikh and coffins were usually covered by a *keswa* symbolic of the dress the *sheikh* had worn during his life. When a holy man is alive, his *jalabeya* is said to absorb his *baraka*, and believers in different parts of the Muslim world touch the *jalabeyas* of sheikhs to receive this power. As in other parts of the Islamic culture area, the people of Dahmit had extended the power associated with living sheikhs to the coffin that symbolized the body and to the *keswa* that symbolized his holy *jalabeya*. The people of Dahmit said: "The *keswa* contains the *baraka* of the sheikh."

The *keswa* procession began with a group going to the house near the shrine where the special *mawlid keswa* was kept. When the covering had been purified with incense it was carried on the shoulders of the men, who paraded around most of the houses in the village chanting the praises of the Prophet Muhammad. Gunshots and cries of joy by the women accompanied this ceremony. As they returned to the shrine, the *naqība* met the procession and joined the singing. The men then marched around the wooden frame that represented the sheikh's burial place, and the new *keswa* was put over the worn one that had covered the frame for the previous year.

Not all sheikhs had a *keswa*, and not all *mawlids* had a *keswa* procession. In Dahmit at the time of the study only three sheikhs had *keswa* processions and the *keswa* procession of Hassan and Hussein was a matter of great pride for the Mehannabs. The Gerbabs had a procession but not with a *keswa*, parading from one village to the other holding their walking sticks upwards. The Fagarabs had a *keswa* for their tribal sheikh, but since the shrine had been inundated in 1933, on the day of the *mawlid* their *keswa* was posted on four poles and participants of the *mawlid* visited it.

During *mawlids* some men visited the interior of the shrine where they touched the *keswa* and walked around it, leaving some *ghalla* as well as a piaster or two on the *keswa* or on the shrine itself. The visiting and donations to the sheikh at this time are called *ziāra*, like the visits and donations at other times.

At about four in the afternoon of the *mawlid* the dance master ended the dancing with the phrase, *"daima, kol sana daima,"* after which a ceremonial meal was offered. A procession of women carrying bowls full of *fatta* approached the place where the men were sitting in rows. There they were met by young male members of the tribe, who took the food and distributed it to the men, each bowl being shared by a group of three or four persons. Following the *fatta*, meat was distributed, with each person receiving his share in his hands. While the men ate the women sang:

Lead Singer	Chorus
Al-loun, ya loun, louna, ya di louna	
(O color, O color, color, O this color!)	
awal badina badina!	*iyo!*
(Now we are going to start!)	(Go on!)
'al al-nabī sallina!	*iyo!*
(Pray on the Prophet!)	(Go on!)
ya Gamal ya Nasser!	*iyo!*
(Oh Gamal Abdel Nasser!)	(Go on!)
Abdel Hakim ya Amer!	*iyo!*
(Abdel Hakim Amer!)	(Go on!)
ya rigal al-thawra!	*iyo!*
(Oh men of the revolution!)	(Go on!)
Essi kannanga al-louna!	*iyo!*
(The color of the water is green!)	(Go on!)
Essi jamil al-louna!	
(The color of the water is beautiful!)	

Following their day-to-day pattern of eating, the women had their meal after the men, when what remained in the men's dishes was collected and given to them.

Washing the Keswa

In most *mawlids* of Dahmit, after the *fatta* was offered, the ceremony was regarded as ended, and people began to leave. In the *mawlid* of Hassan and Hussein, however, the ceremony was continued after the *fatta* meal, and the departure of the guests. Members of the Mehannab tribe made another procession, called "washing the *keswa*," in which the new *keswa* was carried on sticks by some of the young men of the tribe and young girls and boys joined processions of men. Singing the *madīh*, the procession moved towards a particular spot on the shore of the river where annually the *keswa* was washed. To reach this spot they had to pass through two villages and as they passed each house, the owners came out to offer them dates or lupines. These gifts were put into a basket carried by the daughter of one of the needy women of the tribe. At the river the *keswa* was washed. People splashed their faces with the drops shaken from it and women filled their tins,[16] for the Nile water in the vicinity of the *keswa* was believed to have special *baraka*. Most sheikhs were believed to possess *baraka* for ensuring the fertility of women and one of the reasons that women touched the *keswa* was to ensure having children. Since washing the *keswa* in the Nile also insured the fertility of the agricultural land, there was often disagreement among members of the tribe as to exactly where the *keswa* should be washed, each member wanting it next to his land. Such conflicts had been resolved in the Fagarab tribe by choosing a central place for the washing of the *keswa*.

After the ceremony of washing the *keswa*, the procession of the Mehannab tribe returned to the village of the *mawlid*, passed by it, and continued to a nearby village where other members of the tribe lived. They received offerings from each of the houses, and finally returned the special *keswa* to a house chosen because it was near the shrine, where it would be kept until the following year. In the final phase of the Mehannab *mawlid* all members of the tribe gathered at this house to sing and dance. Here they were offered a special *fatta* of milk[17] and tea by the owner of the house, and this ended the celebration, at a very late hour of the night.

Because the *keswa* was said to have the *baraka* of the sheikh, people continued to bathe in the Nile nearby for several days after the *mawlid* in order to acquire its special blessing. After several months the old worn *keswa* was cut into small pieces, which were placed in the children's ears to protect them from the Evil Eye.

After the Mawlid

Two or three days after a sheikh's *mawlid* the *naqīb* and the representatives of the tribe held a meeting to discuss the expenses of the celebration. Each head of a lineage paid for all the families of the lineage, including those in the city. Payment ranged from one piaster to two piasters for each male, regardless of age. Each representative of a lineage deposited the sum he had collected, e.g., the sugar from the *nadr* vows, and the price received for the animal skins. What remained after the expenses of the *mawlid* were covered was kept by the treasurer of the tribe to help defray the expenses of the *mawlid* for the coming year or for other purposes such as entertaining government officials or other visitors.

Children's Mawlids

The month of the *mawlids* was an exciting time for the children of Dahmit; afterwards they were often stimulated to organize similar celebrations of their own. Usually the idea of having such a *mawlid* began with a group of children who had built a shrine or who had decided to keep up the tradition of celebrating a *mawlid* started by a relative from their group who had since grown up and gone to the city. There was apparently no pattern in the choice of a particular sheikh by children. They might select the sheikh of the tribe, a dead relative, or another sheikh they had only heard about.

Usually a children's shrine was constructed by more than one child and the *mawlids* were supported and financed by a group of them with the help of their mothers, who supplied them with dates, bread, and tea. Guests at the children's *mawlids* were usually the girls and boys of the local school rather than children of a particular tribe or village, and all were between four and twelve years of age.

Children usually celebrated their *mawlid* on a Friday, their weekend, and the whole celebration did not take more than two or three hours. It might be celebrated in the morning or afternoon, and the actual number of children participating in such a *mawlid* generally did not exceed twenty-five.

They sang the same songs as the adults and they danced the *kaff* dance beside the small shrine just as the adults did. They did not use the *noggar* but borrowed a *tar* or two from their mothers to keep the rhythm. Usually in these children's *mawlids* girls did not enter the *kaff* circle but sat in a nearby place singing and beating the *tars*. On hearing the singing, adult women of the village came to the place of the small shrine to observe and encourage the children.

When the children tired of singing and dancing they would eat whatever they had collected for the *mawlid*, sometimes one date for each child or perhaps two or three oranges to divide among all of them. Frequently, an adult woman in the *naja'* would offer the children some *asīda* (bread soaked in milk and butter) or rice cooked with milk. Such a donation was often given when the children celebrated a *mawlid* for a sheikh's shrine that had been built by a woman's sons who had grown up and migrated to work in the city. Children were thus encouraged to continue *mawlid* celebrations for sheikh shrines built by other children.

Sometimes after a child had built a shrine with the assistance of his mother or female relatives, he celebrated a *mawlid* for it immediately after finishing building. In such a case the adult female who helped him usually supplied the *mawlid* with sweets, tea, *sharbat*, or cooked rice.

Extent of Social Participation in the Mawlid

To a large extent, the success of a tribal *mawlid* was judged by the number of participants. The more people there were, the higher the prestige of the tribe. However, for various reasons everyone in the vicinity could not attend. All of the seventy women of the interview sample were asked about the reasons they may have had for not attending any of the five *mawlids* held in the district of Dahmit during the year 1963. The frequencies of the reasons given are shown in Table X. Being newly married, the major reason for not attending, was due to a taboo; these women were not permitted to go outside their village until after giving birth to a child or at least until one year after marriage. Distance also played a very important role in determining women's attendance at a *mawlid*. Sometimes the celebration might be held in a *naja'* several miles away, entailing a walk or donkey-ride over barren or rocky areas of the Nubian desert. The third reason is closely related to distance since a weak or sick person could not travel to a distant place, though when *mawlids* were at nearby villages, informants stated, they often attended despite illnesses. In some cases, finally, husbands simply forbade their wives to go to distant places.

TABLE X
Reasons Given for not Attending Mawlids

Reason	Frequency
1. Newly married	218
2. Distance	102
3. Health Condition	55
4. Death in the Family	43
5. Husband forbids	10

Conclusion

Sheikh veneration was certainly not unique to the community of Dahmit, but is an important part of religious practice and belief among the masses in all Muslim countries. There is great similarity in beliefs between the sheikh cult in Dahmit Nubia and those in other parts of the Muslim world. The veneration of the shrines and the concepts of *baraka, karāma, nadr, ziāra*, and *mawlid* are all common throughout the Middle East, and studies of the belief in sheikhs in different countries of the Muslim world have been made by a number of investigators. Trimingham's *Islam in the Sudan* (1965), for example, includes the Nubians among other groups in the Sudan, and Westermarck (1926) dealt with saint cults in Morocco, while both Blackman (1927) and McPherson (1940) described the phenomenon in Egypt. These investigators were usually concerned with describing the nature of the sheikhs themselves, the avenues or paths that lead to sheikhship, the sacred hierarchy or *ṭabaqāt* of sheikhs, the *baraka* they were thought to possess, and the miracles associated with them. They tended to emphasize the religious aspects and origins of the sheikh cult, relating sheikhs to various religious orders, such as the Mirghanniga or the Senusia, or to primitive paganism. The cults described in this literature therefore seem quite different from those in Dahmit where the status of a sheikh was clearly determined by the activities of those responsible for him and by his social significance to them as a center of those activities, irrespective of any real-life exploits that might have given rise to his veneration after death.

From a theological or historical point of view these approaches may be justified, but from an anthropological point of view they seem incomplete, since these investigators generally do not attempt to show the relationship of a cult to the social structure of its community, even though according to Radcliffe-Brown, "Religion must also vary in correspondence with the manner in which the society is constituted" (1952, p. 181). The differences in points of view represented by these other studies of sheikh worship as well as their lack of relevant social data make it impossible to compare them systematically with the analysis made here.

Some Functional and Dysfunctional Aspects of the Sheikh Cult in Dahmit

Malinowski speaks of function in terms of "needs" of the individual, and "needs" of the society and culture, while to Radcliffe-Brown the function of any recurrent activity is the "part it plays in the social life as a whole and therefore the contribution it makes to the maintenance of the structural continuity" (Ibid, p. 161). The concept of function, as I have dealt with it earlier in my discussion of the sheiks' hierarchy, includes both these notions as well as the idea of the interdependence of social institutions.

We may now ask: How does the sheikh cult satisfy individual and societal needs? In what way does it contribute to the maintenance of continuity of Dahmit social structures? What other relationships are there between the cult and other social institutions? To begin to answer these questions it is useful to distinguish among the various societal levels and units, for what is functional at a certain level may be disfunctional at another. For purposes of this analysis I am mostly concerned with the four main social units in Dahmit; tribe, district, village and the individual. What is functional on the tribal level sometimes appears disfunctional for the *nahia, naja'*, or individual.

One of the problems of concern to functional analysis is the problem of social integration, i.e., what Radcliffe-Brown calls functional unity. "It is a condition in which all parts of the social system work together with a sufficient degree of harmony or internal consistency." (Ibid, p. 181). Dahmit was a community exposed to potentially radical social change, due to the economic effects of the flooding of the land by the Aswan dams and the consequent labor migration. Thus the problem of social integration was acute there for many years before the complete removal to Kom Ombo.

The Cult and the Integration of the Tribe

One of the main characteristics of the Dahmit sheikh cult is that tribes tended to have sheikhs who were of more concern to tribal members than to any other people or group. Members of the tribe shared the belief in the *baraka* and *karāmas* of one particular sheikh and a sense of possession of these traditions, as well as of the shrine itself. The *mawlid*, aside from its many other functions, had the effect of uniting the tribe and of maintaining its solidarity. The records of *mawlid* attendance are good indices of the socially integrational importance of this ceremony at different social levels In any *mawlid* the tribe giving the *mawlid* composed the largest percentag of the participants and the tribal *mawlid* was the occasion where the largest concentration of members gathered at any specified place and time. This brought members of the tribe from the city and the village together, at a special time for reaffirmation of tribal solidarity. All members also indicated loyalty by contributing to the expenses of the *mawlid*, members in the village giving money and bread for themselves as well as in the names of those of their relatives in the city who could not attend. Members in the city actively participated as a group by sending the *keswa* and the *beyrag* every year, as well as by making gifts to individual relatives to defray expenses.

Members of the tribe in the city frequently sent *nadr* to be fulfilled on the day of the *mawlid*, and those leaving the village to return to the city after the *mawlid* usually took some bread of the *mawlid* to distribute among those in the city, in order that they too might partake of the *baraka*. Before and after the *mawlid* there was a flow of individual and tribal letters between members of the tribe in the city and those in the village. General plans such as setting a day for the *mawlid* or postponing it had to be discussed on the tribal level. On the individual level of communication the *mawlid* was a suitable occasion for a migrant in the city to send money and clothes to his family in the village. Thus, it is clear that the cult rituals had great integrative functions for the persistence of tribal unity under conditions of dispersion.

Minority tribes could not support a tribal ceremony for their tribal sheikh, so they usually affiliated themselves to another tribe which could do so, apparently a step in the process of incorporating one tribe into another, a process that historically seems to have gone on continuously in Nubia. In these cases the cult might be viewed or disfunctional for the annexed tribe, since it gradually loses its identity. In another sense, however, this incorporation process could be considered functional for the smaller group, since without sufficient numbers and without ceremonies, the symbolic social functions and economic support necessary to tribal unity were difficult, and the psychological and spiritual satisfactions which the cult afforded its group would be lacking.

The Cult and the Integration of the Village

These integrating functions of the cult for the tribe are closely related to those for the village, since in many cases tribes tend to concentrate geographically in particular *naja's*. If the total population of a certain village belonged to a single tribe with its tribal sheikh, there would be no problem of integration, since the *naja'* would tend to be a homogeneous and cohesive group. But this ideal situation actually did not exist in any village of Dahmit.

There were always individuals from other tribes, usually females, moving to live permanently in other villages as a consequence of marriage, and they were not easily incorporated into the cult of the other tribe, because allegiance to a particular sheikh usually followed a patrilineal line, and an individual was considered to be a member of the cult of his own tribal sheikh from the day of his birth. Therefore all male members of a particular tribe, irrespective of their age, were obliged to share the expenses of the *mawlid*. Females were exempted from financial obligation on their own behalf, but adult members of the family present in the village, males or females, paid for their male dependents as well as for male relatives living in the city. Thus, a mother who had married in from another tribe would have had to contribute the bread and money of her children and absent husband, who belonged to another tribal sheikh than she, though at the same time, being a female, she did not have to pay obligatory allegiance to her own tribal sheikh. The fact that she kept her belief in her own tribal sheikh meanwhile meant, however, that she could not generally accept the superiority of her husband's tribal sheikh. Such a situation again shows how the cult had integrative powers at the tribal level but that it might not be integrative for the individual woman or for the village, since the conflict of structural elements created divided loyalties among the inhabitants of each village.

One possible means of resolving such conflicts for the individual was through *nadr* making. If a woman was interested in showing her belief in her husband's tribal sheikh, she might make a *nadr* to him. There were also many women who partially resolved this difficulty by contributing for their children in both *mawlids*, i.e., through double expenditure. To the degree, then, that the cult was integrated on the level of the tribe and lineage, it was disintegrative at the village level.

The Cult and the Integration of the District (*Nahia* or *'Omodiyya*)

The *mawlid*, or ceremonial aspect of the cult, contributed to bringing the people of the total *'omodiyya* together. Though the Nile acted as a barrier and relatively few people crossed from one side to the other during a year, yet, if it were not for the *mawlid* this minimum of interaction between the east and the west would not have taken place at all. The patterns of attendance I recorded are evidence of the strong integrative pull of the tribal *mawlid* for the entire *'omodiyya* (see Messiri 1965).

Though the *mawlid* had one kind of integrative function on the level of the district, however, in terms of bringing diverse people together in interaction, in a more profound sense it appears to have been dysfunctional. In Dahmit, tribal affiliation was the strongest mechanism of social grouping, and it split the administrative *nahia* into several "real" communities based on kinship. For example, in comparison with the leaders of the different tribes, the *'omda* of Dahmit, a government appointed official of the district, was relatively powerless to enforce his will upon the tribes, and the cult, with its emphasis on tribal sheikhs, helped powerfully to strengthen this tribal feeling. To the degree to which the tribe was strong the *'omodiyya* was weak, in spite of the national government's attempts to strengthen it as the administrative unit.

Economic Functions

The economic functions of the cult were of great importance. For example, the *nadr*, besides relieving anxiety and helping the people of Dahmit to cope with their isolation, had its economic value. In many cases the *nadr* is a form of charity to the *naqība*, providing some support for some aged members of the tribe, while an animal *nadr*, given by those who could afford it on the day of the mawlid, increased the quantity of meat offered to the guests, and thus served as a minor mechanism for the redistribution of scarce economic resources.

The *mawlid* was one of the few occasions where members of the community had a chance to eat meat. A guest may have come late to the ceremony, but he seldom would leave before the meal was offered and one of the reasons given for serving the food at the end of the *mawlid* was that it helped to keep the party lively to the last minute. But meat had more importance as a symbol of the influence and status of the tribe and other *nadr* givers than as food. It was a special and costly dish usually eaten on special occasions, not at an everyday meal, and its presentation in the *mawlid* thus symbolized the value of hospitality and the importance of the occasion. Indeed though many other relatively expensive dishes were prized by the Dahmit Nubians, whenever there was a special occasion such as a *mawlid* or a wedding, it was always meat that was offered, since it traditionally best indicated the generosity of the giver as well as his affluence.

The *mawlid* also provided a market place for small goods, a service rendered for individuals of the community whether they were consumers or producers. Merchants gained financially by travelling from *mawlid* to *mawlid* and selling their goods, while participants in the *mawlid* had a chance to buy things not readily available under ordinary circumstances.

A final economic function which should be stressed again in the *mawlid*'s role in channeling resources back to the community from the city. Not only were people drawn back with gifts and necessities for their relatives, but the ceremony was a tangible symbol of continuing economic obligations.

Psychological Functions

The *mawlid*, the most important joint ritual of the Dahmit sheikh cult, was characterized by singing, dancing, and a generally joyful atmosphere that seems to have been characteristic of the gaiety of the people of Dahmit. It also served the status function of giving women a chance to exhibit their gold jewelry, which symbolized their wealth and relative social positions.

The dancing and singing on the day of the *mawlid* were a great diversion from the people's ordinary routines of life and were therefore eagerly awaited. They also seemed to serve as an opportunity for relieving or expressing tensions and desires. Most of the songs of the *mawlid* were love songs. The dancing women exposed the beauty of their figures and the grace of their movements to the eyes of men returned from cities; the dancing men showed with their faces and their energetic jumping and clapping their interest in the women dancers. This erotic aspect of the cult seems to have been closely related to the conditions of life in this Nubian community: the separation of the sexes in daily activities and the great sex imbalance due to labor migration lent the excitement of frustration to the other motivations of the *mawlid* festivities.

Notes

1. According to hadīth, marriage "completes" one's religion.
2. The Nubians of the area use the term *ghalla* to mean grains of wheat or maize. It is an Arabic term for all grains collectively.
3. In Dahmit twins were deemed to have certain magical characteristics and though they were not feared, they received special treatment. At night one of the twins' souls could turn into a cat and roam around the *naja'* looking for cooked food. Therefore cats were never supposed to be mistreated, for whatever was done to a cat which had the soul of one of the twins would show on the twins' bodies in the morning. The Kenzi term for twins is *barassi*. Several sheikhs of Dahmit are twin sheikhs and there is a tribal sheikh named *Barassi*, whose shrine is said to embody seventy-seven sheikhs. There is also the family twin sheikh shrine of 'Amr and Omran.
4. The Arab tribe is composed of a group of Ababda Arabs who settled in Dahmit some time in the not too distant past. In terms of tribal structure and various cultural elements they were different from other tribes of Dahmit and con-

stituted the majority of the population of the *naja'* al-Bogaa Gibli. They identified themselves more with the Arabs of Atmur, Khatara, and Daraw than with the Kenuz Nubians, but they participated in the ritual and economic aspects of the cult of Dahmit.

5. The discussion here applies to either one nuclear family or to a group of consanguinally related nuclear families.

6. The writer was able to gather information about only four family sheikhs, though there were many others.

7. In the *mawlids* of neighboring Dabout this host role was more institutionalized. There the hosts are called the *amīrs* or "princes" of the *mawlid*.

8. An Arabic term meaning, "Give me something for the sake of God."

9. A Turco-Persian formula meaning "with your permission."

10. In addition to its beautifying functions, henna is used for many other occasions. The henna tree is one of the trees of paradise and the use of henna is supposed to ensure happiness.

11. Three women of the sample were unmarried.

12. One of my informants owns a family book which contains the life history of Sitt 'Aisha and her *mawlid*.

13. Although McPherson assumes that some of the Egyptain *mawlids* retain certain practices which have come down from Pharaonic times, he points out that the *mawlids* in their modern form date from the death of Sayed al-Badawi in the seventh century of the Hijra (Thirteenth century of the Christian era). He also gives the dates of the hundred mawlids in Egypt that follow the Islamic calendar. Thirty-nine of these occur in Sha'ban and twenty-one of the thirty-nine occur on the fourteenth Sha'ban.

14. An Arabic phrase meaning "May we always have this feast annually."

15. This song was recorded in 1963. According to a Nubian informant the introductory phrase has no significance.

16. In recent years the usual water-carrying container in Nubia has become the five-gallon gasoline tin.

17. Bread cooked in milk.

Chapter 5

The Angels in The Nile: A Theme in Nubian Ritual

FADWA al-GUINDI

Of all the areas on the long course of the Nile of the barren and rocky land of Nubia was probably the most desolate. Nineteenth-century European travelers rarely failed to mention the change of landscape they encountered south of the first cataract at Aswan or to comment upon the smallness of the fields irrigated by the numerous cattle-driven water wheels. They frequently described the pressing closeness of the harsh, if beautiful, desert upon the narrow strip of palm trees and grain. Even more than most other peoples along its banks, the Nubians were forced into an intimate relationship with the all-important Nile, the source of their life sustenance. With such close dependence upon the river, it is not surprising that they evolved close spiritual relations with it.

Allusions to the Nile spirits are made in the chapters on the Saint cults and the *mushahara* concept. The following two chapters describe the two major classes of supernatural beings in the Nile: the beneficent "water angels," and the dangerous and ugly "water monsters." It is logical that in this work the major contributors to our understanding of these beings are women, since it is among Nubian women that beliefs in them are most clearly conceived and strongly held. As women, both Fadwa al-Guindi and Armgard Grauer were involved in the actions and concerns of their informants with the river beings throughout their separate sojourns in the district of Dahmit. Grauer also gathered stories and materials on the river beings from other districts of Nubia, particularly Tushka, a Fadija *'omodiyya* with a large enclave of Kenuz.

The river Nile played an important role in the life of the Nubian people and it is no overstatement to say that without the Nile sedentary life in the region would be impossible. The cultivatable land itself was almost entirely composed of silt brought down by the Nile during thousands of years. There is almost no rain; crops depended entirely upon irrigation by Nile water. This remote region lacked any ordinary means of long-distance surface transportation, making the river the only means of human transport, commerce, and communication.

The Nile had other uses which are both obvious and important. Since the people had no other access to water, the river was the only source of water for drinking, washing, bathing, and fishing. It was the center of many daily activities and of the communication exchange which accompanies them. While the women filled their tin cans with water they were also transmitting all the daily news. It would be difficult to overstress the importance of the Nile to the people of Nubia.

Our research among the Kenuz of the district of Dahmit,[1] Nubia, shows that within the religious belief system there existed a subset of beliefs and rituals focussing on a community of supernatural beings existing in the river Nile and associated with goodness and benevolence only. These beings were called *malayket-al-bahr*[2] (river angels).

The significance of this river-related subset is twofold. First, it embodied an integral set of relations within the Nubian belief system as a whole. It was, therefore, an important complement to other areas of religion covered in this volume, though for analytic purposes it is separated here from the total religious experience. Second, although beliefs associated with *malayket-al-bahr* have been shared by the Kenuz people in general, they were mainly related to the women's domain of ritual experience. It should be repeated that the female population in Dahmit was significantly larger than the male population by a ratio of three to one. Understanding the religious experience of Kenuz women, then, is indeed central to the understanding of the society of Dahmit and in the degree to which these beliefs were universal in the area, they are also critical for the comprehension of Nubian culture.

Malayket-al-Bahr

These river beings were largely anthropomorphous. Such human characteristics as sex, age, and offspring were ascribed to them and, in some cases, their kinship was known and recounted. Their tangible human characteristics were human interests, emotions, culinary tastes, moods, and languages (both Arabic and Nubian), as well as individual names. They lived in underwater castles in the river.

According to native statements *malayket-al-bahr* were both males and females,[3] and were sometimes visible. The females were called the *banāt-al-Sālehīn* (daughters of the virtuous or pious) and appeared naked, with long straight hair, vertical eyes and eyebrows, and very long breasts thrown crosswise over their shoulders. The males were called *welād-al-ṣālehīn* (sons of the virtuous or pious) and no definite picture of them could be given by informants. *Banāt-al-ṣālehīn* were said to outnumber *welād-al-ṣālehīn* because the river "favored females."

River Practitioners

Some persons dealt with the river beings by acting as their spokesmen while in a state of possession. The person possessed, the male sheikh or female sheikha, had in most cases become so as a result of a supernatural sign consisting of some sort of unusual innate trait or odd experience. A large variety of departures from the commonplace were given this interpretation.

A local man was said to have a wife and children in the river and to go down into the river to visit them and come out again dry, sometimes taking hot bread with him while bringing dates and sugar from below. He was also able to walk on the surface of the water. This man was known as a sheikh; such feats as coming out of the river dry or walking on the surface of the water were cited by informants as indications of his supernatural powers and signs of his superhuman relationship with the river beings. Succession to such positions could be hereditary, and when this sheikh died, his wife became a ritual leader in the community. She then served with equal legitimacy as a link between the human community and the superhuman one of the river beings.

Any seemingly miraculous escape from death might also be taken as a sign of such a relationship. For example, a girl in Dahmit accidentally fell into an oven and came out without having been burned or in any way injured. People predicted that she would be a sheikha. And indeed, when she grew up she became possessed by one of the river beings called Abu Sirwal, a name which remained attached to her even in her old age.

Theoretically, the river beings, males and females, sought incarnation in both men and women; in fact, however, the only two river practitioners living in Dahmit during the period of our research were women. The women of Dahmit were active believers in the existence of river beings. The men although they shared the belief with the women, seldom participated directly in a river-related ritual. A man indicated his belief by sending with a woman relative an article of his clothing or a lock of his hair, or "anything with his smell on it," along with a sum of five piasters[4] for the sheikhas. In this indirect way he would seek the fulfillment of a wish or treatment for an illness.

The Zār

A sheikha in Dahmit usually gave a zār (exorcism ritual) twice a week. Only women, coming from all naja's on both the east and west banks of the river, attended it. The zār was a public ritual performed by the sheikha and attended by twenty to forty women from twelve to fifty years of age. It was held every Thursday and Sunday in the evening "because the Prophet favored these two days."

The seance usually took place in the sheikha's house, with the assistance of women attendants (usually kin) whose duty it was to help the sheikha change her costumes in correspondence with the river creatures that were possessing her in turn. Female relatives also assisted in serving tea to all the attendants, spraying perfume on each woman's head, and passing the incense pot to the women who sat on the ground around the sheikha.

The performance began in silence. The sheikha sat on a quilt laid on the ground with a pot of incense in front of her and sprayed perfume all over her hair, dress and face. Then the incense pot and the perfume bottle were passed around for the women attendants' blessing.

The sheikha then put her hands on her knees, elbows outward, in deep concentration. The first signs of the oncoming trance were deep and extensive yawning, interrupted by moments of silence and followed by her fixed stare; she then twisted her arms and neck in a cramped and unnatural posture. Suddenly she jumped up, greeting the women with "*Salāmu aleykum, ya sittāt!*" ("Peace on you, women!") and while some women beat on a tambourine drum and sang, she also sang, jumping up and down. All her movements were conspicuously violent.

In a state of possession, the sheikha then began to talk in a forced falsetto with the voice and manner of one of the river creatures, according to its sex and age, simulating masculinity when possessed by a male creature called Abu Shousha, or childishness when an infant river angel called Mirghaniyya possessed her.

Malayket-al-bahr were associated with four categories of human preoccupations: fertility, cultivation, marriage, and health. Seeking help in those matters, women contacted the river beings through the sheikha who prescribed a procedure, ritual, or charm to avoid or to ensure particular happenings. Orders were given to the sheikha throughout her trance, expressing the likes and dislikes of the river creatures possessing her in turn, and the conditions they set to solve the various problems brought to them.

The possessed sheikha enjoyed certain healing powers. Whenever consulted by a patient or his family, the sheikha went into a trance and discovered the origin and treatment of the disease. Typical remedies included sacrifices, gifts to the sheikha's river creature, charms, baths, and incense. I observed the sheikha spitting into the eyes of a sick woman to cure her, and ordering the mother of a feeble-minded man to feed her son a wolf's brain so that he might recover. For cases such as divorcée whose husband had returned, a childless woman who had had a first baby, a sick man who had recovered, and others, the sheikha received such gifts as pieces of cloth, veils, chickens, or eggs, in addition to the monetary gifts given her before and during the *zār* ritual.

Private Ritual

Not all the people sought the help of river creatures through the sheikha's susceptibility to possession. Some performed private rituals. These direct attempts to secure supernatural aid sprang from a desire to secure good fortune, to ask for aid, or to avert evil. For example, whenever any Nubian from Dahmit crossed the river he recited the *Fatiḥa* to the river beings.

According to informants, many women "visited" the river beings every morning as they filled their tin cans with water from the river; they threw pieces of candy, lumps of sugar, some perfume, or some henna into the river. One woman cooked food and put it every evening in the *shollag* (a hanging straw or metal food container) for the river beings. Eighteen pots had been placed on top of a hill in a *naja'* at the far south of Dahmit (Naja' al-Khor) to secure the benevolence of river creatures. These pots were always kept full of water and remained untouched except when the water in them decreased. They were then refilled so that the Nile angels could continue to gather there at night to drink and to wash. Another woman went to the river every month before her menstrual period and threw perfume, sugar, and henna to the river creatures. She asked them to help her have her menstruations only two of three days and without cramps so that she should not feel weak.

We have seen that one kind of relationship between the human beings and river angels of Dahmit was that of possession: the belief that a particular spirit inhabits a certain individual, as in the case of sheikha mediums. In other cases the river angel hovered about an individual and influenced his life without ever possessing him. Such individuals might have physical contact with the angel or communicate with it through dreams and visions. In some cases the individual was advised to perform certain rituals. One such case is that of a woman who, while filling water from the river, was pulled off her feet by a male river creature. When she called for help, he asked her to be quiet and invited her down to his castle at the bottom of the river. She was frightened and refused to go with him. A neighbor went to help her up out of the water, but after that incident the river creature always remained in this woman's house, gossiped with her, shared her food, gave her village news, and entertained her.

A single example will suffice to illustrate the prescription of a ritual by Nile angels through dreams or visions. A woman in Naja' Kollodol had had a dream, ten years prior to the study, of river creatures asking her to give them, regularly, a share of her food. After the dream, the woman gave a yearly *karāma*, or sacrificial offering, for the creatures. Each year in the Arabic month of Ragab she slaughtered a goat by the river and cooked it in order to offer a dish of meat and *fatta*. She did not invite people to this *karāma*, but some men, women, and children voluntarily attended it and helped themselves to the meat and *fatta* by the river to secure blessing.

A *karāma* is an individual ritual rather than a regular and culturally institutionalized one. Some wealthy men gave periodical *karāmas* to overcome calamities, to secure their own or their kin's health, or to receive blessing. In cultivation seasons *karāmas* were frequently offered against locust attacks in the agricultural fields. In recent times, such *karāmas* tended to be offered to God rather than to the river angels.

The *nadr* (vow) was a more private ritual, which consisted of an individual's promise that, upon the fulfillment of a wish, certain offerings would be made to the river angels. One woman informant made a *nadr*, offering to slaughter an animal by the river and throw a dish of meat and *fatta* for the river angels every time any of her daughters had a baby, to enable her grandchildren to grow in good health.

Besides *nadr* and *karāma* there was a private ritual specifically associated with *mushāhara* (see Callender and al-Guindi 1971 and chapters 4 and 7 for discussions of this phenomenon). An example of a *mushāhara* ritual took place when people crossed the river to visit a new mother before the *sebu'* of her child. The new mother had to cross the river back and forth in order to avert any evil consequences on the child. A fire was kindled on the river banks, salt was thrown on it, and the mother stepped over it seven times. She then crossed the river in a boat with her child, and while doing so washed its face, hands and feet in the water. Again on the opposite river bank she had to jump seven times over a fire upon which salt had been thrown, and leave a stone by it. These actions shifted the evil of the *mushāhara* to the other side of the river. Then she saild back to her own village.

Life-Cycle Rituals

The river played an important part in most of the life-cycle ceremonies in Dahmit. I will describe here only the river-related features of these rituals (for a description of these ceremonies in their entirety see Callender and al-Guindi 1971).

MARRIAGE AND THE RIVER

On the afternoon of the wedding day the groom traditionally sat on a mat in the middle of the courtyard of the house while his mother or maternal aunt dyed his hands, feet, and forehead with henna. Meanwhile, male and female relatives and friends gave *noquṭ* (reciprocally owed gifts of money which are part of customary ritual obligations). When this was over the groom stood up and ran toward the river raising his sword in front of him. Young men of the village ran after him, attempting to beat him with whips, but they had to stop immediately when he dipped his sword in the river and stooped to wash the henna off his hands, feet, and forehead. Washing in the river helped to ensure the groom's ability to procreate children, since fertility was one of the attributes most persistently associated with the river and its creatures.

DEATH AND THE RIVER

In Dahmit a death ritual related to the river took place on two different days, once at noon the day of death, and once again on *kobar* day, the day on which women visit the cemetery after a death; the custom was to visit after three or five days in the case of a deceased female and after four or six days in the case of a deceased male.

On both days women in old Dahmit purposely went to the river together and washed their faces. This was said to "cool the body of the deceased." After washing they sat for a few minutes by the river, leaving their faces wet. This allowed the corpse to relax in its grave. Then each woman returned to her house.

BIRTH AND THE RIVER

During pregnancy, and when birth seemed imminent, the woman made a dish of *asīda* (bread cooked in milk) and took it to the river where she threw it to the river creatures so that they would ensure her an easy and successful delivery. After the birth of a boy (whose parents were both alive) the mother carried a knife and walked to the river followed by the midwife or a female relative who carried one of the two big stones on which the woman sat when giving birth, the sand on which the blood of delivery had dropped, seven dates, and the afterbirth. On reaching the river, the woman threw all these things in it. Long ago, I was told, the birth cord was thrown into the river with the afterbirth, but when I was in Dahmit, it was saved as a charm for the child.

In Dahmit the *sebu'* ceremony for the baby took place three, five, or seven days after birth. Every day until the *sebu'* anything that was used for the mother or the baby was kept aside in a big dish to the right of the mother, including food given to the mother, perfume, henna, kohl used for the baby's eyes, the string used in knotting the baby's navel, and a cup of water and sugar from which the baby drank.

For the *sebu'* celebration the mother carried her baby and, after crossing seven times over a fire outside the room sprinkled with salt, went with the midwife and some little girls to the river. They took with them all the items mentioned earlier, as well as seven dishes of food. If the baby was a boy, an animal was slaughtered for the occasion and there was *fatta* of meat and bread. For a baby girl they took *belīla* (corn or wheat cooked in milk). Less well-to-do households carried only one dish of *asīda* to the river. However, seven lumps of food were always thrown into the water — either seven lumps from one dish or one lump from each of seven dishes. At times seven lumps from each of the seven dishes were thrown into the river, and the women and children ate what remained. They also threw into the river seven drops of perfume, seven drops of henna, and seven drops of kohl. After applying some of each to the baby, a piece of onion was used with the kohl to widen the baby's eyes. After they had eaten they filled the seven dishes with river water, which was then taken back to the house and sprayed all over the room where the child slept, so that the *malayket-al-bahr* might bless and keep him company.

The river angels normally remained in the house of birth for forty days, until the ceremony marking the end of the mother's confinement took place. (In one instance the fortieth day would have fallen just after the *'id al-kibir* and rite was therefore observed four days earlier, so that the river angels could spend this important holiday at home in the river). On the fortieth day the mother went to the river with the baby, carrying a dish of bread and milk. The remainders of the henna, kohl and perfume, seven drops of each of which had previously been thrown into the river during the *sebu'*, were poured into the river at that time. Seven lumps of bread and milk were also thrown into the water, after which the women and children ate from the dish. Then the mother washed the baby's face, hands and legs in the river and filled five gallon tins with water so that she could have her *arba'in* (forty-day) bath at home, a ritual which involved pouring forty-tins of water over herself.

The water used in that ritual and the food prepared for *malayket-al-bahr* were thought to be blessed. On occasion I was invited to drink from the water and eat from the *fatta* prepared for the river so that I might be blessed with *baraka*.

CIRCUMCISION AND THE RIVER

A boy of approximately seven years or less was dressed as a bridegroom for a circumcision rite. People arrived in the afternoon, an animal was slaughtered, and the boy sat covered with henna while people offered *noqūt*. Then the boy went to bathe in the river. The barber stood in front of him and, as the people gathered by the river, he operated. A two piaster coin was fastened to the foreskin and thrown with it into the river for the angels.

Annual Cycle Rites

As in the case of private ritual and life-cycle ritual in Dahmit, the annual Islamic ceremonial cycle also showed a theme of river-related activities. Two examples are given here.

'ASHŪRA AND THE RIVER

'Ashūra is an Islamic rite held on the tenth day of the Arabic month of Muharram in memory of the martyrdom of the Prophet's grandchildren. Women and children in Dahmit burned ropes after dark and ran to the river. There each put together some stones symbolic of his or her household, the number being equal to the number of family members, to provide them with the river angels' blessing. They also took along dishes of food from which seven pieces were thrown to the river beings. Later they all undressed and swam in the river for blessing.

THE MAWLID AND THE RIVER

The mawlid is an Islamic ceremony on a sheikh's birthday (see chapter 4). On the mawlid of Hassan and Hussein two grandchildren of the Prophet Muhammad, the keswa (cloth cover for the shrine in a sheikh's tomb) was carried in procession to the river. The men dived with it into the river and then the women squeezed water from the cloth for everyone to drink for blessing.

Conclusion

Clearly, just as the river was of focal importance to the Nubian people, the river angels were a central theme in their beliefs and rituals. It is not an unusual phenomenon that such creatures were believed to exist in a river as significant to a people as the Nile was to the Nubians, and this coincides with previous observations made by Tylor (1958) who gave examples of a similar spiritual significance of rivers for American Indians as well as for Africans (Ibid, p. 297). Many examples from all over the world illustrate the same kind of recognition of the river-man relationship. The annals of Egyptologists are, in fact, full of such examples, and many of the practices and beliefs described here may well have their origin in the Egyptian dynastic past. The intent of this chapter, however, has been neither to seek out such "origin" relationships nor to demonstrate a "functional" relationship between the Nile and the Nubians' religion, but to present an ethnographic account of the Nubian subset of river-related beliefs and rituals.

Notes

1. Research relevant to this chapter was conducted in Dahmit from October 1962 through May 1963 and in Cairo with Kenuz migrants between September 1963 and December 1963. This chapter, prepared especially for this volume, is a revised version of an earlier paper presented at the "Symposium of the Social Research Center" of the American University in Cairo (cf. al-Guindi 1966, pp. 239–256).
2. In my earlier paper (1966), these angels were presented as interchangeably labeled sheikhs (spiritual leaders), nās-al-bahr (river people), banāt (or welad)-as-ṣālehīn (daughters, or sons, of the righteous) by native informants. It seems to me that this interchangeability in the labeling of categories by my informants is an indication that these categories share an important set of features and thus form a general class of river creatures with malayket-al-bahr as one subclass, as opposed to the dogīr (monster) (cf. Kennedy 1970 and Grauer and Kennedy in this volume).
3. Women attendants compete in guessing the name of each "being" when the sheikha is still at the early stages of possession. They seem to be familiar with each being's individual characteristics and are able to identify them as they "arrive."
4. I would like to refer the reader to my 1966 paper for a theoretical position which I no longer hold. For my present theoretical position see al-Guindi 1973a and and 1975b.

Chapter 6

The Dogri: Evil beings of the Nile[1]

ARMGARD GRAUER AND JOHN G. KENNEDY

It is to be expected that, in addition to its association with notions of good-ness and happiness, the Nile should evoke emotions of fear and awe. It gives life and creates a green barrier against the arid specter of desert sand and rock, but it is also mysterious. Its source is distant and unknown. At certain places rocks and whirlpools are treacherous to boats and it is dangerous everywhere for swimmers. Some years it is high, flooding the crops, and in others it is low, making it difficult to grow needed food. It therefore is not surprising that in addition to beneficent angels, evil and fearful spirits are also associated with the Nile. In Nubia these are called the *dogri* (singular *dogīr*) and the same word is used in all the Nile Nubian dialects.[1]

Though the principal and basic meaning of the term *dogri* seems to refer to ugly water beings with specific characteristics, in some of the earlier writings a number of related meanings are used in translating it. In the writings of Reinisch, Schäfer, Junker and v. Massenbach, for example, the terms for "sorcerer" and "witch" are often used (*zauberer* and *hexe*). Murray's English-Nubian dictionary (1923) and Armbruster's *Dongolese Nubian Lexicon* (1965) also translate it this way. Samuel, the Western-educated Nubian from Abu Hor, used several terms to translate dogir — the German *zauberer* (Shäfer 1917, p. 190), the Arabic *sāher* (sorcerer) and the Nubian word for "hyena" (see v. Massenbach 1933, p. 157) — while Massenbach also uses the German equivalents for "cannibal," "man-eater," "ghost," "monster," and water spirit." These terms are each appropriate in one context or another. An adjectival form is *dogiren*, while the word *dog-rekka* ("she is a *dogīr*") refers to women who have special relationships with *dogri*. Like the sheikhas who commune with Nile angels, such women can divine and give advice. They may be under the spell of a *dogīr* and be given the *dogīr*'s power to "smell the smell" (i.e., to diagnose or predict), but they are not possessed by them.

Since a major characterisitic of the *dogri* is their capacity to metamorphose, it is difficult to obtain exact descriptions of them. The feature most often

114

singled out as revealing their identity, however, is the long vertical shape of their eyes, as exemplified in a story collected by Grauer in the Kenuz enclave of the Fadija district of Tushka West, the essence of which is as follows:

Once a man had a frog that he kept in a box, and he made it a condition that anyone who wished to marry his daughter had to guard the frog and not let it escape, a nearly impossible task, since the frog had some supernatural power. At length, however, a *dogir* down under the Nile became interested in the girl and decided to undertake the task. He prepared everything for a marriage, painted his water castle, put on his shoes, took human shape, went to the girl's father and declared that he would pass the test. He did so and was accepted as an appropriate husband. When the girl was taken to his river home, however, she noticed his elongated eyes, and was no longer deceived. She knew her groom was a *dogir*, especially when it was clear that he went to a graveyard to collect cadavers for his meals. Terrified, she returned to her home.

The mixing of conceptions about *dogri* with those about the Evil Eye is seen in the belief of some women of Dahmit that the monsters have blue eyes. When Grauer first went to Dahmit she was sometimes accused of being *dogiren* because of her blue eyes, as was Massenbach before her (1906, 1940).

Another frequently mentioned characteristic is long black hair on the head and sometimes all over the body (Schäfer 1917, p. 191). In our accounts this black hairiness was said to enable the monsters, who often come out between sunset and sunrise, to merge with the darkness. Sometimes victims reported seeing only the long burning eyes of the monster when it leaped out of the blackness to confront them. Like the Greek Pan, however, they also like to appear at high noon and informants singled out as additional visible traits their long tails, donkey-like legs, and large ears. Aside from all those physical characteristics, the female *dogir* has the distinguishing habit of carrying her breasts thrown crosswise back over her shoulders.

While the most frightening characterological attribute of the *dogri* is their hunger for human flesh, they are also thought to possess many ordinary human desires. They especially crave dates, the most valued food in Old Nubia, and often come out of the river to steal them. They dislike and will shun milk, however, and this aversion sometimes allows potential victims to detect their identities.[2]

The country of the *dogri* beneath the Nile is believed to be very much like that of the Nubians and the activities and requirements of life there are strikingly parallel. They cultivate the soil, for example, and are hard pressed for taxes, one of their principal motivations for attacking human women being to obtain gold jewelry to pay these levies.

One of the main traits of a *dogir* is a proclivity for attacking, frightening, tricking, and generally harming human beings, who may be so terrified that they go mad. One of the usual aims of an attack is to suck the nose of an individual until he dies of suffocation and loss of blood, the creatures thus absorbing the strength of their victims. They are reputed to eat people, especially small children and since they often loiter in waterwheel enclosures and along river banks, they know the villagers' names and can lure them by calling them individually. One of their favorite places after the building of the first Aswan dam and its subsequent raisings was in the tops of plam trees, which in many areas, during much of the year, stood out above the backed-up water.[3] Even more favored are the tamarind and colocynth trees. The fruit of the latter is used to prepare a powerful cathartic and the fruits of both trees are considered to be favorites of the *dogri*, who enjoy throwing them at passersby.

Certain places along the Nile were particularly thought of as homes of the *dogri*. One of the most famous of these in the Kenuz area was the Bab al-Kalabsha, a forbidding section of the river near the *'omodiyya* of Kalabsha, with large rocks and whirlpools that have given rise to numerous tales of smashed and overturned boats. Many of the accidents are attributed to the tricks of the *dogri*. On one occasion when Grauer was passing the Bab al-Kalabsha with some Nubian boatmen, one of them excitedly pointed to a whirlpool in which he had just seen a huge black *dogir*. He claimed it had been attempting to twist the boat and seemed terrified until the group reached safety at Kalabsha, where he found courage to boast about the encounter. The beasts also notably inhabited the *khors* or long inlets of water separating some villages from one another.

Though most of the *dogri* are anonymous, some of them have had individual names and have been known to inhabit particular locations. One of these was Abu Sirwal, who was reputed to live near the Naja' Amai in the district of Daboud. He had a reputation for capturing and marrying the prettiest girls in the district. It is said that when he tired of a girl he sent her back to her village and looked for a new one, the girl being compensated for her experience to some degree by the fact that she could thereafter operate as a sheikha, since she would have been given the power to "smell the smell" (Schäfer 1935, p. 298). The same name for a particular *dogir* was known in other areas, such as Dahmit and Amberkab.[5]

Like blackness, hairiness and cannibalism, the ability to transform themselves into different shapes for various deceptive purposes gives the *dogri* something in common with another Middle Eastern ghostly monster, the *ghūl*, who also appears in many Nubian tales.[6] The *dogri* have been reported to have changed themselves at will into crocodiles, cats, dogs, hyenas, goats, frogs, rocks, trees, plants, or piles of dates. Most dangerous, of course, are their frequent disguises as men. Even if one of them assumes human or animal form, however, it often reveals its identity through the elongation of its eyes.

The *dogīr* tales are told to children with the explicit purpose of frightening them. The Nubians feel that it is generally dangerous to go out at night, especially near the river, and many reports of encounters with the monsters frequently involve nothing more than having seen one. The Fadija prayer leader of the mosque in Kanuba narrated the following experience to Kennedy: Just after sunset he was walking back to his house from the fields when he saw a huge black goat in his path. He knew that no one in the village owned such an animal and when it moved toward him he recognized that it must be a *dogīr*. He quickly recited the Throne Verse (*āyet al-kursi*) from the Qur'ān, and it disappeared, proving to him that his assessment of the situation had been correct.

Another man reported that he had often seen these creatures at evening around the well near the mosque of Kanuba. Sometimes one took the shape of a small boy or a donkey, which disappeared when he approached it. Once, on his way to the mosque he heard footsteps and saw a man walking in step with him a few feet away. When he called out the other person approached him silently. Suddenly realizing that it was a *dogīr*, the man screamed and rushed home.

Among the Nubians most of the kinds of behavior we would generally classify as symptomatic of mental disorders are thought to be caused by spirit beings. The most serious impairments are believed to be due to the jinn, Nile spirits, or dead saints who occupy the body and control the will. Though the *dogīr*, too, is implicated in some mental problems, it does not act through possession. A Fadija medical practitioner from Diwan stated that a kind of emotional problem called *wasswassa* (which seems to refer to what we would call anxiety states or depressions) is caused by a frightful shock of some sort and that generally such frights were attributed to supernatural causes: jinn, *afarīt*, or *dogri*. This doctor recounted the case of a man who foolishly went out after sunset to gather some dates. He climbed a palm near the river. As he was picking the dates, he felt the tree moving strangely and suddenly realized that the tree was actually a *dogīr* who had assumed that shape. Before he could do anything the monster threw him to the ground, breaking his legs. The experience plunged him into *wasswassa*, which in this case took the form of excessive anxiety and a phobia against going outside. Over a period of several months the man's mental state deteriorated until he crossed the line into complete and hopeless insanity.

In a similar story from the village of Kanuba a man was sitting under a palm tree after sunset when a *dogīr* approached him. He screamed with fright and fainted. People came rushing from all directions and found him lying unconscious. The next day the man was nervous, and from then on was always afraid to go out at night, insisting that other people accompany him outside the house even in daytime. He was taken to a number of healing sheikhs and famous *zār* practitioners, but his anxiety worsened until he too degenerated into unreachable insanity.

An interesting feature of some *dogīr* stories is that the monsters are claimed to be members of non-Nubian groups who were bewitched and transformed into supernatural river beings. Some accounts state that the *dogri* are the original inhabitants of Nubia, who were there before the Nubians occupied the region. In one Fadija version a famous Ṣūfī sheikh, who was traveling up the Nile propagating his message to pagan peoples, bewitched an entire tribe after they failed to become members of his "way," forcing them to live in the river, when it was difficult to secure dates and other human amenities that they continued to desire.

In a Fadija tale collected by Kennedy the *dogri* are said to have been a tribe with territory in what is now the Sudan. When the British arrived in the nineteenth century and imposed taxes upon them they rebelled, but did not have gold enough and were not sufficiently strong to resist the oppressors. Being great sorcerers, however, they transformed themselves into river beings, which did not save them, for apparently in addition to becoming ugly and stupid as a punishment for their use of inherently evil magic, they were condemned to suffer constant hunger for human blood and dates, and continued to be plagued by a scarcity of gold in their adopted country under the Nile, where the taxes turned out to be very high.

In a story collected by Massenbach, a particularly cannibal-like group of *dogri* live near the Kenuz *omodiyya* of Kushtemna whose tribal name is Bogobogochi and who are supposed to have appeared also in the Sudan near Dongola. In other accounts the beings are regarded as Nubian tribes that have been bewitched, as is the case with "the people of Abu Tōgo," who are said to reside around the first cataract at Aswan. Stories recount how they experimented with powerful magic, which got out of control and transformed them into water creatures (Massenbach 1931, p. 203). In connection with this notion of the *dogri* as a bewitched Nubian tribe, it may be noted that some human sorcerers are believed to possess controlling power over them, so that one reason given for the appearance of the monsters in the previously resettled community of Kanuba, which is some distance from the Nile, is that they were brought there by magically powerful individuals who use them for evil purposes.

Nubian brides and grooms and other persons in the supernaturally vulnerable state created by life-cycle crises must take special precautions against the dangers of spirit beings. Most precautionary activities concern the angels of the Nile and the jinn, but the dogri may also be involved. A part of the traditional marriage ritual was the confinement of the couple in a special room for forty days, during which they ate special foods, were attended by a servant, and observed various taboos. In many districts of

Nubia, each morning for seven days the groom had to run to the Nile with his sword, dip it in the water, and then ritually wash himself. In one Fadija story:

A groom was ritually washing in the Nile just before sunrise when a hideous *dogīr* rose up out of the water in front of him. The groom was terrified, but he flung his sword, and the blade passed through the body of the monster, forcing it to fall back into the river and disappear. The sword was never found. Some years later the man was traveling far to the South in the Sudan on merchandising business, and in the house of one of his clients he noticed a sword hanging on the wall. On closer examination it appeared similar to the one he had lost during the wedding ritual. Recalling the incident, he realized that it was the identical one, and he feared that his friend was some kind of spirit. Just as he was ready to flee his host explained the situation. He admitted that he was a member of a tribe which had been bewitched long ago when the British came, and described how his people had been condemned to live in the Nile and to suffer perpetual hunger, always hunting human beings or stealing their food. When he had been pierced by the sword, however, the spell had been lifted and he had been enabled to come back to live as a human being again. In a spirit of thankfulness he embraced the merchant.

The following story, which embodies many of the elements we have been discussing, was told to Massenbach by a woman of the Kenuz *'omodiyya* of Amberkab (Massenbach 1931, p. 208). We produce the essence of it here rather than a translation:

Once there was a rich widow who was afraid to die and who promised her only son all her wealth if he would take her to a country where death did not exist. The son set out up the Nile. At each village where he stopped, however, he found a burial ground. Finally he reached the Sudan and after many days discovered a village where there was no cemetery. He asked the people why and was told, "Here no one ever dies." Happy to have made this discovery, he brought his mother to the village, married a native girl, and settled down.

Some time later he had to leave the village on business, and left his mother in the care of his wife. One day, the mother complained of a headache and the daughter-in-law went to her neighbors. "The old woman is sick," she said, "I give her to you as a present. Eat her up before she grows lean. You can pay me for her later." When the son returned and asked for his mother, he was told what had happened. He realized then that he was in the land of the *dogri* but was too frightened to say anything and even accepted his share of the cannibalistic feast that featured his mother.

When the man's wife gave birth to a son, however, he hid the baby in his donkey's feed sack and fled in the night, travelling forty days until they reached another village where they took shelter for the night in a house, as it happened, where there was another newborn baby. That night, while the father was sleeping, his baby son climbed out of the feed sack and devoured the baby of the house. His hunger momentarily appeased, the little cannibal took the other baby's head into the feed sack with him to eat the next day.

As they were travelling through the desert the following morning the father heard strange noises issuing from the sack. Suspecting that mice were stealing the donkey's hay, he opened the sack and found the child nibbling something. "What do you have there?" he asked. When his son replied, "That's a baby's head," the man was horrified and killed the child on the spot, burning the body to be rid of the evil power which the son had inherited from his *dogīr* mother.

As he was raking the ashes some men from the village approached and asked if he had any knowledge of the missing baby. The poor father related the whole story. Since he was not really to blame, the pursuers left him, returning to their village and he continued his trip back to his native Nubian place.

Many stories locate the original land of the *dogri* in the Sudan and it may be that some of the beliefs are a result of the slave trade. Nubia was a corridor for slaves coming from the south and many Nubians were engaged in the traffic. Most of the slaves were *koffār* (sing. *kāfir*, unbeliever) who were thought of as cannibals and were believed to be possessors of powerful magic. It is therefore interesting to note that sometimes, particularly in tales about cannibals, the term *nam-nam* is applied to the river monsters, a term very close to the name "Niam-Niam," one of the names of the Azande, a Sudanese tribe that contributed large numbers of slaves to Egypt and had a reputation for cannibalism (Seligman and Seligman 1932, p. 497).[7] With thousands of slaves passing through the region it is not surprising that many remained there, and though some undoubtedly became Nubianized, many of their descendants still form distinct enclaves among the Nubians.

The notion of the *dogri* as cannibals seems related to ideas that are similar to the widespread conception of the "werewolf," as seen particularly in the stories of their assuming the shapes of hyenas or wild dogs. In these stories, even though the *dogir* may disguise itself as a human, it cannot get rid of its tail, which may often be detected under its clothing. The way a monster signals its intention to devour somebody, for example, is by first pulling out its tail (Massenbach 1962, p. 763).

Massenbach (1962, p. 14) reports an interesting set of events indicating in some degree the social effects of some of the *dogri* beliefs. In the year 1929[8] a whole series of reports of attacks on people by *dogri* were made, not only in Aswan but in the northernmost Kenuz districts of Daboud and Dahmit as well. In the panic that ensued, the blame for these attacks was placed by the Nubians on the large Sudanese population that occupied a quarter in Aswan. The rumors became so strong that the Nubians rioted against the Sudanese, the local police intervened, and investigation was ordered to examine a number of suspected individuals to determine whether or not they had tails concealed under their clothing. Though the negative results of this inquisition put an end to the worst rumours at that time, it did not improve the generally low opinion in which the Nubians hold their southern neighbors.

In connection with the notions of the *dogri* as werewolf-like beings, one belief is that, in addition to killing people for their flesh, they prey on the corpses of the recently deceased, which they dig up in cemeteries. It is interesting to recall that one of the synonyms given by the European-educated Samuel for *dogīr*, is "hyena," and that hyenas were feared by the Nubians precisely because of this propensity for robbing graves. In fact, the fear of hyenas is the main reason the Nubians give for digging graves so deep and lining them with flat stones (see chapter 11 and Schäfer 1917, p. 202).

The *dogri* are particularly associated with dates and the date season and with the *sāqias*, the cattle-driven water-wheels that came into Nubia during the Roman period of Egyptian history. Nubian land was so sparse and sandy that in order to make a living in most areas the water-wheels were usually run far into the night. Many nineteenth-century European travelers, resting on their river boats by the shore of the Nile, reported hearing the lonely creaking moans of water-wheels coming through the darkness. It is not strange that the boys and men who had to drive the draft animals on those lonely night vigils experienced apparitions of various sorts.

Some Fadija stories about water-wheels illustrate the mischievous and stupid characteristics of the *dogri*. People feared them, but they could also outwit them. One tale concerns a certain Abdu Khalil of Abu Simbel, the district across the river from the famous monument of the same name. Abdu Khalil was known as an exceptionally brave and righteous man who had no fear of the spirits of the night. Once when he was running his *sāqia* alone in the late hours, a being with elongated and burning eyes appeared to him and said loudly, "I want dates!" Since it was a cold night, Abdu Khalil, who realized it was a *dogīr*, told the being it could have all the dates it wanted if it would run the *sāqia* for the rest of the night. The monster agreed, and Abdu built a fire and warmed himself contentedly while his work was being done for him. When morning approached and it was time for the deal to be completed, Abdu quickly grabbed a burning branch from the fire and threw it at the head of the *dogīr*, who fled back into the Nile screaming and shouting and never returned.

Another such story from Diwan tells how Hussein ash-Allah used to have his dates stolen every night as he ran the *sāqia*. He realized from the donkey-like tracks that a *dogīr* was the culprit. One night he hid his son near the *sāqia* and built a fire close by. When he heard a rustling among the date palms he signaled his son to continue running the *sāqia* while he picked up a burning stick, ran after the *dogīr*, surprised it, and burned its head. This one, too, went shrieking into the river and did not bother Hussein again.

Sometimes a *dogīr* was blamed when *sāqias* were broken, and in the Fadija district of Qustel Kennedy was shown one that had been deserted for some time because the *dogīr* who lived in it had frightened away the owners. An interesting adaptation of the association of the beings with broken irrigation devices occurred in resettled Kanuba. One of the more progressive men of the village had worked in Cairo for some years and had saved a small amount of capital. In 1947 he used his savings to buy a gasoline pump to irrigate the previously undeveloped land around what was then the relatively new village of Kanuba. His pump broke down after a short time, however, and his experiment was a failure. A common explanation in the village was that a *dogīr* had been disturbed by its noise and wrecked the machine.

Conclusion

The *dogīr* stories seem to consist of a peculiar amalgam of many of the supernatural beliefs of the region. Like the angels of the Nile, for example, the monsters live in the river, but like the jinn and *ghūl* of the desert and mountains they can also be dispersed by the *fātiḥa*, by invocations of a local saint, or by the steel weapons of armed men. They have many human and animal-like characteristics, however, a fact that places them considerably below the powerful spirit beings. Jinn are dispelled by incense and by salt thrown into flames, but we collected no instances in which they were tricked and routed by fire, as were the *dogri* in the stories above. The appetites of the *dogri* for dates, their cannibalism, and their delight in frightening humans all tend to put them in the monster-spook category, malevolent beings somewhere between men and true spirits. That belief in these beings may be pre-Islamic is suggested by their complete dissociation from Orthodox Islamic practices, though they are allegedly terrified of mosques and saints' shrines, both of which may provide sanctuaries against them.

The associations of the *dogri* with foreign and ancient peoples are interesting, since these associations may be remnant memories of the actual historical events. More historical probing in that direction would be useful, and it would be significant, too, to look for parallels in ancient Egyptian folklore or even in the Greek and Roman stories of water beings. The work of Kriss, Winkler, and Blackman, among others, indicates that the traditions of peoples in other places along the Nile, as well as those of Arabic tribes in other parts of the Middle East, are full of similar concepts that could be fruitfully examined for comparative purposes. The goal here is only to outline a system of belief that is important to Nubian ceremonialism.

Many of the young Nubian men now deride the idea of *dogīr*. They say it is only pagan superstition, or that the stories are only old wives' tales used to frighten the children, perhaps to protect them from falling into the Nile at night. One informant said, "Of course the stories are fictitious and were created from people's fears that their dates would be stolen. They might have invented the monster to cover up their own stealing!" There may be some truth in this explanation, but the *dogri* were apparently very real to many people in old Nubia and fear of them influenced a good deal of Nubian behavior.

Some of the young adult informants, trying to play down present belief in these monsters, said that now that Egyptian Nubians had moved to Kom Ombo they would drop such beliefs, being now too far from the Nile. In spite of this distance, however, we already have several reports of women seeing *dogri* near the new water taps in the resettlement area. It is also noteworthy that though Kanuba is likewise somewhat inland and though it is more than thirty years since resettlement took place, people still encounter the monsters around wells and in the canals near the village. Nevertheless, we suspect that with the accelerated program of modern education now being developed in New Nubia beliefs about *dogri*, as well as those about the Nile angels, may disappear.

Notes

1. In this chapter the Kenuz material as well as the references to the German literature on the topic were provided by A. Grauer. The Fadija material was collected by Kennedy and his field assistants. Much of it is the same as that which appeared in Kennedy 1969–1970. The materials from both areas were integrated into one chapter because of the basically identical quality of these apparently ancient Nubian beliefs throughout Nubia. Grauer wishes to express deep appreciation to Gertrude von Massenbach, who tutored her in the Kenzi language before she went into the field, making it possible for her to work without interpreters. Massenbach worked for more than half a century as a missionary among the Kenuz and she kindly put her knowledge at Grauer's disposal.
2. Milk is an important symbolic substance in Nubia. (See references to it in chapter on the wedding). It is used in various magical actions (Massenbach 1962, p. 86). If one steps on milk he will be punished by spirits and the cows will become dry. The proper response when milk is spilt is to pick up the dirt upon which it dropped and carry it to the Nile.
3. With regard to the frequent association of *dogri* with palm trees, it is interesting to note that in Pharaonic Egypt palm trees were regarded as dwelling places for various gods and goddesses, e.g., Nut, Hathor, and Osiris. The doom palm, so common in Nubia, was a symbol of the god Min (Wallert 1962, p. 133). The palm also has sacred connotations throughout the Islamic world, and is an important symbol in most Nubian ceremonies.
4. Daboud was the first Nubian 'omodiyya south of Aswan.
5. Abu Sirwal seems to be a common name for supernatural beings in the area, e.g., a spirit sheikh with this name was reported to have "possessed" a Nubian girl from Naja' Almanya in Dahmit (al-Guindi 1966, p. 4). Another Abu Sirwal was supposed to live in the Nile near Amberkab (Schäfer 1935, p. 298).
6. For example, see Lane 1963, pp. 233–34 and Kriss 1962, vol. 2:15. There are

also similarities to the *irkābi* or "riding" spirit of the dead (e.g., Reinisch 1879, p. 74; A. R. Blackman 1910, p. 25; and Winkler 1956, passim).

7. Winkler reports similar cannibalistic beliefs about the "Nam-Nam" among the Ababda of the Red Sea coast (1936, p. 71).

8. At the time, Massenbach had been working in Aswan and Nubia for about twenty years.

Chapter 7

Mushāhara: A Nubian Concept of Supernatural Danger and the Theory of Taboo

JOHN G. KENNEDY

"But a little thought soon shows the true import of these taboos."
Meyer Fortes

This chapter focusses on a very narrow set of beliefs within the total spectrum of Nubian religion. It is placed here because the exposition of these beliefs forms a bridge between the concepts and practices of Popular Islam, discussed in the previous three chapters, and the surviving non-Islamic elements, to be described in the following expositions of the crisis rites. *Mushāhara* beliefs play an important role in all these ceremonies, so it is useful to understand them before reading the descriptions of circumcision, marriage and death. Since there is no separate description of birth ceremonies in the book, the abbreviated discussion of them in this chapter will provide enough data so that the total pattern of life-cycle rites can be comprehended. Most of this chapter was presented originally as a paper in *The American Anthropologist* and the last part of it is a theoretical discussion of the Nubian concepts in the light of anthropological and psychoanalytic concepts concerning the nature of taboos.

The taboos of foreign peoples fascinated early travelers and later scholars because they seemed to constitute arbitrary and irrational restraints upon human conduct. They were prime examples of the "primitive mind." Modern theorists, reacting against racist and unilinear evolutionist assumptions, have sought logical bases (functions) in all apparently bizarre customs. Their relativist-functionalist orientation has been fruitful, but, it has also directed interest away from what seem to be important questions about human behavior. However, in the course of examining a complex of taboos and rituals practices by the Nubians, I found that in fact very little attention has been devoted to taboos in recent years. I also found, unlike Fortes, that considerable thought did not convincingly show the "true import" of such customs. This recognition led me to re-examine theoretical ideas about taboo in the light of the Nubian case.

Though the Nubians have long considered themselves devout Muslims,

125

a striking characteristic of their religious system, as of their entire culture, has been its flexibility, its capacity for incorporating new elements. Thus, what are now more and more under attack as "pagan" beliefs exist side by side with new ideas as well as with rituals that have been added to the system over centuries, with the result that distinctions between "pagan" and Popular Islamic concepts are often not clear among Nubians, particularly women. With the passage of time a syncretistic mixing of many ideas has occurred.

1. *Mushāhara* Taboos

Mushāhara is a word derived from the Arabic *shahr*, meaning "month." A basic idea of the customs associated with the term is that if certain actions are engaged in before the appearance of the new moon (indicating the beginning of the lunar month), harm will befall an individual undergoing a "crisis" rite. Consider the following extracts from field materials that illustrate the behavior to be examined.

A woman from Abu Hor (Kenuz), preparing to make an obligatory visit to congratulate a neighbor who has just given birth, takes off her gold ornaments and leaves them at home. Her explanation: "If I wore gold into the room, it would bring *mushāhara* to the mother and baby; her milk might dry up, or the baby might become ill."

A woman from Diwan (Fadija) who had given birth two weeks before has had her milk dry up. It is said that she is *tasharot* (stricken by *mushāhara*). The gold necklace of a neighbor woman is brought on the night of the appearance of the new moon and immersed in a pan of Nile water. The mother and child are then bathed in the same water by the midwife. On another occasion a woman from Diwan bathes in the water that a barber's razor and scissors have been immersed in so that her birth wounds will heal.

A woman of Abu Hor claims that her baby is sick because a few days previously a man who had just crossed the Nile came into her room, causing *mushāhara*. Therefore, on the night of the new moon she goes to the bank of the river and steps across a fire of palm leaves which has been sprinkled with salt seven times. Then she gets into a boat and crosses the Nile. At mid-stream the boat is stopped and she bathes her face and that of her child with water from the river and holds him up to the new moon. On the other side she performs the same fire ritual before returning home.

A woman from Korosko (Fadija) is talking in the courtyard holding a baby in her arms. A knock is heard and the woman goes to answer, but before the guest can enter the woman quickly steps outside the entrance. When asked the reason for her action, she says that she has just weaned her child that day and the visitor, who came from across the river, might have caused her to become barren. Women who want to wean their children do it on days chosen likewise to avoid *mushāhara*.

A woman in the village of Abu Hor is observed collecting dried palm branches with which she makes a fire in the courtyard after sunset. She throws salt on the fire and then steps across it seven times. Then she takes her baby and passes it over the smoke seven times with a circular motion. She does this every evening until the new moon to prevent *mushāhara*.

A man of Kanuba (Fadija) returning from the market at Daraw refrains from going into the room where his wife and new baby are resting. The explanation is that he may have seen blood at one of the butchers' stalls, which would cause *mushāhara* to his wife or child.

A five year old girl is undergoing a genital excision at Abu Hor. She is dressed in white and will wear all the gold ornaments of her mother from the beginning of the operation until the appearance of the new moon. The new moon should appear while the wound is healing in order to facilitate recovery and ensure later fertility. In the days after the ceremony she is taken out to the street in the morning so that no one may endanger her by entering with something that might cause *mushāhara*.

People returning from a funeral in Kanuba (Kenuz) abstain from visiting a new bride, who is still in her forty-day period of seclusion. Their reason is to prevent *mushāhara*.

The *angarīb* bed upon which a corpse has been carried to the cemetery is left outside the house in the street in Diwan (Fadija). If brought inside before forty days, it is said, it would cause *mushāhara* to some of the close relatives, which might occur in the form of blindness, paralysis, or sterility.

On the day after the consummation of marriage a bride and groom at Ballana (Fadija) make a trip to the Nile to bathe. A fire of palm branches sprinkled with salt has been made in front of the door of the bridal chamber (*diwani*) and the newly wedded couple step across it seven times before proceeding to the Nile. The rite is repeated for the first seven days to avoid *mushāhara*, which might prevent them from having children.

A woman from Abu Hor (Kenuz) who was without a pregnancy for two years performed the following ceremony to break the *mushāhara* that she felt was preventing her from having another child: She took an eggplant and cut it into small pieces. Then she made a fire of palm branches and sprinkled it with salt. A girl under childbearing age (twelve) and a woman over fifty were brought and small cuts were made on their arms. They each crossed the fire and then put a little of the blood from the cut on a piece of eggplant. Afterward the bloodstained eggplant was taken and thrown into the Nile.

These are a few of many instances of behavior relating to *mushāhara* that our fieldworkers reported, instances chosen to show frequently occurring themes. It is not easy to find a key to these diverse observances. They are frequently isolated from one another in performance and people usually either could give no explanation for them or replied that their forefathers did it that way. An examination of all such recorded instances yields the following summary list.

Dangerous substances (if brought into a room):
Gold
Razor or knife (barber's implements)
Blood
Eggplant

Actions contaminating a visitor (that is, rendering dangerous one who may enter a room and see the vulnerable person):

Crossing the Nile or an inlet (*khor*) of it
Visiting the market (seeing blood)
Undergoing an incision or operation that draws blood
Having been shaved or had one's hair cut
Visiting another sacredly vulnerable person, e.g., a circumcised child, or
  helping with a birth
Visiting graves, seeing or touching a dead body, or giving condolence
  ('*azā*).
Seeing a scorpion or being stung by one[2]

Other dangerous prohibited actions:
Sexual intercourse of parents within a forty-day period after circumcision,
  excision, or birth

Supernatural punishments to the vulnerable
Sterility
Sickness (undefined)
Wounds that do not heal
Eye disease (infrequent)

Mushāhara-neutralizing procedures (alone or in combination)
Crossing a fire of palm leaves and salt
Ablutions with Nile water
Offerings to the Nile
Rituals involving blood and the offending substances

Times when Mushāhara prohibitions are observed
Birth
Circumcision and excision
Marriage
Death

Mushāhara is strongly associated with "crisis rites," and certain other
aspects of these rites provide important clues to the meaning we are seeking. One of the most important common elements is the idea that individuals undergoing the crisis are in a state of "sacred vulnerability," as I
am going to call it, which makes them peculiarly susceptible to supernatural
harm. It is because of this danger that the vulnerable individual is subject to a
number of restrictions upon his behavior, among which the most important
are restrictions upon movement. He is confined to a room in the house for a
forty-day period, during which time certain foods are eaten and others are
avoided. During this period of confinement, rituals are performed on the
first, third, seventh, fifteenth and fortieth days, while others may be performed on the evening of the first day of the lunar months occurring within
the vulnerability period.

At first glance many of the *mushāhara* customs appear to be magical, pre-dicated on the assumption of impersonal symbolic or mystical causation, but examination of some of the crisis rites reveals that spirit-beings are con-cerned. Most prominent among these beings are Nile spirits, which are not only associated with rituals of birth, circumcision, marriage and death, but were also the concern of many other ritual practices in Old Nubia. The Nile spirits are usually regarded as friendly and feminine beings. They are ordi-narily in contact with certain women, or occasionally a man, who report see-ing and conversing with them. Such people, believed to be clairvoyant, are sought for divination and curing. The women perform regular private rituals for the spirits, usually consisting of offerings of perfume, incense or henna, all of which are thrown into the river, but occasionally requiring sacrifice of an animal and a group ritual. Some of the numerous shrines along the river bank in Old Nubia were built for Nile spirits and were maintained by a care-taker who was in communication with them. In birth ceremonies in particu-lar, many of the observed ritual precautions have specific reference to such river-beings, who have come to spend a forty-day period with the mother and child. It is useful to review these ritual acts because it seems clear that they have a similar meaning when repeated in other ceremonies.

In the first place, the mother, especially if it is her first child, is required to wear clean white clothing and her best gold ornaments. She must also be bathed with Nile water, her face and hands rubbed with henna, and her eyes made up with Kohl, the ancient Egyptian cosmetic eye-liner, for spirits are pleased by the sight of beauty.

During delivery the woman grasps two palm branches which are hung above her, and to please the spirits these are retained in the room for the full forty day restriction period. When she is about to be delivered, a bowl containing oil and cotton is lighted near her head for the same reasons, and a knife or a nail is placed under her pillow to defend her against spiritual harm. An eggplant and some dates and wheat are placed in a bowl near the mother's head; onions and Kohl are kept nearby for the midwife to use on the baby's eyes and to protect it from eye disease, along with a spool of thread to tie the umbilical cord. When delivery is imminent, a special food, called *asīda* is thrown into the Nile by close relatives of the woman to persuade the spirits to permit an easy birth.

After the birth the midwife repeats various incantations and performs such rituals as biting a fresh date and spitting the pieces into the baby's face seven times to ensure beauty, health, and a melodious voice. Immediately following the birth, or sometimes on the third day, the midwife leads a procession of neighborhood women to the Nile; she carries the placenta, the flat stone upon which delivery was made, and the sand upon which fluid and blood have been spilled. Preceding her is a boy holding a knife aloft protectively. At the river she offers the contaminated things to the Nile spirits, along with seven dates, perfume, and seven pieces of Kohl.[3] In former days, a sheep or goat was slaughtered for a ritual meal.

On the fortieth day another such ceremony takes place, which terminates the period of sacred vulnerability and permits the resumption of normal life. In this final ritual the woman and her baby, led by the midwife and followed by neighborhood women and children, again parade to the Nile to offer seven plates (or bits) of *asīda*, perfume and henna. This time a tiny boat, made of twigs and filled with cotton soaked in castor oil, is lighted and set afloat down river to petition the spirits for the growth of the child and to ensure safe travel in later life. The faces of mother and child are bathed again and, after incantations for health and happiness, the group returns to the house carrying containers of water and green palm branches. These palm fronds are thrown into the house, and the water is sprinkled inside "to fill the child's father's house with life." Forty jars of water are poured over the mother as a final ritual cleansing.

Probably the most important thread of continuity running through all these rites is the concept of sacred vulnerability for forty days and the ritual pattern of the first, third, seventh, fifteenth and fortieth days, *mushāhara* constituting the major danger in each of the vulnerability periods. Connected with this concept are ideas of pollution and cleansing, derived from the fear of Nile spirits, jinn and ghosts of the dead. Thus, fear is a central theme in a whole constellation of non-Islamic practices, exemplified not only in these birth ceremonies but also in all other crisis rites.

POLLUTION AND RITUAL CLEANSING

A constant feature of crisis rites is the use of Nile water for purification, while among the most prevalent ideas and emotions involved is the fear of pollution by blood, associated with sexuality and ultimately with fertility. The concept of ritual vulnerability thus seems to be based upon the idea that blood (particularly blood from the sex organs) subjects a person to great supernatural danger because it attracts powerful capricious spirits, who will prove a threat to fertility.

In Old Nubia a sacrifice of animals on the first, third, seventh and fortieth days was a part of the ceremonies, their blood apparently serving to placate the spirit's desires and dispel them.[4] But there are conflicting ideas concerning this powerful substance. For example, one should not enter the room of a sacredly vulnerable person after seeing blood, but a woman who has just given birth is forced to look at a newly killed animal on her first day, only after which does the taboo go into effect. Likewise in the *zār* ceremonies, which in many ways seem patterned on crisis rites, the patient may smear his face and arms with blood of a sacrificial animal.

The rites of birth, female excision, male circumcision, and marriage all involve great pain in the genital area and the flowing of blood from the sex organs. The excision of girls is particularly painful since the goals of the operation are to remove not only the clitoris, but the *labia minora* as well.[5] This operation is said to reduce sexual desire and to increase male pleasure after marriage, while validating womanhood and ensuring health and fertility, but it also has the extremely important purpose in the eyes of the Nubians of preserving premarital chastity by closing the vulva with scar tissue. At marriage it must be reopened, which often requires that a midwife or other experienced woman perform the traumatically painful operation with a knife or razor. Thus at marriage, again, as at birth and circumcision, dangerous spirit-attracting genital blood is involved.

The spirits threaten fertility, which is obviously associated with the genital region. The placenta, the blood from a birth, the boy's foreskin at circumcision, and the excised genital parts of the girl are all thrown into the Nile. That these are offerings to the spirits is shown by the custom of putting a coin with the boy's foreskin when it is thrown into the river, for coins, like gold and blood, are magnets for spirits. The spirit's attraction to blood is revealed again in the custom of prohibiting menstruating women from visiting graves — ordinarily an obligation — for it is believed that their fertility would at that time be endangered.

Actions relating to pollution are not only magical in themselves, but may be motivated by a fear of sorcery as well as by fear of dangerous spirit-beings. Some women said, for example, that the reason for throwing the umbilical cord into the Nile in the presence of neighborhood women is so that all of them may bear witness to the event, so that there will be no opportunity for any barren woman to steal the cord as a suppository charm to stimulate pregnancy, an act that would rob the original mother of her fertility.

The danger of pollution by attracting spirits is also associated with sexual intercourse and the sexual fluids. Washing the body of a dead woman is accompanied by the incantation: "I purify you from birth, menstruation, and intercourse." The washing rituals during marriage ceremonies and the cleansing of the vaginal blood, like the restrictions upon sexual intercourse by both parents for forty days following a birth or a circumcision, are all part of the same complex of spirit beliefs and fears concerning fertility and the genital area of the body. They revolve around the association of blood, flesh and sexual fluids with the dangerous spirits who are attracted to these materials.

One of the main Nubian techniques for protection against supernatural danger utilizes cleansing with Nile water. The end of vulnerability in each of the crisis ceremonies. is marked by a procession to the Nile for ritual cleansing and the presentation of offerings to the spirits of the river, while in birth, circumcision and marriage ceremonies, processions to the river and Nile-water rituals are performed on other prescribed days as well. Frequent libations are poured in front of the house, or in the house, and water is brought to bathe the endangered individual. The rituals of immersing spirit-attracting substances — gold, barbers' cutting instruments, and money — are other evidences that pollution means possible infestation with evil spirits and that Nile-water (or the good spirits of the Nile) dispels them. The same principle is shown in the custom of placing a pot of water near the boy for the small obligatory gifts from relatives and neighbors at a circumcision. When coins are dropped into the water their harmful potential to the recipient is dissipated. In Old Nubia, the whole community bathed in the Nile to receive *baraka* from its spirits during celebrations for the community saints and during *'ashūra*, while during the Large and Small Islamic feasts libations of water were poured on the graves of dead relatives.

An interesting reversal, supporting our conception of the idea of pollution, was the fifteen-day prohibition against washing off the ashes and mud on a widow's clothing immediately after the death of her husband. Similarly, a woman with a newborn child was not supposed to remove her blood-stained garments for three days after birth, and in Old Diwan a newborn baby was not washed for forty days. These customs, like that which forced a woman who had just given birth to view the slaughter of an animal, indicate the overwhelming fear surrounding the immediate events of birth and death: at these times the spirits cannot be dispelled, even by Nile-water, so they must be allowed free rein. If they are permitted temporary freedom, the fertility of the woman may remain unharmed.

Nubian ideas of pollution thus seem to be predicated on beliefs in dangerous spirits. The theory of spirits motivates much of the ritual activity of the crisis rites, and understanding this theory will enable us to comprehend other acts that otherwise tend, both to observer and actor, to be opaque in meaning.

OTHER PROTECTIVE MEASURES AGAINST SPIRITS

Among the more important appurtenances used by the Nubians to please the spirits in all crisis rites as well as in other ceremonies are the following: white clothing, green palm branches, gold, *henna, kohl*, incense and perfume, and ritual foods (*asīda, durra*, and dates). I have already mentioned most of these items in connection with birth ceremonies, and here it perhaps suffices to say that all of them are similarly used in the other crisis rites and in *zār* ceremonies. One uses these ritual appurtenances to make the situation agreeable to the spirits. At the same time the materials themselves may on occasion be dangerous, as when gold enters a room where there is a sacredly vulnerable person. The idea here seems to be that spirits hovering about the visitor's gold will be drawn to the blood of the wound and attack. The gold of a family member of the vulnerable one does not cause this danger, and in fact is worn by children during their circumcision or excision to please the spirits, so it may be that only alien, non-family gold is dangerous. Most of the other appurtenances do not appear to have this double aspect; they do not act as magnets for threatening spirits, but are simply regarded as being pleasing to spirit-beings.

The fire and salt ritual is one of the main defenses against sensitive and capricious spirits, a ceremonial act that we have recorded in connection with birth, circumcision, and marriage and that may have been used by widows, though we have no confirming accounts. The ritual is further prescribed by native doctors for sterility and female troubles. The act of stepping over a fire seems obviously connected with danger to fertility, especially in view of the Nubian concepts of the general efficacy of smoke and incense.[6]

Other ideas consistently found are those relating to sharp iron objects. It will be recalled that the mother has a knife or a nail under her pillow at childbirth to protect her against spiritual harm. The widow in mourning uses an identical ritual defense and as I have here described, the boy leading the procession of women to the river after a birth holds a knife to ward off dangerous beings. For the same purpose, seven needles are sewn into the shoe of a bride as well as into the pillow of a widow. The barber's razor appears to be associated both with the spiritual efficacy of sharp iron and with the fact that in circumcision it draws genital blood.

These uses of knives and other sharp objects lead to the inference that the original meaning of the sword in some ceremonies was also connected with defense against spirits. Several of our accounts of earlier Kenuz circumcision rituals mentioned that during a part of the ceremony the boy sat outside the house while a slave or young adult male relative stood by waving a sword each time *noqūṭ* was given. A ritual in which the groom, dressed in new clothing, carries a sword for seven days, accompanied by a boy with a whip, is still important in Kenuz weddings and was also reported to have been a part of ceremonies in the Fadija area in earlier times. On the groom's first entrance into the bridal quarters after his wedding procession, he taps the door lintel three times with his sword before going in. On the seventh day when the Kenuz marriage couple emerge from their quarters and run to the river for ritual bathing, the groom carries his sword before him; he dips it in the Nile before beginning his ablutions. Finally, in funerals of former days, the widow or mother of the deceased is reputed to have brandished a sword, while the other close female relatives, with mud and ashes smeared on their heads and clothing, waved palm branches as they danced and wailed.

Very little explanation was obtainable for these customs from our informants, most of whom said they were simply signs to indicate to visitors the protagonists of the ceremonies. It seems reasonable to infer from what we know about the associations of spirits with money, doorways, sacredly vulnerable conditions, and defensive uses of sharp steel, that swords too were defensive against spiritual attacks.

SUMMARY

My first task here has been to attempt to unravel the enigmatic data concerning *mushāhara* customs. It is apparent that these taboos are associated with the crisis rites of birth, circumcision, marriage and death. Examination of other elements of the life-cycle ceremonies reveals that the *mushāhara* customs, along with other prohibitions and positive rituals, are aimed at protecting people from dangerous spirit-beings who threaten fertility and life during these temporary states of sacred vulnerability. These spirit-beings for the most part are connected with the Nile and/or the ghosts of the dead, and their main danger is a threat to fertility and to the reproductive areas of the body. Examination of such rites also reveals that the basic meaning of most of the ritual substances, appurtenances, and acts is their association with spirit beings, either through pleasing them or defending against them. Even the concepts of ritual pollution and cleansing have the meaning of neutralizing and dispersing spirits.

2. *Mushāhara* and the Interpretation of Taboo

Many of the practices described here are of the type called taboos in the anthropological literature. I now want to examine some explanatory ideas concerning taboo to see what light they may throw upon the data and, conversely, what the Nubian material suggests for the theoretical conceptions.

THE EVOLUTIONISTS

The idea of taboo was prominent in nineteenth-century travelers' reports of "archaic" societies, and the early armchair anthropologists spent a great deal of ink upon it. Wundt, Hubert and Mauss, Marett, Reinach, and Frazer all discussed the subject at length. Thus Van Gennep was led to react: "Because it is easier to enumerate the things that one should not do than those which one must or may do, the theorists have found among all peoples an expansive series of taboos, prohibitions, etc., and have overrated their importance" (1960, 8–9 n). Most of these writers, assuming a unilineal evolutionary framework, regarded taboos, along with other "primitive" practices, as evidence of former stages of mankind's history. Sir James Frazer defined "taboo" simply as negative magic (1961) representing, like other magic, processes of erroneous reasoning typifying earlier stages of the evolution of science and culture. Reinach defined religion itself as a sum of taboos, and stated that the progress of mankind was effected by progressively more rational selection from among these irrational prohibitions for the establishment of laws, permitting a gradual freeing of society from superstition and a continuing secularization (1930, pp. 3, 22–23).

A major reason for this opinion, and for the focus upon taboos in theories of evolution, was their apparently irrational, arbitrary and supernatural character, which fitted ethnocentric theories of "primitive mentality." Reinach's definition is probably representative:

> The distinctive mark of a taboo is that the interdict is quite arbitrary, and that the confirmation presaged, in the event of the violation of the taboo, is not a penalty decreed by civil law, but a calamity such as death or blindness falling upon the guilty individual (1930, p. 3).

Early definitions often pointed out another important attribute of taboos, their frequent combination of ideas of sacredness and pollution. "The Latin word *sacer* is the exact equivalent of 'taboo' for it signifies both sacred and impure. Everything that was *sacer* was withdrawn from human use." (Reinach 1930, p. 104). Although these evolutionists employed now outmoded theories, they pointed out certain distinctive features of taboo as a type of institutionalized behavior, a fact I mention here because the tendency among many modern scholars has been to overlook or deny these features.

THE FUNCTIONALISTS

With the waning of unilineal evolutionsim, analysts of religion and society have not been much concerned with distinguishing the nature of taboo itself, but have simply included taboos with rituals and other customs in general functional explanations. Probably the most well-known example of this is Radcliffe-Brown's famous Frazer Lecture, in which he used taboo to illustrate his theory of societal function and his method for the analysis of ritual (1952, pp. 133–152). Briefly, this thesis was that all rituals, including taboos, are means for keeping people aware of the values and sentiments that promote the cohesion upon which the social structure depends. For example, he states that:

> By this theory the Andamanese taboos relating to childbirth are obligatory recognition in a standardized symbolic form of the significance and importance of the event [of birth] to the parents and to the community at large. They thus serve to fix the social value of occasions of this kind (1952, pp. 150–151).

He offered this theory as an alternative to Malinowski's conception of ritual as a means of coping with anxiety caused by events beyond technical control:

> If it were not for the existence of the rite and the beliefs associated with it, the individual would feel no anxiety, and the psychological effect of the rite is to create in him a sense of insecurity and danger (Radcliffe-Brown 1952, p. 149).

A recent reiteration of Radcliffe-Brown's position has been made by Meyer Fortes in an interpretation of certain Tallensi taboos. Discussing the prohibitions imposed upon new tenants and landowners, and upon incoming chiefs, he generalizes:

> Taboos are a medium for giving tangible substance to moral obligations. More than that, they are a means of keeping the feelings of moral obligation active all the time, so that whenever occasion arises to translate the duty into performance, we are ready for that ... and what is more, taboos refer to observable behavior, so they serve as a means by which a person can account to himself and to the world at large for the conscientious discharge of his moral obligations (1961, p. 82).

One appeal of functionalist explanations has been that any kind of enigmatic behavior can be explained by this formula. Fortes' statement quoted above, for example, is preceded by the comment that Tallensi interpretations of their own taboos depend upon mystical ideas involving the ancestors, "but a little thought soon shows the true import of these taboos. It lies in their utility as a tangible embodiment of, and a daily discipline for, the moral obligations of tenancy" (1961, p. 82). Behind such an interpretation lies the functionalist conviction (despite disclaimers) that all condoned behavior has social utility, and that therefore apparently irrational or inexplicable behavior really has an underlying rational basis related to societal functioning and survival. In their general theories of religion, functionalists have thus not been concerned with the special or peculiar characteristics of taboos as contrasted with the special character of other kinds of rituals and customs. Whether behavior is negative or positive, whether it involves ideas of magic, pollution, or sacred beings, is unimportant in their explanations. Meaning, for them, is to be discerned in the structure of a society or in the amount of empirical knowledge available to a people.

I now want to consider Nubian *mushāhara* customs in terms of these ideas. As we have seen, the *mushāhara* prohibitions have reference to spirit beliefs which, to the Nubians, are a sufficient explanation for their own behavior. How far are we justified in attributing other "latent" meanings to it?

It seems evident to begin with that the customs cluster around a nucleus of real objective danger to the health of the individual undergoing "crisis," and that this danger is not completely controllable by Nubian medical techniques. Infant deaths were common under the living conditions of Old Nubia. Mothers' milk sometimes dried up, and undoubtedly sterility was caused sometimes by post-birth infections. The ability to bear children could also have been affected by the stringent excision operation or by the subsequent painful defloration at marriage. Occasional fatalities occurred to children after circumcision and excision. Pain, blood, impaired health and possible death, all associated with the reproductive organs, were a part of crisis rites and it was certainly the associated fear that gave these rites their actual "crisis" character for people undergoing them.

This fact seems to offer clear support for Malinowski's ideas that such situations arouse fear and that, in the absence of effective technical means, ritual defenses are erected to help allay the fear. In a culture where beliefs in spirit beings and ideas of supernatural causation predominate, however, these ritual defenses are regarded not merely as anodyne but as being directed at the real causes of danger, for the people in crisis are considered to be under a threat that in its origins is supernatural, that is, in a condition of sacred vulnerability. We also note, however, that much of even the actual physical danger is culturally induced and defined. While it is necessary that for a society to survive there must be births, for example, it is not necessary in any physiological sense to perform excisions and it is only excisions that make necessary the consequent wedding operations. In the Nubian case excisions and circumcisions do not even symbolically mark a transition to adulthood, since they are usually held between the ages of three and six (see chapter 8). Not only are these painful operations culturally ordained, but as Radcliffe-Brown pointed out in connection with taboos, the beliefs connected with them create additional fear beyond any arising from actual physical danger. Periods of fear are arbitrarily limited, moreover, in accord with anagogic numbers.[7]

How then do the Nubian taboos and crisis rituals fit Radcliffe-Brown's theory? At first glance it would not appear that *mushāhara* avoidances bear much relation to social structure, but functionalist analysis leads to certain interpretations. We note, for example, that there are two types of taboos involved in *mushāhara* avoidance: those imposed upon the movements of a vulnerable individual and those imposed upon other members of the community. The restrictions required of others are mostly injunctions to refrain from bringing things into a room, restrictions that are perversely coupled with extremely strong social obligations to visit such a person. Visiting obligations, in fact, are manifestations of the powerful reciprocity principle that is a basis of Nubian social organization (see Fernea 1967). Following Radcliffe-Brown and Fortes, we may therefore infer that one function of the ritual proscriptions is to make people keenly aware of their social obligations, highlighting communal social responsibility by requiring everyone to feel especially cautious. All relatives and fellow villagers are not only obligated to visit, but are also made aware that each holds the fertility and health of his relative or friend in his hands. Thus these taboos, along with the positive rituals, reaffirm the high value that the society has placed upon fertility, keeping people tense during crisis events that traditionally have been defined as significant in upholding that value. The circumcision or excision ceremony, for example, does not mark a change of status, but it does symbolize female chasitity, maleness or femaleness, and other values associated with fertility. These values are impressed upon the child not only by his painful operation but by the ritual attention and fearful restrictions that he must endure.

FREUD[8]

Anthropologists have not shown much awareness of the chapter devoted to taboo in Freud's well-known *Totem and Taboo*, despite the fact that Kroeber's appraisal of it in his otherwise quite critical review of the book as a whole was entirely laudatory (Kroeber 1965, p. 52).[9] Unlike functional anthropologists, who have remained indifferent to the special character of taboo, Freud was intrigued precisely by its peculiar and differentiating character, a character that fitted his theory of neurosis. In his review of the ethnological literature, he noted the arbitrariness and inexplicability that are so often a part of these prohibitions and observed that they often involved the renunciation of such desiderata as sex and freedom of movement, stating that "the basis of taboo is a forbidden action for which there exists a strong inclination in the subconscious" (1938, p. 832). Like compulsion neuroses, taboos were seen as based upon the ambivalence of two conflicting emotions, and their arbitrary character was explained by proposing that one or both conflicting emotions are repressed and unconscious. Thus, for example, the often extreme taboos upon kings and chiefs accompany veneration of their exalted and sacred status, but this veneration conceals a mistrust and envy of their prerogatives, so that the uncomfortable restrictions of the taboos actually act as punishment or revenge; taboos imposed upon warriors conceal the ambivalence created by conflict between the necessity to make war and the unconscious guilt relating to strongly socialized prohibitions against murder; and taboos relating to the dead, as Freud had pointed out earlier in his theory of mourning, stem from ambivalent emotions of tenderness and repressed hostility toward the deceased. The forms that taboos often take, which may seem remote from these conflicts, were explained by the mechanism of displacement, which also characterizes the compulsion neuroses. The "dangerous attribute" which inheres in all taboos, regardless of type, is "the propensity to arouse the ambivalence of man and to tempt him to violate the prohibition." The idea of contagion or contamination that is so often found in taboos occurs because the tabooed person "is in a condition which has the property of exciting the forbidden desires of others and awakening the ambivalent conflict in them." This property must be restrained or society could be dissolved. For example, "if others did not punish the violation, they would perforce become aware that they want to imitate the evil doer" (1938, p. 833).

If both Malinowski's and Radcliffe-Brown's theories appear applicable to the Nubian concepts, how does Freud's interpretation enlighten or confuse our view? What forbidden desires, guilts, renunciations, displacements, and ambivalences may be discovered in the *mushāhara* taboos? Perhaps it would be well to quote two more of Freud's statements, which indicate his view more clearly. In speaking of the ambivalences in taboos, Freud says:

> The king or chieftain arouses envy of his prerogatives: everybody would perhaps like to be king. The dead, the newly born, and women when they are incapacitated all act as incitements because of their peculiar helplessness, while the individual who has just reached maturity tempts through the promise of new pleasure. Therefore all these persons and all these conditions are taboo, for one must not yield to the temptations they offer (1938, p. 832).
>
> If taboo expresses itself mainly in prohibitions, it may well be considered self-evident, without remote proof from the analogy with neurosis, that it is based on a positive desireful impulse. For what nobody desires to do does not have to be forbidden, and certainly whatever is expressly forbidden must be an object of desire (1938, p. 860).

Like the functionalists Freud wanted to know why men perform rituals in general, but he also wanted to understand why rituals take the forms they do. The closest that Radcliffe-Brown came to this kind of concern was in his explanation of the social value of childbirth to the Andamanese, when he remarks that "The simplest form of ritual sanction is an accepted belief that if rules of rituals are not observed some undefined misfortune is likely to occur" (1952, p. 150). But why is this "the simplest form?" To explain why, Radcliffe-Brown falls back upon the notion that such a belief is simply "natural" or an attribute of human nature. Freud attempts to go deeper. He says that society defines an individual as being at certain times in the taboo state, that is, under a series of restrictions, because at these times he arouses the forbidden and consciously unacceptable emotions of envy, desire and/or hostility. Society gratifies these forbidden emotions by denying things to him and at the same time displaces its own guilt for such gratification by showing particular concern for him. The individual under taboo restrictions is thus both sacred and polluted. Basic but conflicting or ambivalent emotions are reflected simultaneously in the "rules," making them powerfully and irrationally adhered-to.

In applying these ideas to the Nubian *mushāhara* practices, we may begin by asking how the forty-day sacred vulnerability period fits this formulation. What is there about a new mother, a circumcised girl of five, or a bride that could arouse envy and incite desire in people of the community? One hypothesis would be that at birth and marriage a woman demonstrates her possession of coveted values. It seems evident, for example, that at birth, offspring testify to fertility, and that at marriage potential offspring testify to probable fertility. This fertility could incite envy, which, following Freud's reasoning, might be repressed and displaced, with resultant restrictions upon the movement of the mother or bride. This same hypothesis would fit all Nubian cases because, as was shown earlier, each crisis situation has been defined by the culture as being concerned with fertility, and in three of them there are actual painful physical molestations to the person, which could be interpreted as more punishments inflicted by society, which in turn call forth more solicitous attentions to assuage guilt, which in turn incite more envy, and so on.

Freud's unelaborated remark that the "peculiar helplessness" of new mothers and babies incites to temptation seems to derive from the hypothesis that everyone has an unconscious desire to regress to a child-like state in which others must show concern for one's helplessness. Disallowed envy would thus be aroused by new mothers and babies because of their relative need for attention.

Freud's suggestion that those undergoing puberty ceremonies incite to temptation by virtue of their promise of new pleasure, however, does not appear to hold for the Nubian circumcision and excision rites — a five-year old child could hardly be regarded as having this effect — though the particularly long and stringent restrictions on young widows could be interpreted as the result of a combination of most of the envy-creating conditions, in addition to newly released sexual potential and availability.

But what about the *mushāhara* taboos temselves? It was noted earlier that a central idea in all these prohibitions is that a visitor has great potentiality for harming the vulnerable person. In Freud's terms, the excessive precautions enjoined by these taboos, which are stated to be for the purpose of protection, would perhaps mask hostility born of envy and the attribution of danger by spirits would seem to fit his idea that demons are simply the personified projections of man's own aggressive emotions.

In summary, our examination has shown that all the theories relating to taboo appear to be applicable to some aspects of *mushāhara* practices. Although the Nubians themselves simply believe that they are in danger from spirits, for example, Malinowski's formulation enables us to see that fears arising from actual dangers uncontrollable by traditional technical means are also being alleviated. At the same time, however, as Radcliffe-Brown proposed, it seems that additional fears are created that would not exist without these beliefs, the complex of fears and beliefs acting to support and reinforce moral norms and values. Meanwhile, during the simultaneous relieving and generating of the tensions which these functional theories reveal, we can infer, following Freud, that socially threatening envies and hostilities are also being displaced, disguised by excessive concern but expressed through the mild punishment of confinement.

The emotional picture created by these ideas seems complicated indeed and the functional load of the customs appears inordinately heavy. There are also considerable difficulties of verification for all theories that postulate the operation of motives outside the actors' awareness as causes of behavior or bases of custom. Norbeck has been among the most eloquent of recent writers in pointing this out (1961, 1963 and Norbeck *et al.* 1962). But because such motives are difficult to verify does not mean they are not present. Such ideas remain the most provocative hypotheses we have, even if they seem inconclusive when matched against the refractory complexity of human behavior. One kind of test that might be applied to them is the observation of changes in customs to see whether they correlate with changes in structure, function, or social values. What happens to hidden motivations or latent meanings when customs change? Though I do not have precisely controlled data at my disposal, I can hazard some speculations based upon a general knowledge of change in Nubian culture.

At the beginning of this chapter, I noted that Nubian ceremonialism has been undergoing changes for some time. It is apparent that in the past an additive, assimilative process was going on. Whole complexes, such as the *dhikr* rituals and cults of saints, were added and integrated into pre-Islamic life-cycle ceremonials. In recent years, on the other hand, there has been a process of simplification, a purging of customs. One drastic example is the fact that because of resettlement at New Nubia, some communities that previously had as many as a hundred or more saints' shrines now have none.[10] Another is the almost complete disappearance of the vast amount of ritual that once surrounded male circumcision. In all non-Islamic rituals, in fact, progressive reductions have been going on for many years, at differential rates in different parts of Nubia. Thus, for example, the traditional seclusion period in crisis rites has been reduced in various places and in various ceremonies from forty days to fifteen days, seven days, three days, and even in some areas to one day. The introduction of modern medical techniques has meanwhile greatly reduced beliefs in supernatural causes and dependence upon ritual curing practices.

Changes in some customs were actually observed during our field work. For example, at a funeral in Dahmit a Nubian leader educated at al-Azhar prevented the women from putting dirt on their heads in the pagan manner. He had already stopped the dancing at saints' birthdays and had reduced other rituals to minimal lengths, using his persuasiveness among the men and the force of his religious authority. Meanwhile a young school teacher of Kanuba attended a funeral immediately after his wife had given birth, deliberately violating *mushāhara* prohibitions in order to demonstrate to the women that no harm would ensue. But the attenuation of traditional practices is often rationalized according to traditional belief. A woman of Dahmit, for example, performed the ritual terminating her seclusion after a birth on the twentieth day instead of the fortieth and the reason she gave was altruistic: she wished to allow the river spirits to return to their homes in the Nile in time to participate in the Islamic Small Feast, which was to be held in three days. Of course she was then freed from restrictions upon her own festive preparations (see chapter 5).

The fact that customs may be banned or broken thus does not necessarily mean that belief in them is abandoned. In the village of Kanuba, however, and, I believe, in most Nubian communities, great differences have appeared among individuals, families, and religious factions in the type and degree of maintenance of religious beliefs and practices. Some families pay no attention to *mushāhara* practices and disavow any belief in them, while others still faithfully observe all the rituals of birth, marriage, circumcision, and death. These variances are indicative of the nature of change. Throughout Nubia, it is pagan beliefs and practices that are disappearing most rapidly; most men now scoff at *mushāhara* taboos, for example, and the meanings of many related customs are becoming lost. Most changes are consistent with the increasing influence of Orthodox Islam and the general trend toward secularization, both of which have accompanied male migration to the cities. The isolation of women in the villages of Old Nubia has meanwhile been a major factor in widening the differences between beliefs and practices of women and men.

Many of the changes have occurred rapidly, widely, and without apparent trauma, and thus pose questions for theories that posit unconscious processes. One is led to ask: If all the latent functions, meanings, and conflicts that we have explored are really involved in *mushāhara* taboos, how have people been able to change their habits and beliefs so rapidly in so many instances? Reaching a definite answer with existing data unfortunately is not simple.

As we might expect, Malinowski's ideas receive the clearest confirmation from the changes. Rituals have faded in the face of advancing knowledge, and it is among women, where such knowledge has been slowest to penetrate, that there has been the greatest retention of older practices. These are held to most tenaciously around areas of their own continuing uncertainty, such as pregnancy, birth, and infant mortality. From this perspective, medical knowledge appears to be an obvious functional equivalent of ritual and belief.

The theories of Radcliffe-Brown and Freud, however, seem challenged by the changes. If taboos and rituals mark social values, does the fact a ritual activity is discontinued or declining then mean that the social value it is supporting has disappeared, or does it mean simply that a "functional equivalent" has been substituted? In the Nubian case, the decline in *mushāhara* beliefs and in life-cycle rituals generally has been accompanied by some parallel decline in the strength of obligations of community members toward one another, but this latter diminution seems much more gradual. The community obligations seem much more durable than the rituals and taboos, and will probably remain strong after the pagan practices have disappeared. The high values placed upon fertility, female chastity and so on, have remained intact in spite of the reduction in taboos and ritual that surrounded them. It might be suggested that these ritual practices were only one among many types of customs supporting social obligations, and were, in fact, merely associated epiphenomena. At any rate, if we look for functional substitutes for these disavowed practices, we find none. The question also needs to be raised as to why other strongly held Nubian values, such as honesty and courage, were given no such ceremonial recognition.

These recent changes pose similar problems for Freud's theory. If the customs disappear, what has happened to the ambivalences, hostilities, and envies that presumably supported and gave rise to them? Freud himself anticipated this and covered himself with an evolutionary assumption typical of his day. He simply postulated that "Primitive Man" had a higher degree of ambivalence than does "Civilized Man." With advancing civilization, ambivalence declined, and taboo, as the "compromise symptom" of the conflict also declined, remaining only at the individual level in neurosis (Freud 1938, pp. 858–862). This solution is ingenious and allows the changes that have occurred to become consistent with his general theory. The only evidence we have that ambivalence was any greater in "precivilized" times, however, is the presence of the taboos that have previously been defined in terms of the ambivalence of which they in turn are the only evidence. Thus we are offered unilineal evolutionary assumptions coupled with tautological reasoning.

Another hypothesis derivable from Freud's conceptions is that the sudden dropping of such customs might result in the uncontrolled release of the tensions for which the customs had provided controlled expression. This then might result in deviancy and mental illnesses. The Nubian evidence on this point is slim. It seems true that, as in most situations of social change, there has been some increase in such problems but a major difficulty of verification here, as with the functionalist interpretation, is that as causes of these problems many other factors in the situation of change have much more plausibility.

The theories remain suggestive, but they rely on a number of unverified assumptions and frequently give us uncomfortable feelings of circular resoning. They leave us with serious questions about the ways in which such emotions might become transformed into customs. Concerning taboos, such questions remain as: Why do taboos take the form they do? (Why, for example, should arbitrary restraints be useful for maintaining social values)? What is their relationship to moral norms? Why were they associated with the particular activities they were? I cannot offer definitive answers, but the analysis suggests some concluding reflections on taboo.

Conclusion

One of the strongest impressions gained from examination of the Nubian data is that the taboos take their meaning from situations that have been socially defined as sacred. As isolated avoidances they appear meaningless, but taken together they become comprehensible as a cluster of acts with a common motive or meaning: fear of spiritual powers around particular people, in certain places, for specific time periods, constituting states of sacredness. It is these states that should be our points of reference rather than individual taboos as such. This impression clearly coincides with Durkheim's position and supports it. As part of his attempt to show how the sacred sphere differed from the profane, he said: "Sacred things are those which the *interdictions* protect and isolate; profane things, those to which the interdictions are applied, and which must remain at a distance from the first" (1965), p. 56, italics added). A major concern of Durkheim's was finding an explanation as to why things, people, places, and time periods should have been defined as "sacred," i.e., inspiring awe, respect, and fear. Here, I shall not pursue this still important issue beyond what I have already suggested concerning the possible connection of sacredness and the genesis of fear in Nubian crisis rites. Instead I want to continue with the question of why taboos are so often associated with the sacred. But first, a short digression is necessary.

Some British anthropologists have recently challenged the validity of Durkheim's great insight into the basic difference between the sacred and profane spheres of life. Goody, for example, questions the universal occurrence of the dichotomy, claiming that its apparent universality is an intellectual artifact and that scholars have merely followed one another in equating "sacred" with "irrational" and "profane" with "rational." For him the division of sacred and profane is therefore simply "a division imposed by the European observer" (1962, p. 37), a dichotomy "usually based upon our 'rationalistic' frame of reference" (1962, p. 41). Universality is also disputed by Evans-Pritchard, who claims that ". . . 'sacred' and 'profane' are on the same level of experience, and far from being cut off from one another, they are so closely intermingled as to be inseparable" (1965, p. 65).

The peculiar thing about both of these criticisms is that neither of them adduces evidence of any society where the sacred is not differentiated from the mundane. I would concur with Goody's observation that a distinction between the irrational and the rational is often uncritically equated with a distinction between the sacred and profane, as well as with his apparent intention of stressing the fact that "sacred" ideas may be quite "rational" relative to the conceptual logics of the systems in which they are found. But he is wrong in concluding that therefore the sacred is not distinguished from the everyday in the actual lives of people. I would concur, too, with Evans-Pritchard, in his claim that Durkheim overemphasized the distinction between the sacred and profane. But Evans-Pritchard's opinion that they are so intermingled in experience as to be inseparable seems to be a contradiction in terms, and this statement, itself, like many others of his, shows that he needs the distinction to make any meaningful description of religion (1965:65). Until data are adduced to the contrary, I will therefore assume the domain of the sacred to be a valid category of experience, a category of particular significance in societies possessed of predominantly supernaturalistic world views.

Both Durkheim ((1965) p. 338) and Radcliffe-Brown (1952) wished to banish the word "taboo" from scientific discourse. The former suggested "interdictions" as an alternative; the latter proposed "ritual prohibitions." I think it is not simply from inertia or habit that these proposals have not been widely accepted. The term "taboo" has been retained because it denotes a class of behaviors with special characteristics that the more inclusive categories of these authors do not recognize. The denotation has been intuitively recognized in practice but not explicitly stated. I would define a taboo as essentially an *arbitrary rule of avoidance* of *normal* behavior that is backed by a belief in direct supernatural punishment. Thus, taboos are supported by fear and are found only in relationship to sacred conditions: sacred roles, sacred time periods and sacred places. This definition makes a technical distinction between real taboos and common usage, where "taboo" may refer to any forbidden or avoided topics that may arouse irrational anxiety.

Many activities are avoided or prohibited in human societies, but the outstanding characteristic of taboos is that they proscribe *normal*, acceptable behavior. This characteristic is what makes them distinct from laws or morals, which contain prohibitions against what societies have defined as *abnormal* or *illegal* actions, as well as such bans on dangerous action as are forbidden by common sense. There has been considerable confusion in the literature about the relation of taboo to law. Many of the early writers considered taboo to be the equivalent of law in "primitive" and "archaic" societies. This still persisting confusion derives from a failure to discern that a fundamental characteristic of taboo is its difference from and, in fact, logical opposition to, law and morals.

Freud came close to this position when he asserted that taboos forbid *desired* behavior. It is often true that a tabooed behavior is a desired one. But taboos may quite as well apply to other activities, such as work, that are less desirable, and may often have no apparent reference at all to desirability or undesirability. Many of the *mushāhara* taboos, for example, permit temporary avoidance of responsibility for obligations that are sometimes felt as burdensome. Instead of forbidding a desired action, they actually permit the indulgence of a desire — the desire not to fulfill, for example, the duty of visiting: one may simply plead that one has crossed water or has been to the market. Clearly, it is the suspension of the *normal* rather than of the desired that is the critical characteristic of taboo.

The prohibition of behavior that is recognized as acceptable on other occasions also contributes to the other important characteristic of taboo in our definition: its arbitrariness. This characteristic was, I think, correctly emphasized by the early theorists, but it tends to be overlooked by the functionalists, with their stress upon the "reason" behind the apparently irrational behavior and upon "social relations." My point is that it is exactly their incomprehensibility in terms of daily logic that makes taboos so effective in marking off and preserving the sacred condition. Many authors have noted that *sacred* means "set apart." The universal presence of taboos in nonliterate societies is related to the particular efficacy of arbitrary, hence mysterious, rules of defining sacred states. Of course there is a built-in circularity here. Sacred places, roles, or time periods, once defined as such, stimulate and perpetuate the fears that may bring about taboos.

Taboos are arbitrary not only because they proscribe the normal, but also because they seem, even by the standards of the culture, to have no logical "earthly" reason for doing so. The punishment that is believed to ensue from violation of a taboo has therefore also the baffling qualities of ineffability and awe that are so common to the experience of the sacred and that reinforce it. If a prohibition follows from common logic or from a moral idea, however, it is likely to be backed by permanent community sanctions and thus to be required of everyone in all places and at all times. It therefore cannot effectively serve to mark off a sacred state. As arbitrary avoidances, taboos are further serviceable in defining the sacred because, as Fortes noted, they tend to remain constantly visible for any socially defined length of time. This visibility is brought about simply by the cessation of some ordinary or routine behavior, but is enhanced by the circumstance that a cessation of action is much easier to maintain over a period of time than action is. Rituals also define the sacred sphere, but they require energy, expenditure and time and therefore can only last a short while. Taboos, though usually temporally limited, have an ease of maintenance that makes them particularly suitable for marking perpetual or indefinite periods; and such, for example, are the prohibitions upon sexual activity or upon certain foods enjoined upon members of priesthoods or religious sects. There is no absolute correlation of taboos with sacredness, as Durkheim and Marett held, but without such arbitrary abstinences from mundane pursuits, the mystery that upholds sacredness is difficult to maintain, for symbolism and ritual do not usually seem enough.

Because of their association with sacred states, taboos tend to be found in clusters, a characteristic enhanced by their arbitrary qualities. For this reason, since anything imaginable may be prohibited, they tend to proliferate by analogy. When such prohibitions are found alone, in fact, I could hypothesize that they will usually be found to be survivals and will have lost most of their supernatural meaning by becoming dissociated from their original sacred state. The English belief that spilling salt brings bad luck, an example that Radcliffe-Brown used in his essay on taboo, seems — if it is a taboo — to be a clear case of survival, and his use of it is of interest to the argument here. Why, for example, when he was searching for a Western example of a "ritual prohibition," did Radcliffe-Brown not choose such a supernaturally given and widely held commandment as "Thou shalt not kill"? I suggest that he understood intuitively the special arbitrary character of taboo, recognizing the distinction I have made between taboos and moral norms. That the example is imperfect even from his own point of view is shown by the fact that, although he used this English table custom to illustrate the taboo's nature, when he had to demonstrate its function and social value, he chose Andamanese birth customs as examples. Perhaps this is because it would have required considerable ingenuity to link the avoidance of spilling salt with important social values, much less with the social structure of contemporary England.

In my definition of taboo I noted that the expected punishment for its violation was direct and of this world, another indication of its difference from moral conceptions. An important characteristic of moral norms and social values is that they are internalized by the normal society member as a part of his conscience. When the norm is violated, guilt is felt in addition to fear of social sanctions, which are often experienced as remote. Taboos, on the contrary, in addition to their lack of direct relation to values and goals, have a palpable quality of immediate danger. The danger of sickness, sterility, or death is usually to onself and does not have reference to internalized notions of right and wrong. One does not feel guilt. As when one makes a dangerous and foolish mistake, the feeling is more likely to be fear because an error in judgment was made, not guilt of the sort that arises from violation of a moral norm.[11]

This quality is even preserved in the *mushāhara* taboos where one's indiscretion during a visit may result in misfortune to another rather than to oneself. Blame is not laid upon the transgressor; he is merely considered to have made an error, for the obligation to visit among the Nubians is paramount, and a person who fulfills this duty is presumed incapable of wishing deliberate harm. We might see the situation as a chance for enemies to attack one another. The Nubians do not view it this way; there are occasional suspicions of such malice among the women, but generally evil intentions are associated with sorcery or the Evil Eye and not with *mushāhara*.

The difference between taboos and moral or legal prohibitions is one recognized by the analyst rather than by a society's actors, yet it seems an essential one. If the distinction is valid, as I think I have demonstrated, it enables us to view institutionalized nonrationality more objectively. It aids in understanding many changes that have gone on in the secularization of the world's societies, and in the clearer evaluation of functionalist interpretations of religion. The rationalistic assumptions of the functional approach presuppose important relationships between customs and positively evaluated moral norms and "social relations." An analysis of taboos, however, which are among the most nonrational of man's institutionalized behavior patterns, highlights the fact that these functional links may often be illusory artifacts of the investigator's assumptions. A different kind of evidence is needed to prove that these often plausible links are more than secondary associations without determining significance. What is defined by the taboos imposed upon an incoming chief, for example, is the *sacredness* of his office, not his moral obligations or his power. Secondarily and by chance association the taboos may remind the group of its moral, legal and social obligations. A decline in the sacredness of the chief's office would result in a parallel disappearance of arbitrary restrictions, with some perhaps remaining as survivals for a time, but moral obligations and social power are much more durable. Social significance, in other words, is not a requisite of sacredness and vice versa.

Though they correctly discerned the nature of taboo and its relation to sacredness, the earlier writers were blinded by their evolutionary assumptions. Laws did not evolve from taboos, as they thought, for moral and legal interdictions have always existed side by side with taboos. One source of confusion lies in the fact that in societies with supernatural world views, morals also tend to have supernatural sanctions attached to them. With the increase in knowledge and secularization that have accompanied the development of many societies, however, moral norms, being rooted in more enduring social needs, have often lost their supernatural sanctions and become institutionalized as laws. Taboos, on the other hand, have either persisted to help define remaining areas of sacredness or became isolated survivals in a process of gradual extinction.

Being essentially nonempirically derived, taboos are among the purest expressions of self-fulfilling prophecies or, as Goldschmidt has more properly called the social principle involved, the self-validation of social attitudes (1959, p. 103). Although human beings do not usually change their "definition of the situation" overnight, they may do so most easily for those aspects of experience that are least tied to reality-testing or to social needs. This is one reason why, with the decline of the fearful sacredness surrounding life-cycle events, Nubian taboos are disappearing.

History has shown that taboos are among the most dispensable of man's social creations, but the study of them should reveal a great deal about the large role that institutionalized nonrationality plays in human society. The beginning of this study should be a reappraisal of the insights of the early scholars and a critical but unprejudiced view of the functionalist and psychoanalytic hypotheses. Certainly the psychodynamics of taboo should be investigated by field research directed at the emotional correlates of the beliefs and practices among peoples where such customs persist. Comparative and diachronic studies should be made of their forms and of their associations with other institutions. Meanwhile, more than a little thought is still required to comprehend the "true import of these taboos."

Notes

1. This is the one life-cycle ritual for which all of our information comes from informants' recollections. Circumcision is now a simple operation, unattended by ceremonial fanfare (see chapter 8).

2. Scorpions are identified with jinn, the dangerous ubiquitous spirits of the Islamic world. The identification of them with *mushāhara* is an example of the fusion of old and newer elements.
3. The items offered and their amounts varied from district to district throughout Nubia. The pattern of seven and the form of the ritual were basically the same everywhere. See chapter 5.
4. The killing of animals has lost most of these meanings, and is now done to feed guests invited to ceremonial feasts.
5. There is now a general trend toward reducing the severity of the operation from the Old Nubian or "Pharaonic" type of excision to the milder clitoridectomy so common in Egypt.
6. Smoke, particularly of incense, is used on such occasions as *dhikr* rituals and *zār* ceremonies, where people who are felt to be possessed by spirits inhale it. It is also used at saints' shrines and in rituals to dispel or placate jinn who have caused sickness.
7. Homans (1965) has pointed out that there is no inconsistency between the ideas of Malinowski and Radcliffe-Brown; there may be both primary anxiety due to uncertainty and secondary anxiety if rituals are not properly performed. But it is my belief that Homans overlooked some important points. Although Radcliffe-Brown did say that anxiety would arise if ritual were not performed, his main point was that rituals induce anxiety in order to underscore and re-affirm values (pointed out to me by William A. Lessa in personal communication). Furthermore, taboos, the subject of Radcliffe-Brown's paper, are not "rituals not performed," but are, as Van Gennep noted, a kind of negative rite in themselves.
8. I am restricting my treatment of psychoanalytic interpretations of taboo to Freud because the subject has been largely neglected by psychoanalysts and when it is mentioned, Freud's interpretation seems to be accepted as final. Theodor Reik, for example, one of Freud's students, uncritically applies his master's interpretation of taboo to *couvade* customs with no modification or addition (Reik 1958, pp. 53, 56, 64–5, 68–9).
9. Among other laudatory remarks, Kroeber said that Freud's conclusions regarding the "correspondences between taboo customs and the compulsion neurosis — are unquestionable, as are also the parallelisms between the two aspects of taboo (holy and defiling) and the ambivalence of emotions under an accepted prohibition" (1965, p. 52).
10. See chapter 4.
11. This direct and immediate quality is one that has often been attributed to magic. This is one reason why taboos are often conceived as magical, even though, in most cases, as with the Nubians it is probable that spirit ideas are connected with them, or that they are survivals of such ideas. See Crawley and Besterman (1927, pp. 20–30).

Chapter 8

Circumcision and Excision Ceremonies

JOHN G. KENNEDY

This chapter deals with an important component of the traditional Nubian ritual system, but one which has lapsed into relative insignificance in modern times. In Kanuba, for example, we were sitting on the village mastaba one evening talking with a group of men when one of them mentioned that his son had been circumcised that day, expressing annoyance that his wife had taken the boy to the barber in Daraw while he was away at work. He had not even been aware that the operation was planned for that day. The whole thing had taken only a few moments, the boy had been able to play quiet games for the remainder of the day, and there had been no ceremonial at all, though a few women in the neighborhood congratulated the boy and gave him candy. Girls' ceremonies still retain some vigor, as will be described, but the whole complex, which was of such vital importance in Old Nubia, has diminished to occupy a place of minute significance within the total ritual complex. Though some of the reasons for this diminution are explored in this chapter, the magnitude of the ceremonial reduction still poses questions for social theorists.

How can a group, in effect, jettison an entire complex of beliefs and practices that were of considerable psychological importance to them as individuals, and that were tightly interwoven with many other elements of the socio-cultural system? Much the same thing has occurred with the Nubian sheikh cults such as are described by Messiri in chapter 4, where the same question arises. One answer which suggests itself is that some cultural systems are much more flexible than others — they assimilate or drop customs, beliefs, and even complexes of customs and beliefs much more easily than do other cultural systems. It is as if much of the overlay of learning and tradition sits more lightly upon such groups, or as if, to put it another way, the pattern of socialization had not penetrated their psyches as deeply as psychological theorists tend to assume as a universal tendency. Recognition of such cultural flexibility should have considerable importance for predicting cultural change and adoption of innovations.

It is my conclusion that the Nubians are a group at the more flexible end of the scale, if such a scale could be constructed. Undoubtedly their adaptive ability has been a result of their historical vicissitudes and necessities. But to say

151

this is not enough. A great deal needs to be known about why and how some groups are able to react with flexibility, while others do not survive, or survive by a completely different strategy (e.g. the Jews).

These questions are only raised here, not answered, though these data may contribute to some ultimate answer. The discussion here relates to social science theories of initiation and "rites of passage," but its main burden is the ethnographic rounding out of the traditional Nubian ceremonial complex.

Herodotus found the Egyptians practicing circumcision when he visited their country around the middle of the fifth century, B.C., and stated that either they or the Ethiopians had invented the custom. This conclusion reflects nothing more than the great antiquity of record-keeping in this part of the world, but paintings do attest that in Egypt circumcision was practiced at least as far back as the sixth Dynasty, 2340–2180 B.C. (Ghalioungui 1962, pp. 95–97). Female excision was also a custom of ancient Egyptians, as reported by Strabo (Ghalioungui 1963, p. 96). Other evidence is less clear, but we know that it was customary among several tribes of the Arabian peninsula in pre-Islamic times (Levy 1962, p. 252).

Circumcision of males is still nearly universal in the Middle East. Though not mentioned in the Qur'an, it is an essential feature of the Islamic faith, as it is of Judaism and Coptic Christianity. Female excision is also still widespread in Islamic communities from India to Morocco (Levy 1962, p. 252 and Smith 1903, p. 16f.n.). Both customs are practiced by the Nubian peoples who have traditionally inhabited that strip of the Nile between Aswan, Egypt, and Dongola, Sudan.

In spite of the persisting vitality of circumcision and excision in the Middle East, most scholars attemptimg to account for genital operations or to test "initiation" hypotheses have tended to exclude this area from their samples.[1] Undoubtedly, an important reason for this neglect is that there are few detailed data from the area.[2] A more significant reason is, perhaps, that the ceremonies do not easily fit the theories. For example, most theories are based upon a "rites of passage" model — implicitly assuming that puberty, being the time of transition to adulthood, is naturally marked by such a ritual. As the causal basis underlying the rites, these functional theories postulate society's "needs" for altering the child's personality. Whatever their differences, they rest on the assumptions that children are somehow inadequately socialized for their adult roles, and that the ceremonies are designed to correct these socialization failures (e.g., Cohen 1964; Freud 1939; Whiting et al. 1958; Young 1965). Middle Eastern ritual operations, which are performed on prepubertal children who are undergoing no transition to adulthood, do not easily fit such formulations.

Rather than make a critical analysis of theories of initiation, I wish to provide contrastive data and interpretation that may assist in illuminating the general problem. I shall bĕgin by describing the circumcision rites for Egyptian Nubian boys as they were practiced in some parts of Nubia (e.g., Diwan and Abu Hor) as late as 1933, and excision rituals for girls as they are still frequently performed.

Boys' Circumcision Ceremonies

The Nubians allowed circumcision[3] to be carried out at any time from forty days after birth to ten years after, but they preferred it to occur between the ages of three and five. Older informants insist that boys' circumcision ceremonies, called *balay dawi* "big wedding", were the largest of all Nubian rituals. Though sometimes more costly in complexity, time and organization, however, circumcisions were actually subordinate in social importance to weddings. Circumcisions and weddings were occasionally held simultaneously so that the costs could be minimized, and poorer families might also economize by having several boys circumcised in a single cooperative ceremony. When this happened or when a wealthy man's child underwent the operation, the elaborateness of the communal celebration transcended any other Nubian ritual.

A good show was an important indicator of the wealth and prestige of the family, and arrangements for the ceremony were usually begun long in advance. Members of the patrilineage aided the father in defraying initial expenses and some of the costs were made up during the ceremony through the *noqūt* (small gifts). The major expense was the provision of sacrificial animals; and the required numbers of these varied among the sub-regions of Nubia. In the Diwan-Derr (Fadija) area, the slaughter of four cattle was consdered ideal, but it could only be realized by wealthier families. Costs were sometimes reduced by eliminating certain parts of the celebration requiring sacrifices, and poorer families might substitute sheep for cattle. Other expenses were entailed in the large amounts of grain necessary to provide bread for the guests, the many baskets of dates offered, and the bottles of perfume frequently sprinkled upon the celebrants. New and special clothing had to be provided for the immediate family of the child and the securing of a camel and donkey for the ceremony was often a considerable financial burden as well.

A circumcision was officially inaugurated on the day called *gāwi nahār*. The invitation was signalled by a slave who made the rounds in the village and adjacent villages announcing the event and the schedule of activities. The following day women began gathering at the child's house to help in preparation of special clothing and food for the guests — *sha'reya, durra* bread, dates and *abrīk*.[4] The period of preparation lasted from fifteen to twenty days, and when all was completed, the slave again made his rounds of invitations. Soon after, festively adorned guests began arriving by boat, donkey, or on foot.

The first day of the actual circumcision ceremony was called the *basīm*. Music and dancing, which was to continue almost unceasingly for four days, began that afternoon, a cow was killed, and by evening a feast was ready.

The place of honor was occupied by the five-year-old *'arīs* (groom) wearing his new clothes. If the family could afford it, he wore a red or white *jalabeya*, a green *quftan* and a red fez, decorated with beads and coins of gold and silver.[5] His adult female relatives were dressed in blue *jarjars* (overdresses of sheer material) worn over white dresses; with their gauzy blue veils, they stood out from the other women, who wore their newest and brightest colored clothes and their treasured gold jewelry. The boy's father wore a new *za'boum* (dark brown, woolen, handwoven cloak) over his white *jalabeya*.

The circumcision itself was usually performed on the morning following the first day of dancing and feasting. The boy was often unaware that he was to undergo the painful genital operation. Very early in the morning he was bathed and dressed in a white *jalabeya* of light material that would not irritate the wound, and gold necklaces belonging to his mother or grandmother, called *bandoki* or *farajala*, were placed round his neck. Henna, the red dye used cosmetically and ritually was applied to his hands and feet by an elderly female of the family, and kohl to his eyelids. After the henna had been applied, a woman's veil was put over his head. Such ritual precautions were taken against the bloodthirsty jinns, who were believed to attack fertility and to be more aggressive towards males. Other hovering Nile spirits (*dogri*, *amen*, *nootu*, etc.) were pleased and distracted by the symbols of bridal beauty. While the ritual preparations proceeded within, women were dancing and musicians were playing in the courtyard.

During this part of the ceremony the customary *noqūt* was presented to the family. Money was rare in Old Nubia, and in the nineteenth century *noqūt* usually consisted of dates, sugar cones, wheat and *durra*. Each man's donation to the father, and each woman's gift to the mother was loudly announced by a slave and then carefully recorded in writing. Informants from the Kenuz area of Abu Hor stated that while the *noqūt* was being recorded another slave (or relative) stood by brandishing a sword, shouting "May God give him children."[6] Other *noqūt*, usually in the form of coins, were given to the "barber" who performed the ritual surgery. *Noqūt* coins were dropped in a pan of Nile water so that they might be decontaminated from the dangerous jinns who hover around money.

Several informants recounted variations of the following rituals for the circumcision operation: The boy in ceremonial dress was seated on a mat, his mother and father on his left and right sides. A plate of henna was placed on the mat in front of his mother and a bowl of water was set before the boy. The ritual commenced with the mother sticking a lump of henna to the boy's forehead. The father fixed a gold coin in this henna, preferably a gold pound. The boy then sat quietly as more *noqūṭ* was presented by the guests; the name of each donor was again loudly proclaimed to the gathering. After this, water from the bowl was used to remove the henna from his forehead, and the mother's sister or some older female relative came forward to hold him for the knife.

As he chanted the powerful Muslim incantation, "In the name of Allah, the compassionate, the merciful," the "barber" severed the foreskin. Having been admonished not to act like a girl, the boy restrained his tears. His mother had been holding his face away, so that he would not look at his wound and thereby become sterile. She now cracked three eggs into a small bowl and held it to his nose to prevent fainting. Some of the raw egg she applied to the wound.

The women meanwhile intensified their dancing and drumming, uttering long cries of joy, or *zaghary̆t* and, at intervals, shouted out, "Congratulations to the groom!" Accompanied by the singing and drumming crowd, his mother (or an adult sister) then carried the boy to the Nile. There he was bathed, and the barber or midwife threw his foreskin with an old coin out into the water to pacify the spirits of the river.

After the operation, the entire crowd of villagers and guests began a procession to one of the saints' tombs in the vicinity. In Diwan, Tongala, and other nearby districts, the tomb of Sheikh Shebeika was visited. The boy's father, carrying a sword, headed the procession, followed by the bedecked boy riding on a donkey. A slave riding a camel and beating a huge Sudanese drum came next. This camel also transported two huge sacks of *aslīg⁷* and *abrīk*, which were to be used for the ceremonial meal at the saint's tomb. A cow, which would be slaughtered for the main dish of this feast, followed behind the camel. Following the animals came the boy's mother with the rest of the family. The large crowd of singing and dancing people was spread out along the path.

The dances were essentially the same as those used at weddings. Several lines of men with locked arms danced backwards. They were separated from the opposing lines of women by a dance master. Waving a staff and swaying in rhythm between them, the dance master kept the groups of men and women apart and controlled the progress of the procession. Grouped beside the rows of dancers were five or six musicians beating their *ṭars* and leading the singing. These drummers were either women dressed in white, or slaves. The procession sometimes had to travel as far as ten kilometers, taking several hours to reach the shrine.

Arriving some time in the afternoon, the dancing and singing crowd was greeted by the caretaker of the shrine (naqīb). The cow was handed over to him to be slaughtered, with the help of some of the older men, while the people relaxed and socialized. Under the direction of the naqīb, men immediately began cooking the ceremonial feast. The abrīk, which had been carried by the camel, was used with the cooked beef to prepare fatta. The animal's head, neck, skin, stomach, and legs were given to the naqīb as an offering to the saint.

The singing and dancing were resumed by the crowd and continued uninterruptedly, and while the feast was being prepared, the boy with his father and some of the close relatives circled the saint's tomb seven times. On each circuit, they petitioned the spirit for such favors as health, fertility and wealth. An important part of the ceremonies at the shrine were dhikr rituals in which the men chanted Ṣūfistic praises to God, swaying their bodies in ecstatic rhythmic unison (see chapter 3).

The following afternoon, the ceremonies commenced again. The boy again received visitors and accepted noqūṭ. He sat on his veranda, wearing a white jalabeya and the gold of his female relatives. It was obligatory for the father to serve dates and aslīg to all visitors who came to congratulate the boy. Again, the dancing and singing continued unabated through the day and into the following morning. This joyous but exhausting pattern of celebration was repeated for two more days, making a total of four.

On the evening of each day, a dhikr ritual was held by the men. Thus, while women were dancing to the tambourine drums, men chanted ecstatic praise to Allāh. The event reached its finale when two cows were slaughtered, and a ceremonial feast was served.

Following the celebration, the boy was kept in the house for ten days. Unless infection had set in, he was then considered recovered. Native herbs were applied to the cut to facilitate healing and a small bag of salt was tied to his wrist for the same purpose. On recovery, this bag was removed and thrown into the Nile as an offering to the female river spirits. While the boy was secluded he ate alone served by women of the family. He was given special "strengthening" foods (pigeons, chickens and eggs), the same foods which are eaten by brides and grooms to promote fertility and virility.

For the circumcision, and for forty days thereafter, the boy was required to observe many precautions concerned with mushāhara, the Nubian belief that a person undergoing a crisis, such as giving birth, marriage, or death, is in grave supernatural danger for a period of forty days, or for the period until the new moon (see chapter 7). Since at this time he was also considered vulnerable to the Evil Eye and to jinn, he wore hejabs (charms) to prevent attacks which could endanger his procreative potential.

Girls' Excision Ceremonies

The Nubian excision operation, as still performed, removes a girl's clitoris and closes her vulva with scar tissue and is much more extreme than male circumcision. It is referred to as the "Pharaonic" or "Sudanese" style, and is actually in infibulation.

Though her operation is more severe, the girl's ceremony is comparatively abbreviated and private. It might be scheduled to coincide with a boy's circumcision, but more usually it is conducted privately by women of the neighborhood with no protracted preparations.

On the night before the operation, the small "bride" ('arūsa) is adorned with gold and dressed in new clothes. In the manner of a real bride, her eyes are made up with kohl, and her hands and feet are dyed with henna. On the following morning neighborhood women gather at the house. With little fanfare or preparation, the midwife quickly performs the operation. As several women spread her legs, a bowl is placed beneath the girl to catch the blood and the clitoris, and the labia minora and part of the labia majora are excised with a razor or knife. The women meanwhile chant "Come, you are now a woman," "You became a bride." "Bring her the groom now" "Bring her a penis, she is ready for intercourse." These cries are interspersed with protective Quranic incantations, punctuated at intervals by zagharīt.

According to some informants, this chanting and shouting serves partially to drown the screams of the child. Incense is kept burning during the operation to scare away the jinn and the Evil Eye. Raw egg and green henna are then applied, and the child's legs are tied together.

After the ordeal, the mother and nearest female relatives serve dates, candy, popcorn, and tea to the visiting women, and the hostess sprinkles them with perfume. Everyone congratulates the girl, and some women give her small gifts. The neighborhood women each give "small" noqūt to the mother.

Sometimes the child's legs remain tied together for forty days. More typically, she is regarded as healed seven to fifteen days after the operation. This healing process generally provides the scar tissue for the complete closure of the vulva, except for a small urination orifice, which is kept open by a match or reed tube. To give her strength and to promote her fertility, the girl is fed with lentil soup, chickens, and broth of pigeons. Throughout the healing period, she is treated like a bride or a woman giving birth.[10]

Meaning of the Ceremonies

The Nubians consider that the genital operation is necessary for all normal children, and they readily give several reasons for it. Almost invariably, the immediate explanation offered is that circumcision is a religious obligation prescribed in the Hadīth of the Prophet Muhammad.[11] *Tahāra*, the name of the operation, is a variant of the Arabic for ritual purification, and the Nubians believe that it symbolically purifies the child, making possible his future participation in prayers. The operation is also claimed by informants to be a prophylactic measure promoting cleanliness, as is often implied when they say: "When the child begins to scratch himself, then is the time to arrange for his circumcision."[12] It is further believed to have magical significance in promoting fertility, and in maintaining general body health. And although the idea is vaguely articulated, there is a belief that without circumcision or excision a degree of completeness of manhood or womanhood would be missing, as is also implied in the notion that the operation prepares the person to enter marriage.

Besides excision of her clitoris, the female operation involves an infibulation, which closes the vulva with scar tissue. This severe measure is said to have the aim of preventing the loss of virginity and eliminating the possibility of a shameful pregnancy. Such reasons are direct expressions of the belief that women have an inherently wanton character, which is physiologically centered in the clitoris. The Nubians argue that the only way to blunt the inherent sexual wildness of girls and to preserve their chastity is through this means, though there is no medical evidence that any diminishing effect on desire is actually produced (Barclay 1964, p. 238 and Bonapart 1952, pp. 68–71).

A final Nubian rationale for circumcision and excision is an aesthetic one. Without the operation, the sex organs are disgusting to the marriage partner, both visually and to the touch.

Circumcision and Weddings

Nubian circumcision ceremonies strongly resembled weddings, and I do not believe that they can be understood apart from their connection with marriage. Marriage symbolism was everywhere present, as can be seen in the name of the event — the "big wedding" — in the names of the participants — "bride" and "groom" — and in the form of the ceremony, with its joyful processions, songs, dances, feastings and visits to saints' tombs. In much detail, these ritual patterns duplicate the marriage rituals.[13] Since the form and symbolism of the two rituals resemble each other so closely, a brief consideration of the wedding will help us to understand the meaning of circumcision ceremonies (see chapter 9).

Of the two ritual events, weddings were the more complex. A wedding might last fifteen days instead of four, and there were ritual exchanges of food between the families and an extended series of symbolic customs to bring bride and groom together. Informants report that families felt the need to display generosity and wealth, and that marriage and circumcision both afforded the opportunities to demonstrate these qualities.

Marriage ceremonies usually took place at the time of the date harvest, a time of family unity, when the men returned from the cities, and of abundance. In Old Nubia, weddings were thus deeply symbolic of family and community solidarity. Circumcisions, with their parallel symbolism and spirit, functioned similarly in this respect. In addition, the custom of giving *noqūt* and help at weddings and circumcisions concretely dramatized the network of reciprocal ties of obligation that formed an important aspect of the social organization of the community.

Marriage had extreme importance in the life-cycles of individuals by reason of its validating adult status and ushering each person into full social standing. Islamic sanction backs this notion in the saying that "Marriage completes one's religion." Until marriage, a Nubian is not considered fully Muslim, and thus in a real sense is not a complete social being. Men have no vote in community affairs and women cannot validate their muturity and social worth by bearing children until they have crossed this all-important threshold. Being a prerequisite to marriage, and in many ways a rehearsal for it, circumcision and excision are implicated in this validation of full adult standing and community membership.

Besides the manifold specific meanings and functions in association with marriage, other related but more general associations with sexuality and fertility were extremely important in Nubian circumcision ceremonies. Elsewhere, I have discussed the great significance of fertility to Nubians — the tremendous degree of concern, the symbolism that surrounds everything related to reproduction (chapter 7). The life-cycle crises of birth, circumcision, and marriage all follow a pattern in which the flowing of blood from the genital region entails a forty-day period of "sacred vulnerability." During this time, the person is considered particularly susceptible to spirit attack, which might cause sickness or loss of fertility and potency. Fertility thus symbolizes a most important and emotionally loaded cluster of Nubian values.

Sexuality *per se* is also an important focus in Nubian life-cycle rituals. In the excision and circumcision operations as they relate to marriage, sexuality is given a dramatic focus, its general importance being highly intensified by the anxieties surrounding it. A painful consequence of excision is that at marriage, another operation must be performed to open the vagina. Though it is considered preferable that the groom deflower the bride, this reopening operation is generally performed by the mid-wife with a knife or razor. Usually, since she is only ten to fourteen years of age at the time of her marriage, the girl vividly remembers her excision, but is still largely ignorant of what to expect from intercourse. She is also unsure as to the kind of behavior to texpect from her mate during private moments. She is conditioned to feel shame about sexual matters and often is frightened at the prospects of intimate contact. The fear surrounding the initial consummation of the marriage is magnified by the belief that spirits are strongly attracted to genital blood. Nubian tradition has taught her that those most treasured values — health, fertility, and the welfare of eventual children — are especially threatened at such critical times as birth, circumcision, marriage and menstruation. Many of our informants attested that the consummation of marriage was fraught with terror and anxiety, though fears are slightly counteracted, at an intellectual level, by rumors that the sex act will eventually be pleasurable.

The male is also traumatized to some extent by the marriage situation. On the wedding night, he is honor-bound to perform intercourse with his often hysterical and terrified young bride. In addition to the interpersonal trauma, his fertility, virility, and health are also endangered by the attraction of dangerous spirits to the contaminating blood. Several male informants privately admitted impotence and confusion on their wedding mornings. They described feelings of revulsion towards what they felt was a cruel act, and emotions of fear of the contaminating potency of female genital blood. Several weeks were often needed before intercourse afforded any satisfaction.[14]

The Nubian circumcision and excision ceremonies represented preliminary stages to the marriage complex. Both were community events with social functions relating to community solidarity and identity. They indicate to us, as they dramatized to the Nubians, the importance of marriage and of the particular set of beliefs, motivations and social principles that were to be activated at the person's entrance into full adult status. In some ways, the male circumcision ceremonial suggests a village "coming out party." The family announced a proud possession to the community — a healthy son, who in a few years would be ready to marry. The entire community joyfully lauded this announcement, showed its respects to his family, and took numerous ritual precautions to insure his fertility. The girls' ceremony, though more muted, in keeeping with the lesser status of women and their lack of importance in perpetuating family lines, still possesses many of the same elements and social emphases.

Group solidarity at the level of family, lineage, and community is activated and reinforced by the great focus of activity and concern upon the individual child. Besides the cluster of attitudes and values surrounding the family, kin group, and community, the Nubian social principles of sex separation, male dominance, and age-generation dominance were all overtly delineated and thus reinforced by the roles of the participants, their spatial alignments, and verbal behavior during these ceremonies. The identical symbolism, functions, and patterning of these ceremonies indicate their close association in people's minds. Such facts show that circumcision, excision, and marriage were components of a single ceremonial complex with multiple meanings for individuals and for the community. They cannot be adequately treated as separate ritual entities. Neither can the genital operations be abstracted and explained apart from the total ritual complex, as is so often done in cross-cultural comparisons.

Psychological Effects

In the Upper Egyptian village of Silwa, circumcision ceremonies show many similarities in meaning and content to those I have described for the nearby Nubians; Ammar (1954) has interpreted them psycho-functionally as means for "aligning the child with its sex group." He also proposes the supplementary psychological hypothesis that the operation and ritual help the child to identify with the parent of the same sex, while the drama makes him aware of the social implications and responsibilities of his sex role (1954, pp. 121, 124). Honigmann, commenting on the Silwa ceremonies as reported by Ammar, noticed that their timing coincides with the period of the first Oedipal crisis, and also that during everyday socialization, children are threatened with circumcision to induce obedience. He concludes that: "By this theory [i.e. using the concept of the Oedipal complex], threatening young children with genital mutilations and then carrying them out could be construed as taking advantage of a developmental stage to intensify and exploit such worries in order to enforce docility" (1967, p. 218).

Informants reported that this ritual complex often had a significant impact upon the attitudes and personalities of Nubian children, but enforcement of conformity seems a minor aspect of a complex set of influences. Most circumcisions in Old Nubia were performed between the ages of three and six, and as Honigmann noted, this is the "Oedipal" period — a stage of increased interest in the genitals, masturbation, exhibitionism, and aggression, when children frequently have fears concerning damage to the valued sex organ and guilty fantasies about the mother. It is during this period, too, that much of the superego (conscience) formation is completed.

This critical period of sexual awakening, when the child is also mastering language, locomotion, and learning his potentialities for manipulating the environment, was just the time that the Nubians chose to traumatize him with a genital operation. The operation forcefully and painfully drew his genital area to his attention. Particularly the male child could not help but be impressed by the great ceremonial drama centered upon him and specifically upon his sex organ. The numerous ritual precautions against *mushāhara* and evil jinns maintained awareness at high level, as did the congratulations and constant jokes concerning the operation.

The Nubian girl's drama was more limited, but she was subjected to much more severe genital pain and much longer confinement. As she lay with her legs bound together from fifteen to forty days, her mind was continuously on her genital area. Old women vividly remembered this period of misery even fifty to sixty years later. Genital awareness and the fearful ramifications of sexuality were verbally reinforced by continuous admonitions concerning chastity and marriage. Even more affect and meaning were instilled by a myriad of taboos and ritual precautions having the purpose of repelling danger from hovering jinns, who were believed ready to attack her genitals. A sense of the mystery and importance of sex, a vivid fear of the evils of unchaste behavior, the great responsibility of child-rearing, and an intense awareness of his or her genitals were all powerfully impressed upon the consciousness of the circumcised or excised child.

These ceremonies thus had an ambivalent psychological impact. On the one hand, they were ego-supporting and future-oriented; on the other, they were punitive, painful, and fear instilling. Such a situation might be interpreted as ideal for intimidating a child, suppressing sexual and aggressive Oedipal desires, and inculcating docility — thus reinforcing superego development. The behavior of the actors during the circumcision operation itself, however, suggests other considerations.

It will be remembered that the mother and father are both present in supportive roles throughout the boy's operation. The mother, or a surrogate, gives him support by holding him, applying herbs to his wounds, and so on. It is the barber, moreover, not the father, who inflicts the pain. Contrary to Freudian interpretations, the principal effect here is not the suppression of aggressive drives towards the father nor the enforcement of docility, for in view of the fact that the Nubian father typically has been away working in the city for long periods of his life, it is particularly difficult to presume strong Oedipal hostilities towards him. Neither is there anything to imply that incest desires are directed away from the mother. If anything, her physically supportive role in the ceremony would tend to increase the boy's dependence on her.

The evidence suggests that a principal effect was to create in the child an intense awareness of his sexuality and to arouse anxiety concerning its social significance. He was subjected to pain, surrounded by taboos and precautions against damage to his genitals, and imbued with fear of the mysterious "life-force" fertility — the symbolic and social implications of which he could not possibly understand. Marriage loomed ahead as a dimly comprehended though joyful event. Yet it was also vaguely foreboding, dangerous, and somehow related to his sex organ.

Ammar is, of course, correct in one sense when he states (1954) that the Silwa child was being "initiated" into a sex role. But the uncritical application of van Gennep's passage rite model in the Nubian case would mislead by oversimplification and preconceptions of function. By physiological criteria the Nubian child is actually considered a member of a sex category from birth. There is never any question of feminine characteristics which must be eliminated (as suggested by van Gennep 1960, and Whiting et al. 1958, 1961). The birth of a boy is a time of rejoicing and congratulations, and from that time forward continual references to his gender along with behavior patterns relating to it are made in his presence. In the ceremonial operation, his already unequivocally assigned sex identity was publicly recognized and celebrated. The ritual was a part of the social process by which a family asserted its social presence and ranking, and reaffirmed its solidarity. At the individual level, the boy was given symbolically a collective stamp of approval and a vote of acceptance by the community. He was simultaneously identified on at least four levels: (1) as a member of a sex category; (2) as a member of familistic group; (3) as a legitimate community member; and (4) as a member of the vast Islamic religious system. This dramatic demonstration that he especially was important to the group was an effective means of helping to establish the strong and confident self-image and sense of sexual identity which are so marked among older Nubians.

But it must be emphasized that while group membership was recognized, there was no role-transition or "passage" in the sense usually assumed by analysts of such rituals. The uncircumcised child was laughed at and mildly teased by the already circumcised children, but afterwards he assumed no new role behavior. He was still looked upon as a child and treated by adults in accord with his chronological age. The ritual was a preparation for the really significant role-change to come later — marriage.

The feminine wedding symbolism, in which the boy's eyes are blackened with *kohl*, his hands dyed with *henna*, and a bridal veil ritually removed, might superficially appear to be matters of symbolic "passage" to male status. Ammar makes such an inference from identical practices at nearby Silwa, and states that his inference was stimulated by the following comment by the circumcising "barber": "Let us put this female cloth around you, and by making you look like a girl tonight, you will be able to avert the Evil Eye" (1954, p. 122). I do not see how the inference of a change from female status may be made from such evidence. The Nubians explicitly deny such a meaning. They do not regard the boy as being in any way feminine prior to his operation. Rather, the symbolism conveys a temporary assumption of female attributes in order that his maleness can be recognized and celebrated. The removal of the veil, by dramatic contrast, reaffirms his well-known masculinity, at the same time underscoring the general value of maleness in Nubian culture.

There are complicating factors for any easy interpretations of the symbolism here. As in the Silwa Barber's statement, the stated Nubian motivation for this part of the ritual is simply protection against hostile spirits. Since these creatures are believed to be more threatening to boys, it is safer to disguise the male child. But why is he dressed as a bride and not simply as a girl? Girls wear the costume of the bride in their own excision ceremonies, women giving birth dress in this same costume to please the river spirits, and males may be similarly decked out on the occasions of their marriage and during participation in *zār* ceremonies (See Chapter 10). It thus becomes clear that to interpret this ritual behavior as having the purpose of divesting the child of female identity would be a gross misunderstanding of the situation. Females undergoing the same ritual actions as males obviously do not want to change their sex identity, and if they did, they would not go about it in this way.

Contrary then, to such hypotheses as those of Whiting et al. (1958) and Young (1965), which postulate masculine socialization as the basic function of such rituals, the Nubians have no notion of erasing opposite sex attributes in the children. The child is to them an incomplete human being, and it devolves upon the adult community to complete him as a person through magical and symbolic means. It is incomplete masculine personality and incomplete feminine personality which require ritual attention. The notion that such practices imply changes from prior membership in the opposite sex category is unwarranted here. When the child is circumcised, he is surgically purified. His nascently existing sexuality is thus magically perfected and he is ritually endorsed as a social person belonging to the appropriate sex category.

From the child's point of view, it seems clear that his developing ego was bolstered by this circumcision or excision ritual. Much of the cultural value system, which had been previously absorbed without awareness, was now crystallized for him by the ceremony. At the same time, his own sex identity was forcefully impressed upon his consciousness, he was clearly shown that he was a male with masculine prerogatives, and it was powerfully dramatized how he fitted into the scheme of both cosmos and community. Together with these character-structuring impacts, however, were the anxieties aroused by intense pain and fear of supernatural threats. The ritual expressed a structural ambivalence through the simultaneous association of good and evil, pleasure and pain.

A clear difference in social status between the sexes, which reflects prevailing cultural attitudes, is evident in these Nubian rituals. In the male ceremony, positive ego-reinforcing elements predominate over the anxiety-producing ones. The female rite also possesses some elements of positive reinforcement, but its emphasis is primarily upon punishment and social control. The ceremony makes it plain to the girl that she has a tremendous responsibility for bearing children. There is also a clear implication of woman's natural lack of self-control in regard to sexuality. It becomes very obvious to her that she possesses an organ which is attractive to men, with potentially dangerous social consequences. All through her early socialization, she learns that women are sensual creatures, lacking in intellect and moral control, second-class Muslims in effect, who are generally excluded from the mosque and not permitted in at all while menstruating. She finds out that because of her "weakness" and sexual propensities, she is a threat to the family honor. There is no doubt that what Antoun (1968, p. 672) calls the "modesty code" has great importance in motivating girls' excision rituals, but in the girl's mind honor and social validation are secondary to punishment and pain. Sexual fears, anxieties concerning fertility responsibility, and a clear-cut impression of her social subordination to men are forcefully stamped into a young girl's consciousness.

There are some ego-supporting ritual elements, too, in the emphasis upon the female role in procreation and the focus upon sexual attractiveness, though the importance of the attractiveness of the sexual organ to feminine self-esteem shows the considerable cultural anxiety in the area of sexuality. Other evidence of this anxiety can be seen in the fact that if the husband were leaving the village to work in the city, even long after marriage, women would often gladly submit again to an infibulation operation and might prove their faithfulness in this way two or three times. Several cases were also reported to us in which young unmarried girls were subjected to a second operation when an older female relative judged that the first excision was not complete enough to please a potential husband aesthetically or to give complete assurance of chastity.

These differences between the sexes in ceremonial emphases reflect the principles of sex-separation and sex-dominance, which are so important in Nubian social organization. Perhaps few places in the world have more rigid norms than the Middle East regarding the separation of the sexes. Nowhere is sex differentiation based upon a more clear assumption that men and women are two different orders of human beings. Nubians share these general Islamic ideas and practices. Nubian men and women live the greater parts of their lives within groups of their own sex, and the differences between the sexes are dramatized by numerous behavior patterns and symbolic markers. The distance between the social and experiential worlds of the sexes has also been widened by the Nubians' long pattern of labor migration, which used to take most of the men to cities for much of their adult lives.

It was thus a rigidly dichotomized and hierarchical adult social world into which the Nubian child was moving. For the community, the circumcision and excision ceremonies dramatized and reaffirmed the importance of this structure. For the child, they emphatically inculcated its form and meaning, while placing him clearly at a certain point within it.

Changes in the Rituals

Of all Nubian ceremonies, those concerned with male circumcision have probably changed most in recent years. The operation has become a simple religious necessity and, as in other parts of Egypt, is privately performed by a "barber". In boys' ceremonies there has been a large-scale reduction of the rituals and they are no longer the occasion of great ceremonial feasts. On the day of his operation he is still given a few presents by relatives, and the parents offer dates to guests. A few protective precautions against the Evil Eye and *mushāhara* have been retained. The reason given for these changes is that the costs of the ceremonies have become too great in the face of the diminishing resources of Nubia.

Girls' excision ceremonies have continued much in the form described. This is probably related to women's greater isolation from acculturating influences, as well as to the fact that their ceremonialism was much more meager in the first place. The major change in the girls' ritual has been towards a lessening of the severity of the operation. There is an increasing tendency to substitute the "Egyptian method," a simple excision of the clitoris, for the inflbulation, eliminating the necessity for a special "opening" operation at marriage. This change towards moderation is justified by Islamic authorities, e.g. "Circumcise, but do not go too far." (Trimingham 1965, p. 182). Changing attitudes are also reflected in the frequent Nubian comment that the Egyptian method permits the wife greater pleasure in sexual intercourse.

In support of the argument I have made, there is evidence that these ceremonial changes are consistent with other changes in Nubian culture. As Nubian men have been progressively forced away from their villages, they have been more consistently in contact with urban values, values that have been changing rapidly in the direction of those characteristic of the urban variant of Egyptian national culture. With the loss of their palm trees and agricultural resources, and with rising dependency upon monetarily recompensed labor, land has decreased in importance as a Nubian focal value.

This change has been accompanied by a corresponding decrease in emphasis upon lineage-continuity and its accompanying values and attitudes. These changes have been most pronounced in the southern part of Egyptian Nubia. Studies made there just prior to the recent resettlement showed that the social structure in some parts of the Fadija area was based almost entirely upon nuclear family households and upon their individually developed reciprocal relationships rather than upon the lineage and tribal structures of the past (Fernea 1967, pp. 260–286).

Such changes, along with increased education and accelerated communication with the outside world (e.g., through transistor radios, magazines, newspapers, and transportational mobility) have produced alterations in the meaning of marriage and in the status of women. In spite of conscious attempts to preserve traditional custom, it is no longer as meaningful to marry a cousin or to have a great many children and there is evidence that many such customs are weakening or breaking down. As would be expected in such a case, the multiple supports underlying the intense emphasis on fertility have been undermined. Though still of considerable importance to the Nubians, this value is losing its previous importance and meaning. The hierarchical principle of male dominance is also diminishing in the face of "Western" egalitarian ideas, which are spreading in the cities. These ideas are becoming much more widespread and even dominant through the increasing proportion of men who take their families to live with them in the urban areas (Geiser 1967a). Such changes have also decreased the pattern of extreme sex separation in daily life.

Since all these social principles and social values were obviously supportive of, and linked to, the complex system of circumcision, excision and marriage rituals, it is not surprising that the social changes have tended to empty them of their emotional content and meaning. Such an interpretation is reinforced by evidence of sex differentials in change. Men's ceremonies have all but disappeared, remaining largely as token markers of religious identification, but women's customs have continued relatively unchanged, though they, too, show signs of responding to changing feminine roles.

Conclusion

On reflection, the gross inadequacy of the present state of theory about such rites as have been discussed in this chapter become obvious. Nubian circumcision and excision ceremonies cannot simply be categorized as "rites of passage" or as "initiation rites." They embody a complex constellation of interrelated beliefs, values, and principles of social structure — all of which must be examined in order to comprehend their form and existence.

Furthermore, though the rituals had important effects on the social aware-ness and identity formation of children, they had no obvious relationship to gaps or failures in the socialization process — such as are assumed in the modern theories of Whiting, et al. (1958), Cohen (1964), and Young (1965).

The emphasis was not upon a present passage or initiation, but upon the future (marriage and procreation) with all its social implications. For the child, the manifest stress was upon social preparation and spiritual protec-tion. He was prepared for later participation in religion, marriage, and pro-creation. He had taken a large, necessary step prerequisite to an adult life which would not be activated for a number of years.

In the circumcision and excision rituals for individuals, the community celebrated and thus reaffirmed many of its vital anxiety-laden concerns and values. Communal solidarity and continuity, family prestige and con-tinuity, sex separation, male dominance, and male superiority were all ex-pressed, as were the most specific fears related to fertility, sexuality, and gender identity. With such a complex of concerns and anxieties, and under conditions of a supernatural world view, the genital area of the body was a natural point of ritual focus. There appears to be no need or reason for invoking such Freudian notions as that circumcision represents a castra-tion threat by the fathers which is designed to quell rewakening Oedipal desires in their sons. Nor is there any justification for Bettelheimian ideas of opposite-sex imitation (1954).

My interpretation and the widespread structural similarities of such rituals suggest that these same values and principles may well be at work in similar fashion in societies where the operation actually does take place at puberty and where it does mark a status transition to adult life. Since such values and principles form a complex of concerns that is not limited to a stage of life, however, the same complex of concerns could produce such rituals in societies that practice infant circumcision or in those groups that circumcise long after puberty.

The analysis suggests that the relationships of genital operations to the larger marriage complexes of such societies require more investigation. It also leads to the inference that those older theories emphasizing fertility, sexuality, and gender perfection should not be discarded, and are probably more useful in understanding such practices than are some of the newer ideas, which give great explanatory weight to concepts of identity and personality change. A more general implication is that the interrelation of psychological and social processes in these rites is much more complex than later theorists have assumed.

Attempts thus far to formulate a theory which can account for all customs of genital operations seem doomed to failure. Many kinds of motivation and social forces might have the same end result and the common categorizations, which assimilate all these customs under the wider rubrics "rites of passage" or "initiation," will certainly bear reexamination. The wide variations in timing, and the great diversity in practice of customs that theorists assume to be psychologically and functionally "equivalent" vitiate our confidence in the validity of all cross-cultural studies so far undertaken. It is now appropriate to abandon the search for a simple one-factor theory and to seek multiple explanations dealing with larger complexes of determinants.

Notes

Since the ceremonies connected with boys' circumcisions no longer have the traditional form described here, data concerning them are from informants' memories. Reports of varying lengths were gathered individually from sixteen older informants (eleven males, five females) who had participated in the ceremonies as children. Additional checking of details was carried out in tape-recorded group sessions with older men in Kanuba. Most of the information concerning boys' ceremonies refers to the Diwan *'omodiyya* (Mahas-speaking). Other details are from the Kenzi-speaking *'omodiyyas* of Abu Hor and Dahmit. Girls' ceremonies survive almost intact to the present, and two of these were witnessed by Sohair Mehanna (Kanuba) and Fadwa al-Guindi (Dahmit).

1. For example, Cohen (1964) and Whiting et al. (1958) do not include the area in their samples. Young (1965) and Brown (1963) each use one Middle Eastern monograph (Ammar 1954). Young spends most of his discussion of this example in trying to account for its apparently anomalous data for his hypotheses (e.g. 1965, pp. 74–75; 82–83; 102; 143). Brown's inclusion of Silwa is also dubious because the case does not fit her age criteria (1963, p. 838). In any event coding of it is completely wrong. See tables on pp. 840, 844 and 846, in which she codes Silwa as not having female rites. Freud (1946) and Bettleheim (1954) do not mention the Middle East except for reference to Jewish infantile circumcision.

2. Some information exists, e.g., Lane 1908, pp. 56–60, 511–515; Ammar 1954, pp. 116–124; Barclay 1964, pp. 237, 243.

3. In most other parts of the Islamic world the classical Arabic word *khitan* is used (Ghalioungui 1963, p. 96).

4. *Sha'reya* is spaghetti-like ceremonial food, eaten with sugar and milk. *Abrīk* is paper-thin bread made of *durra*. Among other uses, it is an ingredient in *fatta*, the typical main dish of all Nubian ceremonial occasions.

5. This costume is very similar to that described by Lane (1908, p. 58) for Cairo in the early nineteenth century.

6. The sword apparently wards off evil spirits which are threatening to fertility and health at this time (see chapter 3). Similar customs are reported for the Diwan area (Mahas speaking) weddings at an earlier period. I presume they were found in circumcisions there as well.

7. *Aslīg* is cracked roasted wheat, or popped corn.
8. In the Diwan area, a second such procession was made on the following day to another saint — Sheikh Saad. His shrine was across the Nile, making it necessary to collect a fleet of boats from surrounding villages.
9. There appears to be no evidence that infibulation of this type was practised by the Pharaonic Egyptians (Barclay 1964, p. 238).
10. The present tense is used in this description because the customs regarding girls' excision appear relatively unchanged.
11. "To be a Moslem, it is believed, is to be circumcised ... However, there is no text in the Koran [sic] that enjoins circumcision upon Moslems, and it is only mentioned in the prophetic tradition ... Another prophetic tradition says 'Circumcision is my way for men, but is only ennobling for women'" (Ammar 1954, 120).
12. "They (the Egyptians) circumcise themselves for the sake of cleanliness, preferring to be clean rather than comely" (Herodotus describing the custom about 430 B.C.).
13. Similarities between circumcisions and weddings are not restricted to the Nubians. They have been remarked for other groups in the Sudan and Egypt (e.g., Ammar 1954; Barclay 1964; Lane 1908; Trimingham 1965).
14. The adjustment process of the partners was facilitated by the Nubian custom of confining the bride and groom to the bribal chamber for forty days, where they were served by a slave, ate special foods, and were under many taboos. This was a period when all other activities were suspended, and all attention was devoted to learning about the new life partner (see next chapter).

Chapter 9

Changes In Nubian Wedding Ceremonials

SAMIHA aL-KATSHA

This contribution by Samiha al-Katsha describes the traditional wedding ceremonies of one district in the Fadija area of Nubia and the changes evident thirty years later among a group of migrants from that district. Comparisons with Callender and al-Guindi's description of the wedding ceremony in the Kenuz district of Dahmit and with Barclay's account for Buurri al-Lamaab in the Sudan reveal a basic similarity of pattern for this culture area. However, there are many differences of detail. For example, the Kenuz have the *arosoki*, a young male relative of the groom who accompanies him everywhere during the week prior to the wedding. His role is to "guard" the groom from the pranksters who try to upset his equilibrium, as well as to run errands, and perform necessary duties (Callendar and el-Guindi 1970, pp. 53–54).

The Fadija of Diwan have no such role now nor the memory of one in the past, and Barclay does not record such a custom for his Sudanese village. On the other hand, Barclay does describe a number of wedding customs involving the *rahat*, a skirt of fine leather strings which apparently was worn as a sign of virginity in pre-Islamic times by young Nubian girls (Herzog 1957). These customs are not found either among the Kenuz researched by Callender's group or the Fadija of the districts we studied.

There are many more examples of this sort. I mention them only to indicate the complexities of the picture in this area and to point out the difficulty of finding out what is old and what is lately introduced. It is difficult to make generalizations, but certain similarities of quality and emphasis are evident. One of these is the great stress throughout this region upon gift-bearing processions between the houses of bride and groom. Another is the sense of delay and the great amount of symbolic obstacles put in the way of sexual consummation. Both these sets of customs emphasize the extreme social importance of marital union to the families involved and also create what seems to be an inordinate degree of anxiety around the question of sexuality. These motifs appear again and again in Nubian ceremonial.

Weddings symbolize happiness to Nubians, and these rituals constitute a kind of prototype or model of Nubian ceremonialism. By this I mean that many other ceremonies, particularly birth ceremonies, circumcision, and *zār* ceremonies,

171

were modeled on weddings, and all the basic symbols of Nubian ritualism were brought together at the event of marriage. No other ceremony contained so many of these symbolic elements. In Old Nubia weddings often took place around the time of the date harvest, a time when men returned from the city to look after their interests. Young men utilized the opportunity to negotiate for their own future brides, and the dancing at weddings gave them an opportunity to see girls they might desire. But the roles of males were muted, for these were times when Nubian women were indulged and allowed to shine. Older women looked back upon their weddings as the happiest events in their lives, and as young girls prepared their trousseaus, they dreamt of their own chances for a moment in the sun.

Wedding ceremonies and festivities connected with marriage were among the most important public events in the social life of the Nubians. These activities had several different purposes in addition to uniting two families and cementing bonds between kin groups already related through previous marriages. Among these purposes were the assurance of a happy and prosperous life for the bridal couple and the provision of happiness and entertainment for the village and district. This chapter is a description of the celebrations and an analysis of changes that have occurred in customs connected with marriage in the resettled village of Kanuba. These changes are best seen when compared with the traditional form of the ceremonies described by older informants who still remember them. The baseline for the comparison was developed from structured and unstructured interviews made over a period of ten months with five older Kanuba women who had lived in Diwan in their early lives and who were married there, and from interviews of briefer duration with a number of older women in the village of Diwan itself. Wedding customs in Diwan adhered largely still to the traditional pattern at the time of study, so several new brides in Diwan were also interviewed. A wedding of the traditional type was also observed in the nearby village of Korosko during our visit to the Old Nubian district of Diwan in 1963. The material on modern customs was obtained from recent brides and their families and from observation of weddings and extensive interviewing during a year of study in Kanuba.

The social organization of Old Nubia was based primarily on patrilineal tribal structures that were distributed in several villages within each 'omodiyya. Thus, any one village might be found to be dominated by families of one tribe, but households of some other tribes could be living there as well. In the past, the tribal organizations were of prime importance, but in recent times this importance was only retained by the Kenuz (Callender 1967). In the Mahas-speaking area the tribal structures had lost political importance before the time of resettlement, but the patrilineal extended family remained strong in all areas, and was the main group that exercised authority in the regulation of marriage.

For a boy the preferential choice for a spouse was the father's brother's daughter; for a girl it was the father's brother's son. This is the pattern of patrilateral parallel cousin marriage typical of the Middle East. Thus, marriage meant no break with one's own kin group by either party. If a paternal cousin was not available the next choices were the maternal cousins, followed by more distantly related members of the father's lineage and the mother's lineage. Tribal endogamy was the ideal norm, but inter-marriage between members of tribes living in the same district seems to have been fairly common (e.g., see Callender 1971, p. 45 for a Kenuz district). To marry a non-Nubian as a first spouse was highly reprehensible and tant-amount to an abdication of Nubianhood.

Of course, this pattern of preferences referred to ideal norms, but they were only strictly adhered to in first marriages. The Nubians, being Muslim, had plural marriage, and additional wives often fell outside the normal pattern of prescriptions, as did secondary marriages after divorce or death of spouses. The strength of these marriage prescriptions can be seen from the following sample of two thirds of the first marriages of women in the resettled village of Kanuba.

Female point of view	*Approx. %*
to father's brother's son	10
father's sister's son	8
mother's brother's son	3
mother's sister's son	7
mother's father's brother's son	7
other traceable relationships	11
distant but unknown relationships	13
no relation or unknown	8
	67%

Male point of view	
to father's brother's daughter	15
mother's brother's daughter	12
father's sister's daughter	4
mother's sister's daughter	11
father's brother's daughter	11
other traceable relationships	16
distant but unknown relationships	18
no relation or unknown	12
	99%

This table reveals that the traditional norms of marriage remained quite

strong even in a situation where migrants from six different districts of
Nubia and from twenty-nine different tribes had been together for about
thirty years. In this same village about one half of the marriages were between members of the same tribe and about half were between members of
different tribes. There were no marriages in this village between Kenuz
and Fadija, and only one man married an Egyptian (his second marriage
after his first wife had died). There was only one polygymous marriage in
the village at the time of study: one man had two wives whom he maintained
in separate households with their families. If such strong preservation of
the endogamous rules obtained in a situation of social change, it seems
reasonable to assume that in Old Nubia they were even more strongly
adhered to.

In the past, the parents and relatives of the young people arranged the
first marriage and little choice was possible. There was even a strong
prohibition against the engaged couples seeing each other. If they foresaw
from a distance that they might meet they had to turn away in another
direction and often they did not know what their partners looked like until
the night of consummation. The fact that in this century most of the young
men worked in the city during late adolescence and early adulthood made
avoidance easier and accentuated this attribute of surprise. In the last two
or three decades this pattern has been changing, and males have been demanding more choice in first marriages, but at the time of study most of
them (even those in cities) still chose from the "Nubian lists" made up by
members of their village and urban associations. Mothers, particularly,
still play prominent roles in the selection of marriage partners.

For at least forty days after marriage, the couple customarily resides
with the bride's family. After this they may then move to the father's house
or into their own dwelling. In our sample of seventeen Kanuba women
from the Fadija area who had married in Old Nubia, fifteen (or about 90
percent) of them lived matrilocally for at least forty days after marriage.
The two who did not said that it was because their parents were not alive
at the time of the wedding. In many parts of the Kenuz area even until
recently, however, the period of uxorilocal residence was usually at least one
year, or until the birth of the first child. In the strict families the bride did
not even leave her parents' compound until the birth of the first child. These
Kenuz patterns strongly reflect the older matrilineal–matrilocal pattern
that existed throughout all of Nubia before the Islamic conversion in the
fourteenth century. Other vestiges of this older matrilineal pattern are
the persisting strength of mothers' roles in arranging marriage and the
numerous rituals and customs of respect for mothers-in-law of both families in the wedding ceremony itself.

Under the older custom of arranged marriage the age of brides was extremely young, and most of our older female informants who had been married in Nubia prior to the 1933 raising of the dam were married before the age of fourteen. Several of them reported being wed at nine or ten. Thus, in Old Nubia the tendency was for marriage to be a puberty rite for girls. Boys, on the other hand, married at about sixteen or seventeen. The marriage age has steadily risen among Nubians; now men do not marry before their mid-twenties or later, while sixteen to twenty is the common age range for girls, in compliance with present Egyptian law.

Before resettlement marriage had increasingly become a problem for many Nubian girls due to the changing attitudes of the modernizing men, many of whom came to prefer brides with at least some education, a criterion which was more and more difficult to meet under the isolated village conditions of Old Nubia. At the same time, their longer periods of residence in cities such as Cairo, Alexandria, and Suez have made many Nubian young men restive with the old marriage prescriptions. There were numerous cases in which men divorced their Nubian wives of some years in order to marry non-Nubian women from the city. Some of them brought Egyptians back to Nubia as second wives and a few even took Egyptians as first brides. All these changes were creating a number of husbandless or husband-deprived Nubian women in the villages and consequently producing much anxiety among those who still possessed husbands. (Some of the responses to this stress are described in the chapters of this book on saints' cults and *zār* ceremonies).

The traditional Pattern — Diwan

In Old Nubia weddings were usually held during the summer. All festivities had to be held outdoors and good weather was necessary, but another reason for choosing this season was that most of the males working in the cities had vacations during the summer months and could return to the villages.

Wedding celebrations in Diwan usually lasted from fifteen to thirty days and involved three main stages:

1. *Pre-wedding festivities and ceremonies*
   1. *firrgar* (betrothal), the official negotiation before marriage.
   2. *adisimar*, which marked the beginning of the official wedding preparations.
   3. *tingodyendibi*, the day of slaughtering the cow or sheep (usually the day before the wedding festivity).
   4. *koffare*, the bride's and groom's festivity, centering around the *henna* application on the night before the wedding.

2. *Wedding day activities*
   1. *balay*, centered around the official wedding day.
3. *Post-wedding celebrations*
   1. *ṣabāhiyya*, the celebration on the morning following the wedding.
   2. *barkid*, a Nubian term for "blessing," or *tiger*, meaning "sitting", both terms interchangeably referring to a festivity taking place on the third day following the wedding.
   3. *kolod*, a Nubian term for "seventh"; in weddings it marked the end of the wedding festivity on the seventh day.

FIRST STAGE: PRE-WEDDING PREPARATIONS

Firrgar (betrothal). In old Diwan the betrothal was an important part of the process of marriage, and there were several forms of it. When a girl reached puberty it was the duty of her parents or guardian to find her a suitable mate from among her nearest male relatives. Betrothal negotiations were generally started by the boy's family as soon as his parents thought it the proper time for their son to get married. The proper time depended to a great extent on the maturity and the economic standing of the boy (i.e., whether or not he had a job or was working in the fields).

It was very important to have negotiated an agreement before the official betrothal between the families of the prospective bride and groom; the *firrgar*, or official day of betrothal, followed shortly. This occasion involved primarily the male members of the groom's immediate family and his friends. The latter assembled in the groom's house, from where they all, with the exception of the groom, proceeded in a group to the bride's house.

The formal procedures then started with the father or male guardian of the groom approaching the guardian of the bride: "We come to ask for a favor. We come to ask for the hand of your daughter for our son." The guardian replied: "The honor is ours. The girl is your daughter and the boy is our son." Since there had usually been a prior informal understanding, agreement was quickly reached and all those present read the *Fātiḥa*. The visitors were then offered popcorn and dates from mat plates.

Throughout the negotiations the bride was not told in advance nor consulted directly regarding her future marriage. According to Nubian standards, no well-bred girl would object to a mate who was suitable to her parents or guardian. From the time of her official betrothal she was not, under any circumstances, to be seen by the groom until her wedding day. This custom led to many elaborate precautions to avoid the embarrassment and even danger of chance meetings, since it was believed that such encounters might endanger the future happiness of the marriage or even the fertility of the couple. The wedding day took place after the official betrothal at any time convenient to the families. Sometimes the waiting period was several years, particularly if the girl was officially betrothed before she had reached puberty. This made avoidance difficult unless the groom was a labor migrant, and away from the village. There are many jokes indicating that, at least in recent times, this custom was observed more in spirit than strictly according to the rule.

Adisimar. The *adisimar* was the day marking the official beginning of the wedding preparations; it was generally a month to fifteen days before the event. Since women and young girls living in the same village and nearby villages were expected to help with the preparations, a slave woman was sent around the district to announce the day for starting preparations for the festivities.

When they had assembled to begin work on that special day, the women and young girls were offered *madīd* (a mixture of *durra* flour, butter, molasses, and milk). The bride was offered the *madīd* first, since it symbolized prosperity and insured happiness to her and to her marriage.

Parents of the bride and groom took the initiative in the organization and conduct of the wedding preparations, with the groom's family bearing most of the financial burden. The bride and groom remained out of the way, though the girl was present to observe (a) grinding and cleaning of the wheat to be consumed during the wedding festivities, (b) the making of *sha'reya*, (c) the making of bread, and (d) the painting of the quarters to be occupied by the couple during forty days after the ceremony.

At an ordinary wedding one hundred to one hundred and fifty kilograms of wheat and *durra*, necessary for bread and *sha'reya*, were ground manually by the women and then processed with a special millstone (*gaw*, *Mahas*). The time spent in grinding varied from four to six days, depending on the quantity of the grain.

Sha'reya, a spaghetti-like food which the Nubians eat with cream and sweetening on such festive occasions as sheikhs' *mawlids*, the Prophet's Birthday, and during the nights of Ramadan, was one of the main dishes served to the guests and to the bride and groom at different times during the wedding period. The hard work of processing it took an additional one to three days. *Shaddi* bread, a local variety, was also made beforehand since it was easy to store. This bread was offered to guests with the festive meals, and to the bride and groom at specified times.

The preparation of the wedding quarters for the couple was the final preliminary task. Young girl friends of the bride undertook the decoration of the room. For the walls they usually used a brown-red water-soluble paint made from hand-ground local clay. They hung colorful mat plates and rolled *bursh* mats around the room; mirrors, hanging bowls called *shollags*, pictures, and Evil-Eye charms completed the decorations. Though some of these decorations were handed down from parents and other close relatives of the older generation, many of the mat plates and *burshes* had been woven by the girls and were a form of wedding gift. That is, they were one type of *karray* (*noqūṭ* in Arabic), a gift which is expected to be returned some day on a similar occasion. *Karray* was a kind of ritualization of the reciprocal ties uniting the Nubians, and each gift was carefully recorded so that the list could be checked in future ceremonies. Unfulfilled obligations of this nature constituted serious affronts and signalled breaks in social relationships.

For fifteen nights prior to the ceremony, people gathered at the groom's house to dance. Each night they danced from late afternoon until midnight, and as the wedding approached the dancing became more animated and the sessions increased in duration.

Tingodyendībī.   This part of the celebration occurred on the eve of the wedding, and featured the slaughter of a cow or sheep for the feast. Usually the families of the bride and groom each killed one or two cows or sheep, depending on their wealth and the size of supporting lineages. The guests assembled first at the groom's house and then at the bride's to dance and to watch the butchers at work.

While the butchers slaughtered and carved the animal, the men sat with the groom on one side of the courtyard of the house. Women and girls grouped together on the other side of the open area. The main attraction on this occasion was the singing, which was generally led by the elderly women. The themes of these songs were centered on extravagant praises of the families of the bride and groom, with the exact words and names fitted to the occasion by the singers. The butchering of the cow was followed by preparations for cooking the food to be consumed that night as well as for the feast the following day. Only the guests travelling from distant areas were served dinner by the hosts that evening. Villagers and people from nearby villages ate at home.

Koffare.   The application of *henna* was considered by Nubian women to be a principal means of beautification. In some cases, this orange dye was applied on the night before the wedding, (the *koffare*), but it might also be applied on the wedding morning. The henna of the bride was considered to be an absolute necessity, and even though it was put mainly on her hands and feet, some was also gently rubbed over her whole body. The application of *henna* had to be performed by elderly female relatives of the bride who had living children. After the bride had been beautified, each of these women took some of the bride's henna and applied it to herself. The customs pertaining to *henna* were repeated on the morning of the wedding and on the third and seventh days following it.

From the "night of the *koffare*" onward, gifts called *noqūṭ* were sent between the houses of the bride and groom. The Nubians presented wedding *noqūṭ* to the bride, the groom, the mother of the bride, and the mother of the groom, and in addition small amounts were given to the barber and to the musicians. On the night of the slaughter and the *henna* application, a former slave delivered the first *noqūṭ* from the bride's mother to the groom's mother in the shape of a deep mat basket plate (*konte* or *omra*, Mahas) full of *sha'reya* with a few cones of sugar on top. The groom's mother returned the basket filled with grain. Traditionally the slave kept a small share of both these *noqūṭ*.

SECOND STAGE: THE WEDDING DAY

Balay. On the morning of the official wedding day (or sometimes on the night of the *koffare*, like the bride) the groom also had henna applied to his hands and feet by an elderly female relative. After this ritual and just before sunrise, taking his sword in hand, and accompanied by his male friends, the groom went to the Nile to bathe. Women who lived within the neighborhood followed the group down to the river and while the groom dipped his sword in the water and washed off the henna, offering it and some other gifts of food to the Nile angels, they remained at a distance singing wedding songs of future happiness and joy. These rituals ensured the groom's future virility and fertility.

The bride also traditionally went to the river with her companions to bathe on the morning of the wedding, and sometimes at this time her lips were tattooed. The visit to the Nile and the use of the Nile water in other rituals was mainly for the placation of the Nile angels and protection from evil jinn.

Considerable importance was given by the Nubians to the wedding clothing worn by the bride and groom, as well as to that worn by relatives of both sexes and of varying ages. According to informants from the district of Diwan, the groom traditionally wore a special new and distinguishing attire which consisted of a white cotton under-*jalabeya* and a striped silk *quftan*. He carried a red shawl over his shoulder, and his headdress consisted of a turban over which a white shawl was draped. On his feet he wore red slippers called *markūb* (Arabic), and for ornaments he carried a whip, a sword, and a knife. The sword and knife were said to be symbols of strength and authority and to be defenses against evil spirits. Some informants stated that the sword, the knife and the red shawl were worn only to distinguish the groom from the others and that the main function of the whip was to frighten away the groom's friends when they tried to crowd into his bridal room. It is probable, however, that these accoutrements had deeper multiple symbolic meanings as well, some of which related to protection from spirits and to symbolic dominance over women. It should be remembered that the whip was a symbol of force used by the slave owners of Egypt and the Sudan until the abolition of the slave trade around the turn of the century.

The bride's clothes for the occasion were all new; most brides wore similar attire except for some variations in the color of the dress worn under the traditional dark blue *jarjar*. Three different veils were worn, a coloured one over the head, a second of sheer material over the face, and a third veil of heavy white material over the first two, which covered the head completely. The girl's hair was braided into tiny braids by a special female attendant called a *dewinsha* (Mahas) or *mashāta* (Arabic).

On the second day of the wedding, the bride wore a variety of gold ornaments, some of which were given to her by her parents and some by the groom, the rest being borrowed for the occasion from relatives or friends. The jewelry was typically Nubian in the sense that most of the women in Nubia wore similar kinds of ornaments, but some variety was possible in the necklaces of flat gold, which were styled in different shapes and sizes and were called *jakit* and *baya* in Mahas Nubian. The bride usually wore two earrings (*bartawi*) on each ear, one on the upper part and the other on the lobe. A similar ring called *zomam* was worn on the nose, and silver anklets (*hoqol*) completed the bridal attire.

The guests at weddings also made it a point to wear new clothing sewn especially for the occasion. Women in the Mahas- and Arabic-speaking areas wore special blue *jarjars* instead of the black ones which they used daily, and replaced their black veils with brightly colored ones, while Kenuz women dressed in colorful gowns (*jalabeyas*) with their customary white *shoggas*. Men too dressed in their best *jalabeyas*.

In old Diwan, both the marriage payment, called the *aba* (Mahas) or *mahr* (Arabic) and the signing of the marriage contract, or *katb al-kitab* (Arabic), were generally completed on the same day as the wedding. After the group of visitors, relatives, and friends had eaten the noon meal at the groom's house, the marriage official, the *maazūn*, (or *maadhūn*) (Arabic) formed a procession with the groom's family and friends and moved to the home of the bride to present the *aba*.

The families concerned had previously agreed upon the sum to be transferred, and the average *aba* in the early twentieth century consisted of about fifteen to twenty Egyptian pounds in addition to some clothing, pieces of cloth, and silver bracelets. The money was usually paid in silver coins so that it would appear as heavy and generous as possible, thereby impressing the guests. In cases where the family was well off, the groom sent bolts of new cloth and silver or gold jewelry (bracelets, necklaces, head ornaments) in addition to the money. Generally a small part of the *aba* was designated to be reserved for the bride as a kind of insurance in case of divorce or the death of the husband. This part of the *mahr* or *aba*, was called by the Arabic term *moakhar*, and its function seems to have been largely symbolic, since the two to five Egyptian pounds set aside for this purpose could not have provided much economic help for a deserted or destitute family. The *aba* should by no means by considered a bride price. It was primarily a consideration legalizing the family agreements and providing a small amount with which the young people could begin married life.

On the arrival of the procession at the bride's house, the mother of the bride served the visitors a second lunch similar the the first meal. Afterwards the guests returned to the groom's house where they were met by the young man dressed in his new attire. At this point, in the presence of all the guests, the *maazūn* proceeded to examine his knowledge of the Qur'ān by asking him to recite some well-known verses, a task easily accomplished by men who had gone to the *kuttāb* schools of that period. Following the recitation, the *maazūn* told the groom's father or guardian, "Your son knows the Qur'ān well, what reward will he have for this?" The customary reply was an extravagant statement, such as: "We will give him ten *sāqias* in the such and such district." These gifts were largely symbolic of goodwill, since few Nubians owned that number of water wheels, and few possessed more than a few palms. On some occasions, however, shares in a water wheel or a share in a cow or other property were actually promised to the young man. Most such property passed on at the death of the parents or others of their generation according to the Islamic laws of inheritance, however, and these extravagant statements of bestowal functioned primarily to symbolize the beginning of a new family within the continuing lineage structure. At the conclusion of the ceremonial transaction, the *maazūn* was presented a deep mat plate full of *durra* and a piece of white cloth.

Nubian wedding celebrations were held in both the bride's and groom's houses. On the morning of the *balay*, food preparation started early in the morning, first in the groom's house and then in the bride's, with male volunteers from the village doing most of the cooking. The main dishes were *fatta* and plates of seasonal vegetables. The lunches were served on big round trays to visitors sitting on mats in groups of six or eight. Men ate first, followed by the women and children.

Around noon the guests and the *maazūn* walked in a procession back to the bride's house for the ceremony of signing the marriage contract, but towards sunset the festivity was resumed at the groom's house. This was the time when all the guests and families of the bride and groom donned their best attire and joined the rest of the crowd in singing, eating, and general rejoicing.

The main form of entertainment was dancing and singing led by slave musicians. This joyful activity, in which most of the guests took part, went on continuously until very early the following morning. Between 2:00 a.m. and 3:00 a.m. another procession started from the groom's house to that of the bride, led by the groom with a slave walking next to him carrying a pitcher of water from which he could drink whenever he felt thirsty.[1] On his other side, a young male child carried a censer, the smoke from which afforded protection against evil spirits. Another young friend of the groom carried a chair for him to rest upon whenever the group stopped to dance at one of the houses along the procession route. The groom and his group were followed by the musicians, who continued to lead the singing and dancing. Close after the musicians came family members, male guests, immediate female relatives of both the bride and groom, elderly women, young girls of marriageable age and, finally, children.

The procession passed every now and then in front of neighborhood houses where a session of dancing was carried on for the special relatives or friends of the family who lived there. Then it continued on to visit all the major saints' tombs in the vicinity of the village. At each one, the groom and his friends, along with most of the village crowd, circled the shrine seven times asking blessings on the marriage. Singing and dancing went on for as long as four hours at a stretch, continuing after short rests by the musicians and dancers.

During the groom's procession, a few women waited with the bride, who dressed in her bridal gown with her veils completely obscuring her face, was seated on a mat. On his arrival at her house, the groom was met by her mother or a female member of the bride's family. He was offered sweetened milk to drink to insure a happy and prosperous life for the couple. (In some accounts, these women splashed him with milk and demanded *noqūt.*)

The groom then ceremoniously "sneaked" into the bridal chamber with two of his close friends, where he attempted to unveil the bride. Generally he could not succeed, and when, as the ritual prescribed, he realized that he was circumvented, he pulled off the first heavy white veil, dropped it to the ground and knelt down to pray upon it. Subsequently, he scattered dates and *durra* over her head, which remained covered by the inner veils, and then left the room, still frustrated in his attempts even to see her face. (In some

areas, he pulled off the veil with the tip of a sword, which he carried throughout the wedding, and after tapping her forehead three times, made several
tiny incisions in the calf of her leg.) The groom spent the rest of the night with
his male friends; the bride likewise spent the night in her room with her
companions. Typically, the marriage was not consummated on the official
wedding day, or *balay*.

LAST STAGE: POST WEDDING FESTIVITIES

Ṣabāhiyya. The term *ṣabāhiyya* denotes the morning after the wedding, and since the marriage was generally consummated on that day, the
activities of *ṣabāhiyya* were considered an especially important part of the
wedding celebration. To begin the *ṣabāhiyya*, both the bride and the groom
went separately to the Nile early in the morning in the company of friends
and relatives who had spent the night with them. Again offerings were made
to the angels of the river, who would then protect the fertility of the couple.
As the groom returned from the river, he quietly entered the bride's quarters
accompanied by the midwife and the *dewinsha*, whose role it was to serve
the married couple for seven days after the wedding.

The bride, still veiled, sat on a special mat. Traditionally, she would
under no circumstances talk to the groom until he had paid her a sum of
money (varying from sixty piasters to two pounds). The Nubians referred
to this ritual, and to the money itself, as *agbanyed* (which in the Mahas
dialect means "the opening of the mouth"). After a period of feigning
reluctance, which might last as long as half an hour or more, she finally
accepted the money, and spoke to her groom. This signal permitted physical
consummation to proceed, but due to the fashion in which Nubian girls
were infibulated (the "Pharaonic way"), it was usually necessary for the
midwife to perform an operation to open the vagina. Sometimes this was so
frightening and painful that defloration could not be accomplished on this
day and had to be attempted again later. Usually there was little difficulty,
however, and the bridal couple were then left alone for their first intercourse.

While the "opening of the mouth" ceremony was going on, much joking
and loud laughter issued from both the groups of women and men. Sometimes, peepholes had been made into the bridal quarters so that watchers
could report to the group how long the girl was able to bargain and thus
delay consummation. Giving in too quickly was regarded as evidence of
undue interest in sex, which did not bode well for the future. It is said that
in days gone by, consummation sometimes did not take place until the
kolod, seven days after the wedding day.

Among the Fadija, no public displays of virginity were made, though the information was relayed by the *dewinsha*. Because of the complete closure of the vagina through the infibulatory excision operation, there was usually no doubt about the bride's premarital chastity.

Later in the morning, guests again began to assemble in front of the bridal couple's quarters, and though no one specifically mentioned consummation, the main purpose was to congratulate the couple for success-fully completing it, thereby embarking on the road to family life. The groom met his friends in the outside section of the bridal quarters while the bride met the female guests in the inner section of the wedding chamber. All the guests assembled were offered *sha'reya* to eat for this occasion, and the groom sent *sha'reya* to houses in the neighborhood as a gesture of generosity and thanks.

Towards evening, the groom's guests assembled once more to visit him. Dancing and singing led by the musicians were resumed, and later a supper supplied by one of the immediate family members of the bride or groom, was served to the male guests. This festivity again lasted late into the night. The bride was confined to the *diwani* (bridal room) for forty days, the first seven of which she remained on a mat behind the *kaled* curtain. The groom stayed in seclusion with her for at least seven days until the *kolod*.

Barkīd (or *tigīr*). The term *barkīd* comes from the Arabic word *baraka* or blessing, while the Nubian word for the occasion, *tigīr*, meaning "sitting", emphasizes the period of waiting to receive gifts. Both words are used by the people for this occasion. The *barkīd* or *tigīr* was held on the third day after the *balay*. The main purpose of the occasion was for the bridal couple to receive *noqūṭ* (also referred to as *tigīr* in Mahas), which most commonly consisted of sugar cones, although some of the visitors offered gifts of pigeons, eggs, tea, or wheat. Only men and the bride's friends gave their *noqūṭ* in the form of small sums of money. A *noqūṭ* given to the couple in any form was recorded, however, in order that it could be repaid in the same or a greater amount on similar future occasions.

The *noqūṭ* received on the day of *barkid* was given to the bride's mother. She in turn served a *sha'reya* breakfast to neighbors and relatives, and the guests who came in during the day were offered popcorn and dates. The festivity lasted for a few hours in the morning and included some singing and dancing by the women. The day of the *tigīr* or *barkīd* was also the traditional time for the mother of the groom to visit and congratulate the bridal couple in their quarters for the first time, but the groom's father still did not visit them.

Kolod. The *kolod* was the day of ritual marking the end of the wedding celebrations. The word means "seven" in Mahas and the *kolod*, like the *sebu'* of Egyptian weddings, was celebrated on the seventh day after the wedding. On this day, a sheep was usually slaughtered at the bride's house and the meat sent later with the groom to his parents' house. Towards noon he dressed in his bridal attire and, accompanied by the musicians, guests, and family members, proceeded in another *zeffa* towards his parents' house. The women walked at the end of the procession carrying trays of food from the bride's house and once they reached the groom's house, everyone joined in eating it. This was the first time for the groom officially to come out of his period of seclusion with the bride and to leave his temporary new residence to visit his parents.

One of the principal activities of the *kolod* was the offering of *noqūṭ* to the groom's mother. The women presented their gifts either in kind (wheat, dates, or sugar cones) or small sums of money. In return, the mother of the groom handed them two loaves of local bread that had been prepared previously.

After the noon meal, the groom returned to the wedding quarters. The containers that he had brought filled with food from the bride's family were refilled by his own family with grain or dates, and on top of each container was placed a roll of cloth. These were the presents for the bride herself from the groom's immediate family. Towards sunset, yet another procession was made to the groom's parents' house, and in this one the groom was supposed to stop at each house on his way to collect his presents. Other trays of dates were also sent individually to the bride's house by members of the groom's family from their own households. All these gifts were regarded as forms of *noqūṭ*, and were recorded.

General Remarks on Wedding Rituals

For the first forty days after the wedding the bride was not supposed to leave her quarters; the groom, however, was expected to stay in the bridal quarters only during the first seven days. During this period the couple ate their meals alone in their room, served by the special attendent or slave woman. When the bride went out of her quarters for the first time it was customary for her to dress in her bridal gown and pay a visit to her in-laws. The parents of the groom were expected to slaughter a sheep for the occasion and to invite the families in the neighborhood for a mid-day meal.

Incense was burned throughout the wedding festivities. For example, it was burned during the groom's processions, and a smoking brazier was passed over the bride at least twice daily to keep away evil spirits. Visiting the Nile was also important, for purification and for keeping away spirits which could harm the fertility of the bride or the virility of the groom.

MUSIC

Folk dancing and singing were the most important forms of entertainment in any Nubian communal festivity. The immediate families of both the bride and groom were expected to take leading roles in the wedding dances, but organized singing and dancing were led by musicians from slave families who were considered to be specialists in that field. This entertainment usually lasted from seven to fifteen days before the wedding, and throughout the week following it. All visitors, men, women and children, were expected to take part in both singing and dancing.

Three prominent dances were performed during the wedding, and there were a number of traditional songs. The musical instruments used were the *ṭār* and the *dakalaka*. *Zagharīt*, the frequent piercing female joy cries lent an extra air of excitement to the drumming and singing.

DANCING

The three principal dances were the following:

Kumba gash.   This group dance provided most of the entertainment for weddings since it gave a chance for everyone to participate and for each to take part as long as he or she wished. All visitors, including men, women, young girls, and even children, were expected to join the dancing for at least a short time.

In this group dance the men formed several rows of ten or twelve, and were faced by the women in similar rows. The front lines were usually reserved for the close families of the bride and groom while immediately behind these were the elderly women, who usually wore much gold jewelry for the occasion. Marriageable girls were allowed to dance only in the back rows where they were farthest from the men.

Several slave musicians provided the rhythmic beat on their *ṭars*. They usually stood at one side facing the center area where the male and female groups of dancers approached each other. There was little movement in this dance; keeping to the rhythm of songs and music, the lines of men and women with locked arms swayed from side to side in unison, taking a few steps forward, then a few steps back. Everyone joined in the singing. This dance was performed for several hours at a time, with people joining and leaving the group to visit at various points. A dancemaster generally danced between the front rows to women and men holding a palm stick in his hand. His role was to maintain order and control the general form of the dance. Occasionally one of the elder women would be moved also to take a stick and dance between the rows.

Ollin (Mahas) or *Käff* (Arabic) *aragīd*. The clapping dance. While slave musicians provided background music on the *tambour* (a stringed instrument), a group of men stood in a semi-circle and clapped rhythmically. One or two women, usually members of the immediate family of the bride and groom, entered into the clapping semi-circle and danced in small steps. Later, slave girls or other women danced, moving around the circle to the rhythm of the clapping, swaying back and forth with their whole bodies in a suggestive and seductive manner. Since so few people could participate, the *ollin aragīd* generally did not last more than ten or fifteen minutes. This dance and its rhythmic clapping also required much more special skill than the *kumba gash*.

Firry aragīd. The musicians and men stood lined up on one side facing the women, who were again placed in long lines. The elderly women of the immediate families of the marriage then danced in the space between the two groups. The steps were similar to those of the clapping dance, except that the dancers followed a faster tempo. The *firry aragīd*, like the *ollin aragīd*, provided diversionary variation from the main pattern of the *kumba gash*.

Prior to 1933 in Diwan and other Mahas-speaking villages, different songs were sung for each of the different activities of the wedding festivities. The singing was always led by slave musicians known in Nubian as *sharr*. Usually a minimum group of musicians included a singer, a drummer, and a *daiman*-caller. The term *daiman* ("forever") expresses praise or honor which is given to people by calling out their names. For example, the drumming and singing would stop for several seconds while the caller shouted something like: "Muhammad Abdul Khalil — daiman!" Each person so honored usually gave the caller a little *noqūṭ*, generally one or two piasters, or the equivalent. Thus, one way of announcing one's presence was to slip the caller some *noqūṭ* with a name, and it would soon be shouted forth to the gathering.

Some special Nubian songs for various parts of the wedding ceremony were as follows: 1) the henna songs for both the bride and groom, 2) a special song sung while the groom was getting dressed for the wedding, and 3) a song sung during the slaughtering of the cow ceremony. All these songs were usually led by elderly women who were answered in chorus by the other women, and they consisted primarily of repeated chants of praise for the families of the bride and groom.

For example, the henna song for the bride contained several elements which were improvised upon: (1) the naming of the ancestors of the girl, her tribe, her lineage and her family; (2) praises of the bride herself, i.e., statements that she was a lady and that her mother had brought her up so well that nobody had ever seen her in the streets before the wedding, with verses stating that her parents had so spoiled her that she could ask for anything and would be served by slaves; (3) praises of her parents, her father being said, for example, to have land and many water wheels; (4) laudatory statements about all other family members; (5) reiteration of praises for the bride, who was promised that she could walk on and enjoy all her father's land; (6) verses praising the worthiness of the groom; and (7) verses stating that because the bride's father wanted a good match for her, he had inquired seriously about the groom before accepting him, had consulted the sheikh, the, 'omda, and all those who knew him to ascertain that he was worthy of the bride. Such songs of praise were repeated until the henna application to the bride was completed. A similar song was intoned during the application of the henna to the groom, with praise geared to the groom and his family. Other songs similarly praised the two families. The group singing held before and during the wedding-day festivity was centered mainly around the subject of "the loved one", Samāra (the dark one), and was related to the general Nubian life situation. All the songs had stereotyped themes, which were embellished during performances and made specific to the actors.

Kanuba, 1963

The Nubians who built the resettled community of Kanuba tried to maintain the same wedding festivities as those held prior to their 1933 migration from Nubia, but certain changes inevitably took place. Some events and patterns have been altered in their emphases; others have taken on different functions; a few new elements have been introduced. The preferred time for weddings continues to be summer since weddings are still held outdoors, and since most of the men have their holidays from work at that time.

FIRST STAGE: PREPARATIONS

Betrothal.   Kanuba betrothal procedures are less rigid than those of Old Nubia. In some cases the groom even chooses his own mate, but his parents still retain their roles as negotiators with the parents of the bride. Some of the younger married informants reported that they were even allowed to sit and talk to their future spouses in the presence of relatives, and one informant recounted that in Alexandria, accompanied by his sister, she had gone to the movies with her betrothed.

A new festivity following the betrothal, the engagement day, has been instituted in Kanuba. This event usually takes place at the bride's house. For the occasion, the bride and groom wear Western clothes and the groom formally presents his fiancee with a wedding band. Syrup, sweets, and cakes are distributed by the bride's family to the assembled guests, and in some cases, villagers participate in a modified variety of Nubian singing and dancing at this engagement celebration. However, guests are generally limited to inhabitants of the immediate village.

Adisimar. Elaborate wedding preparations continue to be an important part of the wedding festivity, though some alterations and eliminations of customs have taken place. Preparations begin closer to the event, about a week to ten days before the wedding, and may be initiated either in the bride's and groom's houses separately or by both jointly.

A member of the immediate family informs women and young girls of the village by word-of-mouth of the day of the *adisimar*, and *madīd* is prepared earlier on that day in traditional Nubian fashion. Because preparations in Kanuba take a much shorter time than they did traditionally, less grain is consumed during the wedding festivity and less cooperative effort is needed. Instead of the traditional Nubian *shaddi* bread, Egyptian (local) bread is generally used, bought ready-made from the market town of Daraw. *Sha'reya* is not offered as abundantly as before and it is not now made strictly by hand. The process is shortened by using specially fitted meat grinders, and now only requires one to two days' work. Wheat grinding has also become an easy process, and young girls of the village usually carry the grain down to the public mill of Daraw for grinding. This process does not take more than a couple of hours. These tasks have become so simple that young girls of the village can perform them in a brief time, eliminating much of the long and intense conviviality of the traditional cooperative female work gatherings.

Leylet-al-Henna (The Henna Night). The celebrations of slaughtering the cow on the wedding eve, *tingodyendibi*, are now rare and often completely omitted in Kanuba. On the wedding eve emphasis is now laid on the application of henna, as is characteristic of rural Egyptian weddings, though several informants who were recently married in the village stated that a sheep was slaughtered by the families of the bride and groom, who shared expenses. In contrast with the huge gatherings of people coming from up and down the Nile in Old Nubia, neighbors were the only guests.

During the writer's stay in the village, Kanuba inhabitants attempted to reinstate some of their old traditions. In a wedding involving the son of a prominent village man, for example, an elaborate *tingodyendibi* was held. Towards sunset on the night of the wedding, while all villagers were invited to watch, a cow was slaughtered at the groom's house. Those older women who remembered some traditional folk songs were encouraged to sing them. These songs took the form mainly of short praises of the bride's and groom's immediate nuclear families, however, rather than the form previously described. These surviving wedding songs have thus lost their main significance which, in Old Nubia prior to 1933, was based on praises of land, palm trees, families and tribes.

Social participation of the entire neighborhood on the night of the application of henna has assumed in Kanuba a significance equal to the wedding day (*balay*) celebration in Old Nubia. If the ritual form of application of the henna itself remains traditional, however, the amount applied has become a mere token of what it was formerly. Recent young brides stated that only for the sake of tradition had they allowed an elderly woman to apply a little henna to their hands and feet. They preferred to use Western-style cosmetics. In several recent weddings, grooms barely dipped a finger in the henna to comply with tradition, thus eliminating a whole set of ceremonial actions.

A new element has been added to the Kanuba henna celebration. Towards sunset, the guests assemble at the groom's house and all visitors from outside the village are served dinner. The main form of entertainment kept is typical Nubian dancing and singing. This singing, which contains some songs popular in Egypt, continues until early morning hours.

In one Kanuba wedding which I attended, shortly after one or two o'clock in the morning a tray containing henna with lit candles was brought by the groom's family, while the villagers all sang a popular Arabic wedding song, "*El Henna, el Henna.*" Then a procession set out from the groom's house to the bride's house, for the girl was awaiting their arrival in order to have her own Henna applied. While the groom's group danced outside in the courtyard, the application of henna, only token now, was carried out inside in the presence of the women only. Afterwards the rest of the guests dispersed to sleep. On henna day, many women, and particularly the young girls and children who wanted to apply henna, did so with the bride.

SECOND STAGE: WEDDING DAY

Katb al-ketāb and *aba.*   In Kanuba, the *katb al-ketāb* and the presenting of *aba* are no longer necessarily held on the day of the wedding. In some cases, the *katb al-ketāb* has taken place at the nearby town of Daraw with only a few family males attending. In other cases, it is celebrated in a fashion similar to that of the engagement. The *aba* (marriage payment) is now presented on the day of the signing of the marriage contract and the average amount of it has been raised to about thirty Egyptian pounds.

Preparations for the actual wedding day do not follow the fixed pattern of the past, but start in the morning at either the bride's or groom's house, according to what has been previously decided upon. Since no members of the previous slave families migrated to Kanuba, certain village men do the main cooking, while the women help. The wedding feast usually consists of seasonal vegetables, rice, potatoes, macaroni and meat, as well as desserts such as puddings and custards. Thus, this meal is more expensive than the traditional *fatta* and both families of the bridal couple generally share the expenses of it.

The Bride's and Groom's Dress and Ornaments

The Kanuba groom now wears new Western clothes, which are purchased or tailored especially for the occasion (a suit, shirt, necktie, but no turban). The bride wears Western attire as well (fancy long white dress, white veil, high-heeled shoes, gloves, and costume jewelry). Instead of the elaborate tiny braids and hairdress with gold coins and ornaments, her hair is now arranged in Western fashion and she applies commercial make-up to her face.

Female guests wear black *jarjars* (Nubian style overdresses) which are similar to those worn daily, except that those worn at a wedding are generally made of a more sheer material. The sheer blue ones of Nubia are no longer used. Younger women and girls wear costume jewelry instead of the traditional gold. Some also put on a little make-up, and they all have their hair arranged in a fashionable style according to modern urban Egyptian standards. As for the men, some wear Western-style suits, while others still wear traditional *jalabeyas*.

The Wedding Day

Balay. Towards sunset on the wedding day, guests from nearby villages and towns assemble in front of the groom's house. A number of non-Nubian upper Egyptians from Daraw are usually invited by the men. The musicians are no longer traditional slaves; in recent weddings a group of Nubian boys from a technical school in Kom Ombo have been leading the singing and dancing. The group dance called the *kumba gash*, with men dancing in rows facing the women and in which all villagers participate, remains prominent. In contrast with the traditional pattern, however, young girls and men of marriageable age in Kanuba now dance in the front rows instead of the back rows, a reversal of the pattern typical in the Fadija area prior to 1933. The singing is still mostly in Nubian, but most of the songs have changed considerably in tempo, theme, and choice of words. Furthermore, new songs have been introduced.

The main meal for the occasion is now served shortly before the wedding processions to the houses of the bride's and groom's families. The food is placed on tables in buffet style; all the guests stand to eat. Since families are no longer of the extended type, a cooperating group of villagers generally acts as hosts, serving male guests from outside the village first. Then come the guest women and children, the other non-related families within the village, and finally the families of the bride and groom, who partake of what is left.

Meanwhile, the bride remains with one or two female relatives in seclusion at the bridal quarters. As in Old Nubia, she does not join any of the wedding festivities, but as soon as the procession has started from the groom's house, she is informed. Then, escorted by her attendants, she moves to a special place called the *kōsha* which has been prepared in the courtyard. The *kōsha*, a typical feature of urban Egyptian weddings, is a platform on which two large chairs are placed. The background behind it is decorated with palm trees and flowers, and the bride and groom are to sit there together to welcome guests.

Singing and dancing still continue until the very early morning when the groom finally heads a procession to the bridal quarters with his friends, followed by the Nubian musicians, then the men, and the women and children. This *zeffa* stops to dance in front of a few houses on its way to the bridal quarters, but these stops are nowhere near the number visited by the groom's procession in Nubia. No saints' tombs are visited at all by Kanubans, and no former slave or young boy accompanies the groom with a chair and incense burner. Thus, the procession is a much sped-up version of the traditional form and does not take more than an hour or two at most to reach its destination.

Upon the arrival of all guests at the bridal quarters, the groom joins his bride who is already seated on the *kōsha* platform. Visitors congratulate the bridal couple, and swiftly disperse, so that within a half hour the couple withdraws to the bridal room. In recent weddings, the marriage has been consummated on the first night of the wedding, rather than the following day. Changing attitudes are also reflected in the fact that several grooms have refused assistance in deflowering their brides.

Bridal rituals involving the burning of incense to ward off jinn continue to be performed, but those relating to the Nile are no longer practiced. One reason given for this is that the river is too far away now, since Kanuba is nearly two kilometers from it.

For the first seven days, the bridal couple still eats all meals alone, though usually they are served by young girls of the family rather by a *dewinsha*. The bride is still expected to remain in the house for forty days, and the groom is still theoretically restricted for the first seven days. Women recently married at Kanuba all stated that they maintained this tradition strictly, with the exception of one bride who left the village for the city due to her husband's job. In most cases, however, the groom had gone out to resume his work on the third day after the wedding, breaking the custom of a seven-day seclusion.

LAST STAGES: POST WEDDING FESTIVITIES

Ṣabāhiyya. On the morning after the wedding, guests still assemble at the bridal quarters to congratulate the couple, as is traditional. Besides congratulating them on the consummation of the marriage, however, the majority of visitors now present their *noqūṭ* at this time as well and, the many *noqūṭ* of the past have been reduced to a minimal few. The bride is usually clothed in a fashionable nightgown with matching housecoat and she receives guests in the small inner courtyard next to the bridal quarters, which now contains no dividing curtain (*kaled*). The groom ordinarily wears a new pair of pajamas and meets his male guests in another room of the house.

All those assembled for the *Ṣabāhiyya* are served syrup and sweets, while the *noqūṭ* now consist mainly of bottles of syrup used to make sweet-flavoured cold drinks when mixed with water. Candy is also offered, and some of the young girls present small amounts of money (ten to twenty-five piasters) to the bride. In recent weddings, these gifts have not been recorded immediately, but were later written in a notebook by one of the family members. Usually no organized singing or dancing is held on the morning of the *Ṣabāhiyya.* Instead, young girls sing some popular Nubian songs while visiting the bride, but by noon most of the visitors have dispersed.

Barkīd or tigīr. In Kanuba *barkīd* customs have been relaxed. Only in a very few cases did informants report this as a part of their own wedding festivities. On those occasions when the *barkīd* was celebrated, people presented their *noqūṭ* at that time instead of the day of the *Ṣabāhiyya.*

During one Kanuba wedding attended by the writer, the villagers expressed a desire to return to the old traditions, and the *barkīd* celebration was revived after having been omitted for two decades. In this celebration the guests assembled at night, and women walked in procession from the groom's house to the bridal residence to present their *noqūṭ.* The Old Nubian custom dictated that the mother of the groom come for the first time to congratulate the bridal couple and to present her *noqūṭ* on the *barkīd*, but on more recent occasions guests were offered a meal prepared by the parents of the bridal couple.

Kolod. The celebration of the *kolod* continues to be held on the seventh day after the wedding by a few families, but most weddings in Kanuba now dispense with it. Even when a *kolod* is now held, moreover, it serves a different purpose from what it did in Old Nubia. The gathering is now held at the couple's residence, where all the guests are served a meal supplied jointly by the two sets of parents. No musicians are hired and singing and dancing is performed by all the villagers.

The procession of the groom to his parents' house, the gathering of the *noqūṭ* by the groom within the neighborhood, and the meal sent from the bride's to the groom's house on the *kolod* are now completely omitted. Thus, in most cases, Kanuban wedding festivities now officially terminate with the *Ṣabāhiyya*.

Music and Dancing. Traditional Nubian singing and dancing in Kanuba has undergone considerable change, particularly through the introduction of new elements and the dropping of some old ones. Although the same instruments are still played to lead the singing and dancing, new variations in tempo and actual use of the instruments are now popular. One difference is that most of the singing is no longer led by slave musicians, but by a group of young Nubian students from the agricultural school in Kom Ombo. These boys are not all from the same districts in Old Nubia as the Kanubans and they have introduced a variety of new songs.

Songs of praise for the families of the bride and groom have disappeared and new Arabic songs have taken their places. In one wedding, during the *zeffa* with the henna from the bride's to the groom's house, instead of the traditional henna song in praise of the bride, the verses praised the henna itself. Songs which traditionally were sung for the slaughtering of the cow and the dressing of the groom are no longer sung.

In group singing, also, the language remains principally Nubian, but new songs have been introduced with themes focussed exclusively on admiration of the loved one, rather than themes of the traditional family-oriented variety. Other new features are the inclusion of more Arabic words and the introduction of songs relating more to the social changes in the immediate environment with themes about resettlement, the High Dam, national leaders, and so on. The younger generation has enthusiastically welcomed the new songs and learned them quickly, while older informants attributed the lack of traditional songs to the fact that they no longer had water wheels, land, or older family members to name and praise. Some of the more conservative people felt it would be better to omit songs completely rather than institute such innovations.

The dance that has remained popular in Kanuba is the group dance in which all villagers and guests can participate. Although attempts have been made to maintain the traditional *ollin aragīd*, or clapping dance, and the *firry* dance, they are usually given up because the steps are unknown and the attempts very clumsy. The main changes in the *kumba gash* group dance, which remains the predominant dance form, seem to be a faster tempo and a different composition of the rows. In Kanuba, the front rows are now mostly reserved for marriageable young girls, divorcees, and immediate family members of the married couple. This development parallels the wider choice now made possible in marriage. Wedding dancing now acts as a kind of showcase for potential partners and as an opportunity for restrained courtship and display. In weddings held during our field research, several disputes occurred between the younger generation and the old, who did not approve of the way the younger ones danced. They especially objected to their dancing in the front rows, and to the faster, less dignified tempo of the dancing.

Summary and Discussion of Changes in Marriage Celebrations

From the preceding description of the wedding celebration in Kanuba as compared with descriptions of old Diwan prior to 1933, it is evident that considerable alteration has occurred in the thirty-odd years since resettlement. The main changes which have taken place may be summarized as follows:

(1) A new form of entertainment, which was introduced by young people who had been exposed to engagement customs common in urban areas of Egypt, has been added to engagement festivities. The initial introduction of these new features was not met by much opposition from either the families of brides and grooms or from village leaders. The latter were eager to adopt new ways of doing things if they could be interpreted as being in the direction of "progress" for their village. Since most changes of wedding ceremonial do not contravene basic religious beliefs, many of them have been accepted.

(2) With regard to preparations for weddings, innovations were made that have considerably reduced the amount of time necessary for people to be involved. Having access to a public gristmill in a nearby town has resulted in much less time being spent in grinding the grain required for *sha'reya*, for example, while the availability of a bakery has enabled villagers to buy their bread ready-made and almost eliminated the use of traditional Nubian bread. Technological changes have thus reduced greatly the number of happy group gatherings which were so much a part of the older pattern.

(3) The elaborate festivity of the *tingodyendîbî* has ceased in Kanuba, though there is some evidence of feeble revival. This seems mainly due to economic factors; whereas in Old Nubia all food consumed during weddings was cultivated nearby, in Kanuba everything must be bought with cash. The changed conditions brought about by resettlement in Kanuba has resulted in an adaptive reduction of expenses (e.g., slaughtering a sheep instead of a cow, and in the sharing of expenses by the bride's and groom's families).

(4) The entire set of customs related to applying the henna has undergone change. Henna is no longer used as a major adornment or beautification by either the bride or the groom. Instead, a new procession associated with the

henna application and new Arabic songs about this symbolic substance have become one of the main attractions of the ceremony. This alteration, which was introduced less than a year before these data were collected, was brought to the community by a Kanuba girl who had lived in an urban center where the henna night was celebrated in such a manner. All subsequent weddings have included similar processions with the henna.

Furthermore, the bride and groom now refrain from having more than a symbolic touch of henna applied to them. Grooms no longer consider it proper to resume their work with henna stains on their hands. In Old Nubia, they stayed indoors for a long time following the wedding, emerging for work among Nubians of their own villages, among whom there was no reason to feel embarrassed by henna stains. At their urban occupations, such customs are regarded as provincial and *berberi*.

Young Kanuba brides now prefer cosmetics, feeling that they are more "appropriate" and "modern" than henna. If they do apply a tiny amount of henna, it is mainly for the sake of tradition and to make their parents and the older generation happy. The thought of pleasing the Nile angels still lingers, but appears to have little significance for actual behavior.

(5) The *katb al-kitāb* and the *balay* now are not necessarily held on the same day; furthermore, new elements have infiltrated into existing customs. Separate celebrations at the households of bride and groom similar to the engagement festivity are now held for *katb al-kitāb*. This is another innovation introduced to Kanuba by a community member who had considerable urban experience and who had attended Egyptian *katb al-kitāb* ceremonies in Cairo.

Other new elements in this part of the ceremony are the celebrations following the *katb al-kitāb* in the bride's house. All the villagers assemble in the afternoon; men sit with the groom and women with the bride. Syrup, candy, and cakes brought especially for the occasion from Aswan are served to all the guests. The bride wears a colored dress, cosmetics, and some costume jewelry for the occasion. The groom wears a suit or *jalabeya*. In most cases, the groom presents his bride with a present consisting of some gold ornaments.

(6) The sum of the *aba* has also increased, and it is claimed that this is mainly due to the higher cost of living and the increasing financial demands upon the bridal couple (i.e., the felt need to acquire a set of bedroom furnishings, a more extensive trousseau for the bride, and some household utensils).

(7) The ritual of the wedding day itself has also undergone considerable alteration. Some changes have come about gradually while others have been introduced suddenly. The older female informants expressed little dissatisfaction with most of the changes, but many of them strongly disapproved of the idea of the bride appearing unveiled before the guests. On the other

hand, younger informants were happy with these changes. They agreed that they wanted to be "modern", like other young girls from the city. Among the specific changes in the Fadija wedding ceremony in Kanuba were the following:

a. The actual wedding day is now announced by formal printed invitations (in contrast to an oral announcement in Nubia) which are sent to both Nubian and non-Nubian guests who live outside Kanuba. Informants could not recall when they started sending formal invitations; some stated that they began in 1934 immediately after their resettlement in Kanuba.

b. The main meal is an evening dinner instead of the traditional two noon meals. This change was claimed to be based on purely economic grounds. Informants stated that, due to the high cost of living, expenses have had to be decreased and that this was one way of doing it.

Another change is in the manner of serving food. Instead of the visitors being served Nubian style (which meant sitting on floor mats), guests are served at tables. This particular innovation was introduced about ten years ago by one of the grooms who had been working in Cairo for an extended period of time, and who had invited his non-Nubian city friends for his wedding in the village. He thought it more modern to serve food on tables and since then this has become the accepted Kanuban pattern for food service at marriage feasts.

c. Wedding costumes for both the bride and groom have changed to Western clothes instead of the traditional costumes worn in Nubia. This introduction was made some ten years prior to the study by a bridal couple who was raised in the Sudan, and who came to have their wedding in Kanuba. Their intentions were kept secret until the wedding day when they surprised all the guests and many of their fellow villagers by appearing in modern urban attire. The bride wore a long white dress, a veil, had her hair styled fashionably, and the groom wore a suit instead of a *jalabeya* for the occasion. Besides introducing Western clothing, this couple was also the first to initiate the custom of the bride and groom sitting on a *kōsha* in front of all the guests to receive their congratulations. Additionally, this was the first time for a bridal couple to reside from the first night of the wedding in a bedroom newly furnished in urban style.

These customs have replaced the *agbanyed* ("opening of the mouth" ritual) as well as the Nubian tradition that required the bride to sit on a mat behind the *kaled* with a *dewinsha* and other village women to attend her, and so on. Since then, more innovations along the same lines have been brought in by villagers who were exposed to different customs through their contact with urban customs and with non-Nubians.

These modifications, adopted in all subsequent weddings, have met with little opposition from the elders or leaders of the village. Thus, procedures followed in wedding celebrations at Kanuba now tend to resemble in many respects wedding celebrations held in other Egyptian villages and in the city (i.e., the *kōsha*, the henna night, the bride's and groom's attire, the engagement, and the *katb al-kitāb* festivity).

d. In Kanuba the groom spends a maximum of three days with his bride before leaving the bridal quarters. Modern labor conditions have made it impractical for him to remain indoors for the traditional seven days, so the custom was gradually altered as more and more men obtained work outside the village. A few men even leave for the city the morning after the wedding.

e. The choice of guests has also changed. In old Diwan, only Nubians from surrounding areas and relatives in the city were invited to the wedding. The resettled village of Kanuba is surrounded by other ethnic groups with whom the villagers have a great deal of interaction at the market center, at work, in schools, and in different public services. Many acquaintances and friendships have been formed among these other ethnic groups and it has become natural for non-Nubians to be invited to Kanuba weddings.

f. In the setting, there are no saints' tombs in the immediate vicinity that have special meaning for Nubians. This was a reason given to discontinue the tradition of visiting such shrines during wedding processions.

(8) Though serving different purposes, the *Ṣabāhiyya* celebration has continued as an important wedding activity in Kanuba. The main purpose at present is presenting the *noqūṭ*, since in most cases visitors can no longer stay more than two or three days. The majority of visitors now are non-residents of the village who must return to their work within a short time. Another alteration of the *Ṣabāhiyya* is that the guests are now usually served candy and syrup instead of the traditional *sha'reya*.

The bridegroom's attire for this occasion changed at about the same time the wedding dress changed. Informants said that the bride and groom are now more modern. Consequently, their nightwear consists of contemporary night-wear such as a nightgown and pajamas.

(9) As mentioned earlier, the *barkīd* no longer has its previous importance, though changes in this custom came about gradually. Informants again rationalized the changes by the need to reduce expenses and time, stating that since all visitors could present all their *noqūṭ* earlier, there is now little reason for the festive aspects.

(10) The *kolod* is another part of the celebration which is now generally omitted, for reasons allegedly similar to those given for the elimination of the *barkīd*.

(11) With the change of environment from Nubia to Kanuba, the Nile is no longer close by. Consequently, according to informants, wedding tradi-

tions centered around the Nile and its spirits were elminated. This diminution of involvement with these previously important beings also seems to reflect the general trends toward Islamic reformation and secularization that are taking place in the village (see chapters 2 and 3).

(12) Wedding dancing has undergone considerable but gradual modification. Young men and women who have had little contact with Old Nubia have not learned the skills of traditional dancing, though their elders tried to preserve the customary dances. The style of dancing in recent weddings has also been affected by the kinds of musicians who replaced the slaves . For example, a group of young students of Nubian origin, not all of whom were from the same district in Nubia, have incorporated new dancing tempos and steps into modified patterns. No completely new dances have been instituted, but traditional dances have been altered considerably.

In Old Nubia young people of marital age did not occupy the front rows, while in Kanuba these lines were reserved primarily for them. Female informants explained that the new arrangement gave them a better chance to be seen by young marriageable men. This explanation reflects the female anxieties related to greater outgroup marriage by Nubian youths and the consequently greater difficulty in finding husbands, a situation exacerbated by lengthening education, which has conduced to later marriages. One woman stated that the man who later became her husband had been away from the village for a long time and had returned to attend a wedding. When he noticed her dancing in the front rows he inquired about her, and by the end of the following week they were engaged.

(13) Wedding singing has undergone gradual change, mainly through the omission of some old songs, the introduction of new Nubian songs, the addition of Arabic words, and the introduction of some new melodies. New songs generally have been popular with the younger generations, and whenever a new one has been introduced, the Kanubans have picked it up quickly and sung it to perfection. Older women informants did not wholeheartedly approve of these new songs, but said they could not do much about them since the majority of the younger generation enjoyed them so much. On the other hand, there was no point in singing the old songs which were no longer relevant, being primarily praises of former land, tribes, and families.

In spite of the changes observed in weddings, the celebration still continues to be an important event in the life of the Kanuba villagers. Wedding ceremonies have continued to be community affairs, as well as the longest and most elaborate forms of village entertainment. Villagers, relatives, and friends from nearby villages and from urban centers all participate.

After resettlement in 1934, according the many people, though wages in Kanuba have been higher than at any previous time, the cost of living has risen to such an extent that to meet the demands of everyday expenses the Kanubans have had to reduce elaborate festivities in their new surroundings. Men gradually turned to white collar jobs within the province of Aswan, thereby becoming dependent on salaries for their livelihoods. As for wedding expenses, the following example represents very well the changing costs of the ceremony as a whole: in Old Nubia before 1933, the cow that was traditionally slaughtered cost about five Egyptian pounds; in Kanuba in 1963 it cost at least twenty-six Egyptian pounds. Informants emphasized that such inflation was the main reason to eliminate the killing of a cow during all weddings held in recent years.

All the food eaten during the wedding festivity now has to be purchased, moreover, as opposed to previous times when most of it was grown locally. Consequently, there has emerged a pattern in which the families of the bride and groom share expenses of the single meal offered on the wedding day. In other cases as well the elimination of some traditional celebrations in Kanuba (i.e., the *barkīd* and the *kolod*) was also motivated at least overtly by a desire to reduce expenses.

Another obvious change apparently due to economic factors is the increase in the amount of *aba*. Whereas in old Diwan the amount paid was more or less a token due to the limited demands of the bridal couple, in Kanuba the perceived needs of the bridal couple have increased (i.e., a furnished bedroom and more items added to the trousseau). To meet these changed conditions, the traditional institution of *aba* was altered in the direction of more economic significance.

Thus at least partially as a result of the need to reduce expenses, weddings have become much less elaborate. This reduction probably gives the participating families an opportunity to spend a major part of their income on the demands of everyday living instead of lavishing so much of their substance upon wealth-depleting displays. The groom's partial responsibilities for wedding expenses seem to be one of the reasons leading to the stress upon his financial stability before marriage and may be contrasted with the customs of Old Nubia, where the groom's family financed the entire ceremony. The bride is expected to have more items, (i.e., kitchen utensils, bed linens, and clothing) than was customary earlier. But some of the added expense of today's Nubian weddings is offset by the fact that the small amount of cash that young unmarried girls can earn from crafts enable them now to pay for part of their own trousseaus.

The new economic "needs" related to marriage seem mainly to be the result of urban contact and the consequent development of new aspirations and values. During my stay in Kanuba, a big wedding was attended by several relatives living in urban centers who had made the long trip especially for the occasion. Their arrival was an important event in the village:

all villagers were proud of their city relatives who had made good. They looked forward to their arrival, and were eager to offer any possible form of hospitality. The mother of the groom explained that these visitors were important; they included her brother, who was an Army officer and was engaged to a female Nubian doctor, a relative who had a good clerical job in a bank, and two girls who had university degrees and were working. This was their first visit to the village and the Kanuban inhabitants wanted to impress them. Throughout the festivity of the week the villagers went out of their way to present their guests with the best kind of hospitality, not forgetting to mention frequently and proudly the honor the village was enjoying by their visit. This hospitality not only revealed the continuing close relationship built on respect and admiration between the Kanuba inhabitants and their relatives in the urban centers, but also reflected the attitude towards city values that is altering so much of the traditional Nubian life.

We have further observed that many socio-cultural changes that were accepted in the village were introduced by those members who themselves had considerable urban experience. For example, one informant stated that she had witnessed the henna procession, previously described, and had heard the Arabic henna song in Daraw, while several other Kanuba inhabitants had seen such practices among other ethnic groups in their vicinity. The henna song was only adopted by Kanubans around 1962, however, when a young Nubian bride who had been living in the city introduced it in her wedding in Kanuba.

In some cases, innovations have been reinterpreted to conform with traditional patterns. For example, while Arabic words have been introduced in the singing, Old Nubian tunes are still maintained. Another reinterpretation is related to the wedding day eating practices. Although in recent weddings guests ate at tables, the Kanubans themselves ate sitting on mats in groups of five and from the same plate, as they were accustomed to doing.

Ties based on non-kin reciprocal obligation, which are one of the factors strengthening the ties among community members at large, are now activated and reinforced in wedding ceremonies. Kinship bonds previously had served as the main socially unifying force in Old Nubia, but now members within the neighborhood, regardless of their kin relationships, are expected to take active roles throughout wedding celebrations (i.e., they take the initiative in preparations and are hosts for guests from outside the village). Since no slaves migrated to Kanuba, many of their roles in weddings are now carried out by community members. The role of the *dewinsha* has been eliminated and young neighborhood girls have been assigned the responsibility of some former slave roles, including the preparation of meals and serving the bridal couple during their period of confinement and first few days after the wedding.

The duration of the total wedding celebration has been gradually decreased, even though other types of entertainment have been introduced in the village at the same time. Village entertainment now centers largely around dramatic programs sponsored through the village rural club by young men of the community. These programs have been initiated to serve as a means of recreation for the total community. Sports events (i.e., volley ball, soccer, and relay races or tournaments) are now held between students of the community and those of the neighboring schools in the area, and during these events the total community participates as members of the team or as spectators.

In Kanuba, kinship roles now have less significance during the wedding due to the alterations brought to some of the festivities; whereas in Old Nubia close kin played dominant roles in entertaining and throughout the celebration. Since application of the henna has become only symbolic, for example, the roles of the mother or older sister who attended to it have ceased, and the bride's mother, her maternal aunt, or her paternal aunt have now assumed the roles that formerly belonged to the slaves who carried out ceremonial preparations of the bride for the wedding night (i.e., the bride's bath, incense burning, and the application of henna). In Diwan close relatives wore special costumes that were different from those of the other guests and occupied the front rows during the folk singing and dancing, but in Kanuba they wear attire similar to that of the other guests and the front rows are occupied by young unmarried men and women.

To conclude, it is evident that the changes occurring in the Nubian wedding ceremony as practiced in the resettled community of Kanuba are products of many social drives. Changes in economic conditions and secularization of attitudes have provided underlying general stimuli and a climate of readiness for innovations in many areas of life. The visible mechanism for most of the wedding changes, however, has been the simple process of cultural borrowing. New ideas were introduced from the cities and upper Egyptian towns, and they were quickly adopted.

Notes

1. If the family was wealthy the groom rode a camel, was accompanied by a a boy or donkey, and was followed by a drummer or another camel. See the description of Old Nubia circumcision ceremonies (chapter 8).

Chapter 10

Nubian *Zār* Ceremonies as Psychotherapy

JOHN G. KENNEDY

The ceremony described in this chapter is not a part of the main Nubian ceremonial cycle. I have found no direct evidence of its antiquity in Nubia, and since nineteenth-century travelers did not mention it, I am inclined to accept the opinion of informants that it is probably a fairly recent phenomenon in the area. The acceptance and spread of the *zār*, in fact, is probably related to the substantially increasing privations inflicted upon the Nubians since the building of the Aswan dam in 1902. The ceremony is of interest in the way it reflects the major patterns and symbolism of the life-cycle ritual pattern. At the same time, it shows a great similarity to those curing rituals throughout the world which feature possession by spirits, and which may have powerful therapeutic properties.

The term *zār*, referring both to a ceremony and to a class of spirits, is usually associated with Ethiopia and may be of Amharic origin. The ceremony of *zār* is found along the Nile, however, from Alexandria to at least Khartoum in the Sudan, and similar rituals are common much farther south (Harris 1957 and Seligman 1914). For other recent accounts of variant types of *zār* rituals, the reader may refer to Messing 1957 (for Ethiopia); Barclay 1964; pp. 196–209 (for a Sudanese village); Fakhouri 1968; Nelson 1968 (for Cairo); and Modarressi 1968 (for S. Iran).

In Egyptian Nubia[1], the main purpose of a *zār* ceremony is to cure emotional disorders or interactable physical ones, through contact with the possessing spirits believed to cause such maladies. Though the Nubians possess several methods for dealing with psychological disturbances, the *zār* is a last resort, one that has powerful therapeutic effects for several kinds of ailments. It seems particularly tailored for alleviation of the hysterias, anxiety-produced problems, and psychosomatic ailments apparently related to living conditions in Nubia. The technique has also been used, however, in treatment of depressions and obvious psychoses. This chapter describes the form and content of the Nubian *zār* ceremony and attempts to account for this therapeutic effectiveness. The analysis suggests that the concentration and combination of symbolic and emotional elements in such prolonged dramatic ceremonies might be studied for possible applications to the often fragmented, intellectualized therapeutic techniques of Western society.

Theory and Purpose of the *Zār*

The Nubian *zār* ceremony is essentially a means of dealing with the demonic powers of evil, variously called *gour* (Mahas Nubian), *shayṭan* '*afrīt*, *iblīs*, jinn (Arabic) or *zār* spirits, who may cause illness. The whole direction of the ceremony is towards propitiation and persuasion of spirit beings rather than coercion of them. Before trying the *zār*, most patients have already been to healers such as the sheikhs of the *hejab* (charm makers), who use the Qur'ān to exorcise jinn; they may also have visited diviners or other native doctors who use herbs, blood-letting, or various other physical techniques. Sometimes they have tried Western-trained doctors.

Since it is used when other curing methods have failed, it is, in a sense, an acknowledgement that the evil entities have won, for if it is determined that demons are indeed causing the disorder, the patient often becomes inextricably associated with the particular spirits for the rest of his life. Resort to the *zār*, therefore, has overtones of an alliance with evil powers. The person may go through a marriage ceremony with his or her *zār*, and, to satisfy this spirit, in many cases, a perpetual responsibility is assumed, with a special performance at least once a year, as well as an obligation to attend the *zār* ceremonies of others. Orthodox Islamic opinion condemns the *zār* for dealing with devils, but opposition is generally not strong since jinn are mentioned in the Qur'ān, in which some verses may be interpreted to connect them with illness.

Nubian disease theory recognizes many purely physiological illnesses, which are treated with a variety of herbs and physical manipulations, but certain types of sickness that do not respond to such treatment are assigned supernatural causes. The Evil Eye of envy (*'ayn al-hassad*), the breaking of taboos, and sorcery (*'amal*) all produce illness and are often associated with spirits. Breaking a taboo is sometimes felt to bring a kind of automatic, almost mechanistic punishment, while at other times it is linked with a punishing spirit (see chapter 7).

In Nubian theory, jinn and other spirits are the most important causes of mental disease. The earth is believed to be inhabited by a host of invisible spirits that parallel the human population. Many are angels, or good spirits, but people seem more aware of the demons that descended from the Devil and began propagating at the same time God created the prophet Adam. Although demons tend to cluster in certain areas (such as along rivers or canals or in mountainous and desert regions), they are quite mobile. They like to occupy rooms and houses while residents are absent and are particularly fond of filth, garbage and ashes. Their preferred dwelling is human bodies, however, and therefore they are always a threat to people. It is possible to dispel demons by saying the first line of the *Fàtiḥa* or opening of the Qur'ān, and people use this incantation frequently, but the jinn hover in unsuspected places and sometimes individuals forget to say the preventive words before they are attacked.

There is an implicit idea of pollution and purification in all *zār* rituals, but it is notable that no confession is involved, and that in general mental or other disorders are not bound up with overt moral stigma. It is said that an angry or aggressive and violent person is more susceptible and attractive to the jinn, but blame for erratic behavior usually falls on the possessing spirit rather than upon the individual.

Form and Variation of the *Zār* Ceremony

Zār ceremonies vary considerably in detail according to the idiosyncrasies of the practitioner or "sheikh of the *zār*" and to the type of illness being treated. For example, a ceremony intended primarily to cure a seriously impaired psychotic who is diagnosed for the first time is longer and more elaborate than one called for by a trance-prone woman as the required annual placation of her *zār* spirit. Although some *zārs* focus heavily on social, entertainment, and divination activities, their major concern is mental illness, and certain features are common to most of the ceremonies.

When a *zār* is requested, the sheikh (male) or sheikha (female) begins by asking questions about the patient. A sheikh of Ballana (who supplied our most complete information on the topic) said he first asks whether the ill person has an appetite and sleeps regularly. He also asks about behavioral symptoms. If the eating and sleeping habits of the patient are not disturbed, he says that he usually decides the *zār* is not needed. After the initial interview, comes the *aṭṭār* to establish a diagnosis by various forms of divination. A common form of the *aṭṭār* is for the sheikh to request a piece of patient's clothing, which is said to possess the sick person's smell, and is generally brought wrapped around ten piasters, the diagnosis fee. The article is placed under the sheikh's pillow and if, during the night, he is disturbed by some sort of discomfort (usually reported as a shaking), he knows what class of ailment the patient has, i.e., whether or not he is possessed by the kind of spirit that may respond to the *zār*. Another sheikha in Abu Hor threw seven dates into a plate of sugar. According to their pattern, she would either prescribe her *zār* or some other form of treatment.

Some sheikhs may make a second diagnosis in some cases. If in doubt after the first interview, they may visit the patient again and ask for certain ingredients (henna, mastic and clove), which are then ground up and dissolved in a potion which the patient must drink. The practitioner may also pass a special incense beneath the clothing of the sick person. Certain responsive spirits may then cause the patient to quake uncontrollably and desire to dance. This reaction indicates that a *zār* is called for.

Another kind of diagnosis, made during the *zār* ceremonies themselves, does not concern the principal patient: people in the audience may request the spirit-possessed sheikh to tell them the causes and cures for ailments from which they or their families are suffering. Such requests are also accompanied by ten piasters wrapped in a piece of the patient's clothing.

After the trouble has been diagnosed, a proper *zār* should be held for seven consecutive days, excluding Friday, since the jinn stay under cover on Orthodox religious occasions. The ceremony may be restricted because of financial inability, quick recovery, or mildness of illness to two or three days or even to one. A two-day *zār* usually occupies the afternoon and evening of one day, finishing at noon the following day. A full-scale seven-day ceremony goes from morning to late evening each day, ending at noon on the seventh day.

The *zār* is primarily a female activity, though males often play the principal roles of leader and musicians, and the core of the typical *zār* audience is thus composed of women who regard themselves as having been helped or cured and who are obligated to attend in order to placate their spirits. Each member of this group of initiates puts on at least one annual *zār* to keep her spirit satisfied. The remainder of the audience come to lend support to ill relatives or neighbors, to get answers to pressing questions, or simply to be entertained. Theoretically, anyone may attend the *zār*, but it is felt that men should not attend women's ceremonies, and *vice versa*. None of our informants had heard of a public *zār* with an all-male audience, but our principal informant recalled several men he had treated secretly because they wished to avoid public admission of their participation in such practices.

The setting of the *zār* is usually a house with a very large room, since the audience will number from thirty to a hundred or more women. A cleared "stage" area in the center is needed for the sheikh and his (or her) helpers, with enough room for the dancers. Doors and windows are closed and the only light comes from lanterns. Room temperature should be high, since " the jinn are more likely to jump from the body when it is sweating." It is important to keep the room filled with the fragrance of incense and perfume, and a censer is passed around the audience several times during the performance.

On entering the room, each woman leaves her shoes at the threshold and places five or ten piasters on the sheikh's tambourine. All those attending the *zār* wear new or clean clothing to please the "masters," as the inhabiting spirits are sometimes called. The main patient usually wears a white gown (*jalabeya*) and a white veil (*tarha*). Her hands and body are dyed with henna, and her eyelids are blackened with kohl. She also wears as much gold jewelry as possible, is heavily perfumed, and sits like a bride, looking neither to left nor to right. If the patient is a man, he also is adorned as a bride. Other members of the cult who have permanent relationships with spirits usually also wear white, though sometimes they are commanded by the "masters" to wear garments of green or other colors while the ceremony is in progress. The sheikh himself usually has several costumes for changes during the performance, according to the personalities and desires of various spirits.

Music and dancing are invariable elements of the Nubian *zār* ceremony. An Arabic proverb is often quoted: "Songs are the life of the soul, and music helps to heal the sick." Important qualifications of a *zār* specialist are his knowledge of special songs for summoning spirits and an extraordinary drumming ability. If the ceremony is small, a single *tar* (a kind of tambourine) may be used, but large performances require more *tars* and perhaps a *dabella* (a type of tambourine). The sheikh may also drum on a *tisht* (large metal washbasin), which has an especially powerful effect on spirits.

If the person for whom the *zār* is given is very disturbed, some special ritual preparation may be made before the singing commences. The patient's silver bracelet may be placed on the overturned *tisht*, while on her head grains of *durra* or sugar are sprinkled three times, followed by seven dates, dropped one by one. Another preparatory act is purification by incense. For example, the patient may be made to inhale the smoke before and during the ceremony.

The sheikh begins the ceremony proper with songs and drumming. The form of the songs adheres to a typical Nubian pattern of verse and refrain, with the latter often being the name of the spirit called e.g., *"Haji Jabillo"* ("Holy Man of the Mountain"). Each song is addressed to a different spirit. When a spirit associated with some person in the audience is called, that person begins to shake in her seat, then makes her way to the central dancing area, sometimes dancing and trembling till she falls exhausted to the floor. Before the spirit consents to leave, it usually demands special favors such as jewelry, new clothing, or expensive foods. The commands may be more bizarre, however, such as orders to wear a green veil or dunk one's head in a pail of water. It is the duty of the relatives and friends to gather round the prostrate woman and pacify the spirit. The patient may lie for some minutes on the floor, "as if dead," with only her hands twitching, before a special song by the sheikh brings her back to consciousness.

Some of the songs sung by the sheikhs in the Fadija area of Ballana are addressed to "masters" called Abd al-Sīd al-Sudan, Safra al-Bahr, and al-Maghrabi (Slave of the Lrd of Sudan, Emissary of the Nile, and the Westerner). The fact that several people may be moved simultaneously by one of these songs may indicate that a class of spirits may be involved. The extremely flattering, even erotic imagery and tone of some of these songs are exemplified in this song to a feminine spirit:

> Sherifa! Sekina! Sherifa!
> You pure daughter of the Imām!
> You beautiful sailing boat!
> You beautiful guide!
> Your lovers are ten!
> Oh Sayyida, you pure daughter of the Imām!
> How sweet you are, you flower of the bath!

The audience's enthusiasm may be low at the beginning of a *zār* performance, or may flag at later points during long sessions. At such times, the sheikh of the *zār* usually demonstrates his own supernatural abilities. He becomes possessed by a series of often quite different spirits, each demanding elaborate costume changes. The following examples suggest the nature and range of these performances.

One sheikha in a Kenuz hamlet in Dahmit is known by two names. In everyday life she is called Zeinab, but during her performances she becomes Defaya, dresses in a fancy satin dress, and behaves erratically. After assuming the identity of Defaya, she may be possessed by various spirits. One of these, a river spirit named Abu Shusha, causes her to jump hysterically to the music and to act destructively. On one occasion, the women in the audience had to restrain her from breaking and throwing away her jewelry. Abu Shusha then caused her to take off her satin dress, complaining that it was ugly and should be white. The sheikha finally allowed herself to be restrained by force from tearing the dress before she was brought a white one, which calmed the spirit and permitted the dance to proceed. The sheikha then demanded a cake made with milk (things made with milk are especially liked by the river spirits). Next, she was possessed by a female Arab spirit who wanted a husband, saying "I am pretty. Who will give me her husband?" Finally she became Mirghāniyya from the Sudan, speaking with a different tone and accent and apparently unable to understand *rotān* (Nubian dialect), for informants claimed that Mirghāniyya spoke only Arabic. Mirghāniyya scolded the sheikha's mother and others present for being inhospitable to her. When she demanded milk and gold, the women tried to humor her and comply with her wishes.[1]

In another ceremony, in a village of the Kenuz *'omodiyya* of Abu Hor in New Nubia, the sheikha and another participant were possessed by the spirits of a bride and groom. One of them wore a man's green *jalabeya* and a veil (green is never seen in weddings or in women's daily dress). They sang about a bride and groom desiring *henna* and perfume, while dancing suggestively. When *henna* and perfume were brought to them, they distributed it to the members of the audience, who rubbed it on themselves. During this same performance, another of the spirits possessing the sheikha was a wild *Bishari*[2] tribesman who waved a staff aggressively and shouted. Then a male spirit who wanted to smoke cigarettes possessed the sheikha and made her pass them around to other women in the audience. They all smoked together, though women's smoking is frowned upon, especially in public.

Another kind of behavior was observed in another performance at old Abu Hor. The sheikh, in one of his identities, wielded a long whip which he cracked aggressively, forcing some people to get up and dance and chasing others who laughed at him. This man also became possessed by a ferocious cannibal. With great gnashings of teeth and snarling noises he tried to tear a baby away from a screaming mother, causing all the young women with babies to flee the room.

Fortune-telling and prescribing cures for people in the audience are other frequent features of *zār* ceremonies. A typical example is afforded by the woman who asked what was ailing her infant son. The spirit replied that she had neglected her son by leaving him alone. In her absence, a man passing by had given the boy the Evil Eye. The prescription was to pass incense throughout the room in which the boy had been left alone and to rub a substance called *mahlab* over the bodies of both boy and mother. Many questions put to the spirits concern family members absent in Cairo or other cities. In one ceremony, a woman was assured that some expected clothing had been sent and would soon arrive. Another was told that her son's injured hand had been healed, while a third was informed that her husband would find work soon. A worried wife was reassured by being told how to offset black magic, which had been used to steal her husband, who had not returned from his work in Suez for many months.

A final set of ritual actions in the Nubian *zār* involves animal sacrifice. The length of a *zār* depends as much on the desire and wealth of the person or family holding it as upon the condition of the patient; the timing and type of sacrifice is decided by the duration of the ceremony. If the sponsoring family is poor or if the *zār* is a relatively routine annual performance, the sacrifice may be a single cock or, perhaps, two pigeons. On the other hand, if the ceremony lasts the full seven days, several chickens may be killed on the first, third, and fifth days, and the final slaughter on the seventh will be a lamb or sheep. The sheikh has determined at the initial diagnosis what the important color of the sacrificial animals (either black or white) will be. In a typical case, a white or black cock (according to the type of illness) is killed over the patient's head on the third day at exactly noon, and the blood is smeared over her face, hands and legs. In the evening or on the following day, this fowl is cooked and the sheikh shares it with the patient. On the seventh day, the patient ceremonially straddles the lamb or sheep holding the slaughtering knife in her hand. After five piasters have been placed in the animal's mouth, its throat is cut by the sheikh. The ritual is continued by wrapping the five piasters that were in the animal's mouth in a piece of cloth and tying it to the patient's right hand. The hot blood of the sacrificial animal is rubbed all over the body and face, and some of it is mixed in a potion with cloves, henna and water. After drinking this potion, the sick person ritually steps across the dead animal seven times.

It is said that usually, at this point of the zār, the jinn is pacified, though the music and dancing continue while the lamb is being cooked for the final ceremonial feast. The dish prepared is fatta, the traditional Nubian ceremonial food. In this commensal meal, the sheikh receives the head of the lamb, an honor which on ordinary ceremonial occasions usually goes to the imām of the mosque or to another holy man. Guests who have not been possessed by zār spirits abstain from eating this feast for fear of demons transferring into their bodies from the food or from possessed individuals. All leftovers and garbage from the sacrificial animals and from the meal must be collected and thrown into the Nile to prevent contamination and sickness to poultry or animals, which might unsuspectingly eat it.

As a final part of the ceremony, the patient leads the other possessed participants of the zār to the Nile where they bathe their faces and legs. Sometimes the patient is then advised to sit for forty days in seclusion, like a new bride.

Social and Psychological Functions

For its audience, the zār obviously serves psychological and social needs beyond the therapeutic purposes for which it is ostensibly held. Most significantly, it is primarily an adult female activity reflecting stressful social conditions of sex-separation, low female status, restriction of women from religious participation, an unbalanced sex ratio, marital insecurity, and relative isolation.

As Muslims, the Nubians teach girls submissiveness to males. Women's feelings of inferiority are reinforced by the fact that they are permitted only half the inheritance of men and are excluded from the highly valued religious activities of the mosque. On all ceremonial and public occasions, men and women are grouped separetely and in daily life communication between the sex categories is minimal. Women's marital choices are much more firmly regulated than those of men and their premarital chastity is zealously guarded. Their activities, particularly any that take them outside the village, are closely supervised. Perhaps as important is the insecurity resulting from Islamic customs of easy divorce and polygamous marriage. Polygamy is not frequent, but its ever-present possibility hangs over most women as a constant threat. This is especially true under Nubian conditions of labor migration, where the convenience of a man's having both a country and city wife sometimes detrimentally affects the economic resources of the family remaining in Nubia. Divorce is an even greater fear than the possibility of another wife, and it is commonly threatened by disgruntled husbands.

There are other anxieties connected with female status that are intensified by migrant labor conditions. In isolated villages populated predominantly by women and children with a few old men, far from medical care and the diversions of a city, it is understandable that the women embrace *zār* ceremonies with enthusiasm. The same anxieties and frustrations that find relief in the *zār* are also expressed in other Nubian ritual activities, thus supporting the hypothesis that for the healthy participant, as well as for the sufferer, such ceremonies constitute a socially sanctioned "safety-valve." We have already described the elaborate saint cults in Nubia (chapter 4) in which people petition spirits for many of the same things which are requested in the *zār*: return of husbands, marriage of children, marital goods, cures and the like. There are also many special rituals centering on the "angels of the Nile" and upon spirit sheikhs who can grant similar favors (see chapter 5).

As is evidenced by the content as well as by the intensity of the acting out, the cathartic discharges of emotions provided by the ceremony provide an ideal situation for the relief of many of the sexual and aggressive tensions that are generated under the stresses of such conditions of life. Through possession by spirit beings, an individual temporarily changes his identity and is thus absolved of responsibility for her actions. The psychological effects of the intense activity and excited emotionality undoubtedly in themselves produce relief from tensions for a great range of "normal" individuals, as well as for those suffering from various types of neuroses. Substitutive release of forbidden sexual desires is obvious in such things as the copulatory movements of the dances, the marriage symbolism, the love songs addressed to the spirits, and the "possession" of individuals by spirits of the opposite sex. While it is possible that some persons of homosexual predilection may occasionally express themselves in the *zār*, most of the transvestite activity appears to be an expression of envy of male prerogatives. This envy is also evidenced in such behavior as the ostentatious ritual smoking which I described as part of one ceremony. It may be hypothesized that even for those members of the audience who do not actively dance, some tension is relieved vicariously through identification, escape and laughter.

The wish-fulfillment aspects of the ceremonies give evidence of anxieties deriving from migration and isolation. Demands by the spirits are for items usually procurable only in urban areas. Typical questions put to the divining spirits are: "Is my husband being seduced by another woman in Cairo?," "When will my daughter marry?," and so on. That the answers and prescriptions do have an anxiety-reducing effect, which makes life more bearable for the ordinary woman, was directly attested to by several informants, and their relief in having their worries paid attention to was evident and overtly recognized.

Zār Practitioners

Sheikhs of the zār usually come from slave ancestry and are, therefore, accorded low status in the community. Faith in their power is increased by this circumstance, however, since the tribes further down in the Sudan from which the slaves came are reputed to know much more about sorcery and magic than do the Nubians. The performance of zārs rewards both male and female practitioners with much higher prestige and more respect than other members of their social categories. Former slaves are generally looked down upon, and there is orthodox religious opinion against zār activities, but even a member of the puritanical Anṣār al-Sunna sect never knows when illness may strike him or his family, and the Qur'ān itself speaks of jinn and associates them with mental derangement. Some of those who oppose the zār speak of fraud and fakery, but often the more salient objection seems to be to the sinfulness of dealing with demons.

Opponents accuse the zār sheikh of economic motives, and it is true that considerable income may be earned. A famous zār sheikh of Ballana charges a three-pound fee, for example, and takes ten piasters from each person entering, as well as ten piasters for each fortune or diagnosis. Some female sheikhas take only five piasters for entrance and for divination, and may net as much as fifteen to twenty pounds for a seven-day performance. Sponsoring a large zār thus entails considerable expense. Not only must the sheikh be compensated, but sacrificial foods, foods for guests, and possibly new clothing must be acquired. Wealth, of course, inevitably promotes the general prestige of the sheikh. He is also able to exercise some power over high-status male members of the community through his divining techniques, for he can raise or lower the anxiety level of believers at will and may, on occasion, prescribe very difficult and expensive procedures for the cure of certain individuals.

Besides the desires for economic gain and prestige, it seems clear that other motivations and needs are often involved in the role of sheikh of the *zār*. These practitioners, like the shamans of many other cultures, are masters of drama who understand how to surprise and thrill their audiences — how to entertain, as well as how to satisfy desires for security and self-expression. They must not only be good musicians, but must also have self-confidence and inspire expectations of hope in others. One famous sheikh informed us that he had been unable to find a successor to train in his art. Two of his young relatives to whom he wished to bequeath his role did not possess "strong enough nerves," as evidence of which he stated that "the incense falls from their hands and they cannot repair the drum during a seance."

An even more important trait of the practitioner is the technique of ecstasy or trance. All of those about whom we have any information also claimed themselves to have been cured of a serious mental disturbance in a *zār* and, indeed, the behavior of some sheikhs seems to indicate that the *zār* may be therapeutic for them, as well as for their patients. As has been suggested for shamans elsewhere, such ceremonies appear to be an institutionalized form for the acting out of impulses considered antisocial or abnormal in other contexts. Aggressive and even sadistic impulses are sometimes exhibited, as exemplified by the whipcracking, cannibalistic performance described earlier. However, the aggression may also be less virulent, as in the case of the sheikha who castigated her mother while in another identity and who in ordinary life was as docile and obedient to her parents as any good Nubian.

The sheikh role seems to contain a range of stable and unstable individuals. In the general motivational structure of these individuals, desire for power, wealth, and social ranking appear to operate along with needs for attention, with exhibitionistic and aggressive impulses, and with expressive, dramatic, or artistic abilities. As in the case of other participants, the tensions and frustrations of the practitioner may be relieved by the *zār*, where he has an opportunity to make use of unique qualities which there is little other opportunity for using in the culture, especially among those who belong to the female and former-slave social categories.

Psychotherapeutic Aspects

The *zār* provides an ideal situation for relief of persistent and regular anxieties and tensions arising from the Nubian conditions of life. In much of the activity, in fact, it is difficult from our data to distinguish "normal" individuals from those who could be classified as emotionally disturbed. The evidence seems to indicate that many, probably the majority, of the *zār* patients suffer from anxiety reactions or hysteria, although these symptoms are difficult to separate.

The sheikh, in his diagnosis, places great importance on the patient's eating and sleeping difficulties. These symptoms are, of course, typical of anxiety-reaction neuroses, but manifestations of hysterical symptoms in the *zār* are even clearer. Psychiatrists attest that "the quality that emerges as the most plausible single feature constant to all cases (of hysteria) is the tendency to dissociation," and dissociative states, are one of the most outstanding characteristics of the *zār* ceremonies. Paralysis, another apparently hysterical reaction, is also described by many informants as being treated and cured by the *zār*. The hysterical nature of such paralysis is suggested by frequent reports that the affliction immediately followed a severe fright or a moral or ritual breach. Although we have no good epidemiological evidence for the Nubians, the data thus indicate that hysterical or hysteriform ailments are closely associated with the *zār* and may be the most frequent type of mental illness in the culture.

We may hypothesize that those who make up the central core of *zār* cult initiates tend to be rather unstable, emotional, and hysteria-prone persons. This hypothesis seems plausible in view of the Nubian theory that possessed individuals are inescapably linked with their demons and must regularly placate them. It also accords well with clinical observations. Mayor-Gross, Slater, Elliott, and Ross aptly point out that "it is the tendency of the hysterical personality to make *excessive demands* which are often met, to obtain, in fact, excessive consideration; the tendency is self-perpetuating" (1960, p. 137 italics added). The wish-fulfillment aspect of the *zār* performance also fits the hysterical syndrome and supports the idea that the ceremony is, in some ways, a cultural form built up in response to hysteria-precipitating conditions of endemic stress.

Direct evidence of wish-fulfillment is seen in the important part of the *zār* ceremony where the possessing spirit demands material items. The demanded goods (jewelry, clothing, fancy goods) are all things that husbands should provide. Some husbands who are opposed to the *zār* in principle claim that such demands are merely a means of extortion by women, and in his discussion of the similar Sudanese *zār* in Buurri al Lammaab, Barclay emphasizes this point (1964, pp. 197, 203); others, too, have suggested that in similar ceremonies such activity is a means of obtaining desired or needed items from reluctant males (Messing 1957 and Harris 1958). In the Nubian case this sort of manipulative behavior certainly does occur, but it should not be overstressed. Often the spirit does not request material items, but requires special activities instead, such as wearing a green veil; and in some cases where jewelry or other material goods are demanded, they are given only temporarily, to pacify the spirit, and are returned after the ceremony. There would appear to be more of a demand for attention than for goods, the goods demanded symbolizing attention. The response of the audience is an affirmation of social support and a temporary indulgence of wish-fantasy.

I have already spoken of the substitutive release of frustrated forbidden sexual impulses. Other kinds of tensions expressed in zār ceremonies not so clearly tied to sex or other deprivation are also clearly of a hysterical type, e.g., the case of the woman whose spirit demanded that she immerse her head in a bucket of water and then eat kernels of green wheat, which was the favorite food of a particular jinn. After the ceremony, this woman reported great relief from tension.

Although a majority of the active participants in the Nubian zār seem to suffer from high anxiety and hysterical types of neuroses, such individuals are not considered especially abnormal and many come to the zār as audience participants rather than as patients. The informants themselves felt that patients most frequently treated are those suffering from what they call wasswassa, a state usually precipitated by the death of a close relative or a frightening encounter with a spirit. The characteristic symptoms of wasswassa are apathy, withdrawal from human company, minimal communication (though with rational communication still possible), refusal to work, a strong desire to die, lack of appetite, and sleeplessness. In these cases, the zār is said to "untie" the wasswassa. Two common and frequently treated psychosomatic complaints are unlocalized pain, and an unaccountable wasting away and progressive weakening, accompanied by listlessness and loss of appetite. Both these conditions are also reported usually to be cured by the ceremony.

In Nubian nomenclature (Mahas dialect) mental disorders are classified in two main categories: witti dowu or dowi (big madness) and witti kodoud (small madness). Disturbances described as witti dowu are the most serious and would probably be identified by Western psychiatrists as psychoses or chronic brain disorders. They are subcategorized according to the type of behavior exhibited, e.g., witti atoji (violent and dangerous). Witti kodoud refers roughly to what modern psychiatrists call neuroses.

One of the most common and most feared manifestations of witti dowu is called ayendanbany ("he who whispers"), a term that appears to be applied to some kinds of what we would regard as schizophrenia, since the symptoms are incoherent talk, confused thinking, speaking to unseen beings, erratic behavior (such as laughing without reason or running at inappropriate times), and non-response to direct conversation. The seriousness of this diagnosis is reflected in a saying: "The whisperer whispers until he dies." Yet several cures of this disorder were reported and Sheikh Muhammed himself was claimed to be a cured whisperer.

Within the limits of their categories and experience it appears that Nubian sheikhs can usually distinguish between minor neurotic symptoms, such as hysteria, and major psychoses. Though most of the psychic ailments brought to the *zār* seem to be neuroses, it is obvious that severe schizophrenia or other psychoses are also treated. The diagnostic techniques of the sheikhs provide a means of excluding the completely psychotic, noncommunicating individual. But motives of economic gain or the importuning of relatives sometimes prevail to allow a severely impaired person into the *zār*, and surprising recoveries are sometimes said to occur.

One reported example of a remission from apparent schizophrenia was Sa'diyya, a woman now about thirty-five years of age, from the village of Qustal. One morning shortly after the death of her mother (ten years prior to the report), Sa'diyya, who was then single and living in the same house with her father and siblings, awoke screaming and ran from the house. Her father caught her and beat her, but to no avail. The neighbors brought her gifts and tried to calm her, but her speech was meaningless and jumbled, and she would run frantically through the village laughing wildly. She remained in this hopelessly incapacitated condition for several months. Her father took her, without result, on long journeys to several famous *hejab*-making sheikhs who agreed that she had the whispering disease, the most feared form of *witti dowu*. Finally, a seven-day *zār* was held for her and she recovered. She has been married now for several years, has two children, and is considered normal by the community. The fieldworkers were impressed by her rational, capable behavior.

Effectiveness of the Zar Treatment

All systems of psychotherapy have as their major purpose the change of socially inadequate or unacceptable behavior patterns to adequate, acceptable ones. Jerome Frank has, perhaps, defined universal therapeutic ends as clearly as anyone by speaking of symptom-relief and improved functioning. At the same time, the great proliferation of differing psychotherapeutic methods and partial theories in the Western world, along with the fact that about the same proportion of individuals are cured no matter what system is used (Kiev 1964, p. 27), suggests the need for more serious study of other culturally determined systems for treating mental illness (see Kennedy 1974). The *zār* often does accomplish therapeutic aims of symptom relief and improved functioning, and it may be therefore of interest to inquire into some of the reasons for its success.

Part of its effectiveness can be attributed to such universal character-istics of therapy as emotional support, intellectual support, and emotional discharge (Alexander 1963, pp. 273–275). Notable in the *zār*, however, and in practices of other non-literate societies, is the lack of rational or insight-based approaches. Introspection, verbalization, or "working through" of early conflicts or traumas are absent. Writers who have noted similar phen-omena in other societies seem to feel that because of these lacks, the cures are not as effective as their Western counterparts. Devereux, for example, makes the questionable generalization that remission without insight is not really a "cure". Kiev points out, somewhat apologetically, that "although primitive therapies are fundamentally magical, that is, non-rational, attempts to deal with non-rational forces, they often contain elements of rational therapy" (1964, p. 10). It is probable, however, that Prince's opinion that Western psychiatric techniques are not demonstrably superior to many indigenous Yoruba practices applies also to other non-Western systems (1964, p. 116). Opler made a similar point concerning the indigenous therapeutic milieu developed in the Ethiopian *zār* and in Ute Indian dream analysis (1959, p. 14).

The factors most often singled out for these emotional, rather than rational or insight-based cures are faith, suggestion, catharsis, and group support. In addition, Frank has suggested that magical techniques give the patient a framework for organizing his vague distresses and heightening his sense of worth. Of course, these elements are also present in varying degrees in Western psychiatry, but they are usually in combination with or subordinated to overtly verbal techniques administered in a two-person situation.

What seems critical in the case of the *zār* is that these emotional factors are combined and concentrated in a mutually reinforcing matrix, which brings emotions to an exceptionally high pitch. This emotion-arousing, heightening and intensification is effected through the dramatization of danger and awesome power in a ritually constructed world where "society" is temporarily neutralized. The situation is so defined that restraints are removed, learned norms are stripped away, and repressed impulses are allowed to reign. This is the kind of situation that a "rational" therapy would have great difficulty in constructing through free association, direct intervention, or other methods; and even psychodrama, which superficially seems to utilize similar techniques, appears "intellectual," artificial and contrived by comparison. It is in this context that the elements that seem to account for the effectiveness of "primitive" therapy may be understood, as may be illustrated by their function in the *zār*.

Faith. Since it is omnipresent, belief alone is obviously not enough to account for the curative effects of the ceremonies. People believe in the supernatural causes of these illnesses, and they will try several methods in the same attitude of faith. The generally high level of faith in traditional curative practices is tempered by a practical skepticism, since (though rationalizations are available) there is clear awareness that some people do not respond to treatment. In addition, everyone is aware of the opposition from religious orthodoxy and from those who ridicule traditional methods with accusations of fakery. Furthermore, in some cases that have responded to treatment, the patient had been functioning too inadequately to establish the effectiveness of faith as a critical fact, at least at the outset.

In most cases, however, immediately during the diagnostic procedure, the sheikh begins to arouse and buttress the patient's faith. The diagnosis is really the beginning of the treatment: the sheikh works to reinforce the patient's belief by entering his weighty, supernaturally-given opinion of cause and possible cure. Faith is also intensified by the fact that possible causes such as Evil Eye, sorcery, and non-*zār* types of spirits have been eliminated by first trying other diagnostic and curing techniques appropriate to these causes. When he enters the *zār*, the patient knows that "this is it." It should be mentioned that the sheikh may reduce the possibility of failure by excluding those in whom he senses lack of faith to respond to the ceremony, or who are hopelessly beyond any sort of communication.

Group Support.   Prior to treatment, the patient has also had the benefit of constant group support. In contrast to the withdrawal response of people in some societies, the Nubians rally around a disturbed individual and try to keep him (and his jinn) continuously diverted. The belief is that he should be given good things to eat, like oranges and dates, and that two or three people should always be present to converse and carry on other activities with him. Since they have been given from the beginning of the patient's trouble, group support and attention are also not unique to the *zār*, and cannot be invoked as sufficient conditions for curing. What is different about both faith and group support in the *zār* is their intensity and combination with each other and other powerful influences.

In the *zār* ceremony, these universal therapeutic features are given new dimensions and a much higher intensity by the drama involved, by the association with powerful cultural forces through symbolism, and by the definition of the situation as one of supernatural power, outside the jurisdiction of social conventions and norms. When people enter the ceremonial place, the atmosphere is charged, the mood is set, and participants approach in a mood of exhilaration. Intensified anxiety and fear and guilt derived from impending contact with dangerous and irresponsible spirits are mixed with anticipation of entertainment and of escape from the daily humdrum. This combination is enhanced by the requirement to remove the shoes, by the wearing of new or special clothing, and the special staging of the room. Therapeutic activities take place in this already-charged atmosphere, from which orthodox religion and God are excluded, in which social rules are suspended, and where the partially unpredictable forces of evil are in evidence.

Symbolism. The emotional effects of the *zār* are to a large degree dependent on stimulation by the symbolism employed. The symbols are those found throughout Nubian ritual signifying goodness, joy, purification, and protection from evil.

First there is an attempt to make the occasion as happy as possible for the benefit of both spirits and patients. Much of the activity is patterned on the most joyful of Nubian ceremonial occasions, the wedding: the patient is dressed as a bride, adorned with henna and kohl, and performs some of the marriage rituals. Music and dancing in general are also most strongly associated with weddings. But the materials used in the *zār* all have much more symbolic significance than merely the suggestion of a wedding. Their uses in other rituals indicate that they evoke a host of other powerful emotions and associations. Henna, for example, is used in practically every Nubian ritual occasion, usually by women. When applied to hands, feet and body, it is considered to create and enhance beauty. It is associated with purity, femininity, sexual pleasure, and protection from evil; it is used as medication for small cuts and as skin cleanser. Its special effects on spirits are shown by its use on the flags on saints' tombs and on the draped coffins inside them, in burial, and as an ingredient in purificatory incense.

The theme of purification runs through the entire symbolism of the *zār*. In addition to the purificatory meaning of henna, the ubiquitous incense and perfume are also thought to have a purging effect, in that they entice out the polluting evil spirits. The potions drunk by the patient and the ritual cleansing in the Nile are acts of the same order. The white required for clothing and for sacrificial animals has a purifying meaning, as does the sacrificial blood itself, which, in addition, placates spirits.

While the purification symbols also have a protective meaning, other symbols and acts are more exclusively concerned with protection from harm, e.g., the color green which is associated with heaven, palm trees, and all good things, as well as the many uses of the numbers seven, three and forty. For instance, the *zār* should last seven days and seven dates are thrown on the sugar in divination or dropped on the patient's head: dates symbolize general goodness, wealth, and health in themselves, while the numbers signify good luck, protection, and the proper way to do things. Gold is another symbolic substance found throughout Nubian ritualism. It gives protection from the Evil Eye and spirits, and signifies wealth and general good as well. Animal sacrifice and the commensal eating of the ceremonial food, *fatta*, also belong to common Nubian patterns, being associated with communal solidarity, generosity, and good will.

All these symbols have a powerful evocative effect, which aids the intensification of faith and awareness of group support. They also represent familiar Nubian themes, probably harking back to pre-Islamic times, and therefore, in addition to their magical potency, they have a purging effect on subconscious guilts and give a sense of appropriateness and correctness to the occasion. The marshalling of these symbols in the *zār* throws the weight of all positive Nubian traditional values on the side of the patient.

I propose that such multidimensional cultural reinforcement is much more powerful than "group support" alone and that it goes much deeper than the simple idea of "faith," which is usually invoked to explain such phenomena. The patient is not only bombarded with symbols and given powerful socio-cultural support, but is also placed in a dramtic context that involves the violent acting out of roles by the practitioner and other members of the audience, as well as by the patient, the person in need of help. Powers of suggestion are enhanced by the focus of attention on healer and patient as protagonists in this drama. The *zār* practitioner not only heightens beliefs and intensifies emotions by legerdemain; he, himself, also acts as a model for dissociative abreaction, which under the hypnotic conditions of the *zār* is readily imitated.

Several kinds of emotional discharge take place, but the one aimed for in the *zār* is that of the hypnotic trance, which frees the patient from restraints imposed by both social norms and superego controls. The situation is defined at the outset as one in which many ordinary norms do not hold, but in trance and the temporary guise of another identity, the patient is permitted even more freedom. It is not only that norms are suspended: there is an expectation of reversal, in itself lending an air of excitement and unpredictability that is appealing to participants.

Abreaction is by many writers associated with the assuaging of guilt, and it is of interest to note that, unlike cathartic techniques in many societies, the Nubian *zār* does not involve confessions. Responsibility is usually projected to the jinn rather than accepted by the individual. The purificatory emphases in the whole proceeding do *imply* an underlying sense of guilt, however, which is indicated in whippings administered to the mentally ill in the *zār* and other non-*zār* contexts, and which may be inferred from the fact, as well, that mental retardation is sometimes considered to be caused by adultery of the parents. The idea that jinn are attracted to individuals who are angry and aggressive is also suggestive of a guilt association, since the Nubians place strong values on non-violence and non-aggressiveness. It is interesting, however, that the symbolic purificatory elements of the *zār* ceremony are carried out in an anti-religious, "evil" atmosphere and that much of the acting out represents behavior that would be anti-social or at least morally undesirable in other contexts. Thus, the patient is allowed to act out his "evil," while powerful symbolism is being evoked to purge him of it. During it all, he never admits guilt, but projects it onto spirit surrogates.

It should be pointed out that physiology plays a role in the abreactive aspect of the *zār*. The patient does not lie on a couch, but is physically and emotionally stimulated by rhythm, music, and body activity to the point of emotional exhaustion, for the cathartic release is preceded by a tremendous *increase* of tension and anxiety. This tension seems to be as important for the inducement of trance as for the degree of catharsis obtained. The patient is also to some degree physically manipulated, i.e., put through a course of symbolically important motor activities: he (or she) is dressed in special clothing, dates are dropped on his head, he is smeared with animal blood, smoked with incense, and so forth. All these actions function to "involve" the patient physically and emotionally.

We may finally suggest the analogy of the *zār*—the whole atmosphere, as well as the hypnotic trance—to a culturally staged dream. As in dreams, the censoring superego is removed and repressed wishes are allowed free expression, the weak and subjugated dominate, the timid aggress, the repressed express strong sexual desires, males become females, and females males. It is as if these were implicit cultural recognitions of the effectiveness of "dream work" and an attempt made to simulate it through symbolic and dramatic means.

Conclusion

In this analysis, I have tried to single out those factors of the Nubian *zār* that could account at least partially for its curative effects on mental illness. It is clear that the essential emphases are on emotional rather than intellectual techniques. The "real world" is submerged; the world of fantasy, the subconscious, or the *id*, are deliberately exploited. The processes involved seem more complex than is implied in such familiar explanatory catchwords as "suggestion," "group support," and catharsis. Their complexity suggests that more intensive research of such techniques as the *zār* might be of some use to Western theories of psychotherapy.

The problems most effectively treated by the *zār* seem to be those of hysteria, which is not surprising since techniques of suggestion and abreaction are often used for such cases even in Western psychiatry. The *zār* may be a more effective technique than others, however, since it combines a whole battery of methods, including hypnosis, which some psychiatrists feel should be investigated and further exploited in such ailments (Mayer-Gross, Slater, Elliot & Roth 1960, pp. 138–46). Such Western treatments as the following are parallel, though in effect much weaker and more artificial in approach than the *zār*:

> The acute hysteria of soldiers often responds to stimulation of the nervous system by the inhalation of small quantities of ether, by inducing the patient to relate the events of the past in a dramatic way, to relive the past, and *by psychological means to induce a state of excitement*.... The abreaction of emotions was a feature of Freud's first successfully treated patient and abreaction in a less dramatic form plays a part in psychoanalytic treatment even today (Ibid, p. 133, italics added).

The symbolism and the removal of repression in the *zār* function to counteract precipitating environmental stress factors, especially if the stress is constant (i.e., non-removable or perceived as such). These techniques may well be more effective than most of the segmented and partial methods of present-day Western psychotherapy. It might even be suggested that long term dependence on the *zār*, shown by the lifetime duties and responsibilities to a spirit, is a viable, and functional adjustment *under conditions of more or less perpetual stress*. The security and stability of such a lifelong relationship seems different from the "sick" dependence that may develop in a situation where stresses are less formidable and can be removed more easily.

Different societies bring different types of stress systems to bear on their members, and Opler's comment on the *zār* is apropos:

> This hysteriform acting out is not just a matter of thwarted wish-fulfillment and safety valves provided in the culture, but these folk-cult forms in psychiatry additionally offer group social supports, which certainly counteract or take the place of isolation and private wish-fulfillment in a very active way. Psychoanalysts and family group therapists do not have such ready resources close at hand. The *zār* cult form is tailored to problems quite different epidemiologically from those we have in our urban populations in the United States with their high incidence rates of paranoid schizophrenia. (M. K. Opler, personal communication).

It is undoubtedly true that these techniques are more appropriate and effective in the cultural settings in which they developed. Yet the *zār* is apparently effective not only with hysterical and anxiety reactions, but with depressive neuroses, psychomatic ailments, and even some psychotic conditions. More research is needed to ascertain how effective such treatment is, but the data suggest that certain kinds of emotional strategies might be exploited by Western psychiatry much more than they have been. Group support and family and milieu therapy are increasingly utilized in the West. The data from the *zār* suggest that cultural symbolism and drama might be more effectively used in such similar Western forms as psychodrama for strengthening group support, faith and suggestion, and helping to enhance, focus, and concentrate attention.

The *wholeness* of the *zār* experience is also suggestive; it is not a piecemeal event like the daily or weekly one-hour session so typical of our own urbanized, fragmented existences. In the *zār* ceremony, seven days may be devoted by the group to intensive therapy. All the techniques, many of which are singly employed in Western psychiatry, are brought to bear in one integrated context. Research might reveal that the emotional therapies discovered by so-called primitive peoples, with their "irrational" belief systems, have greater power to cope with some of the dimly understood forces of the human psyche than do many of our methods, which are still ineluctably tied to the implications inherent in our lingering model of rational Western man.

NOTES

1. Most of the data reported in this chapter were gathered by Sohair Mehanna, Bahiga Haikal, and Zeinab Gamal. The incident recorded for Dahmit was supplied to me by Nowal Messiri.
2. *Bishari* is the singular of *bishariyyīn*, a pastoral nomadic group of *Beja*-speaking tribes living in the deserts between the Nile and the Red Sea in Southern Egypt and Northern Sudan.
3. Mayer-Gross, Slater, Elliot, and Roth 1960, pp. 129–146.

Chapter 11

Nubian Death Ceremonies

JOHN G. KENNEDY

The death of an individual is experienced almost universally as a psychological blow to those socially near him and also constitutes a shock to the structure of social relations of which he was a part. This personal and social damage is everywhere responded to with ritual and ceremony which function to relieve the emotional tensions, anxieties, and fears of bereaved individuals, and to repair the social gap in the interpersonal network of interlocking obligations and reciprocal activity patterns. The Nubian ritual response to death has much in common with customs throughout the Middle East, yet the ceremonies have their own cultural phrasing. A description and analysis of them will help to fill in the picture on the ceremonialism of this group and its meaning within the total Nubian life pattern.

A death in Old Nubia was an event that terminated all but the most basic subsistence activities for the whole village and initiated a set of prescribed ceremonies and obligations centering on the bereaved family. The long and complicated cycle of death-related activities was triggered by women in the vicinity, with piercing ululating wails (called *wigiba* in Mahas dialect), usually first emitted by those who had been attending the death agony. The cries were then taken up in adjacent houses, passed on throughout the village, and echoed between villages up and down the Nile, signalling the name of the deceased so that people who might be involved could know the nature of their obligations. The responsibilities varied with age, sex, status, degree and type of relationship, and mode of death.

The village's normal peace and quiet changed at once to excitement: women's cries crescendoed up and down the river bank, the thud of running feet and the rustle of dresses echoed in the streets, and the background hum of conversation became noticeably louder. Almost everyone in the immediate hamlet or village was under strong obligation to drop everything and hasten to participate, and until the corpse was buried there would be continual movement. After burial the tempo would slow to a measured carrying-out of ritual and social tasks, as attention turned to the observance for prescribed periods of sacred restrictions upon behavior.

The immediate response of women in the neighborhood was to put on black mourning and rush to the house of the bereaved. Women of the bereaved family changed to black garments, tied ropes around their waists, and lashed rolled-up mats to their backs, along with some garment of the dead person. Careful to remove all jewelry and to unbraid their hair, they smeared mud on their heads and their clothing, while a blue dye (*nila*) was applied to their faces. Older women of the immediate family carried green palm sticks in their hands, which they waved above their heads during the death dance and which were said by some informants to have the purpose of distinguishing the family of the bereaved from others in the crowd, though they had symbolic protective significance as well. Those arriving to give condolences (*tafé* in the Mahas dialect, *'azzā* in Arabic) were received in the courtyard of the house. (It will be remembered that Nubian houses were very large and built around ample open courtyards). As each woman entered the courtyard she stooped to take ashes from a container placed near the door. After blackening her face and hands she went to offer condolence to the family and then joined the funeral dance, which began in a cleared area of the courtyard.

Condolence was formally given by stroking hands, embracing, and crying alternately on each of the shoulders of the bereaved: "God exists!" "God will give you patience!" "It is God's will!" "The dead will return to life!" or "The dead will not lack a shroud, the living will not lack bread." As the women joined the dance, they continued to wail, beating their breasts and slapping their faces, shouting out "God bless your children!" "Who will care for your children now?", and other similar exclamations. On the death of a child they might cry: "You left the world leaving no name behind you!" As they danced they scooped dust and poured it over their heads, tearing at their clothes.

According to informants, the tearing of clothing symbolized empathetic temporary rejection of worldly happiness and a sharing of loss with the family. Ashes and dust also had this meaning, but further denoted worthlessness and sorrow and dramatized the transiency of life. The palm sticks, and the dye and mud were said to be related to fear of the spirits and jinn, which were believed to flock around at death: the palm was protective, while the mud and dye acted to confuse the threatening beings.

The whole tone of the women's expected response was unrestrained, an almost hysterical expression of grief; and the nearer one's relationship to the deceased the more extreme was the behavior allowed and even expected. This role prescription often produced ritualistic weeping that could frequently be interrupted at will to allow conversation or the performance of duties.

Under the influence of the Orthodox practice and belief that have been becoming more and more prevalent in Nubia during this century, these extreme outbursts, along with such customs as funeral dancing, smearing the face and hair with dye, and continuous wailing, have been prohibited by the men of more and more Nubian districts, especially in areas where the Reformist sect, the Anṣār al-Sunna, has become influential. The main rationale for eliminating them is that they are not Islamic, and that, therefore, they represent sacrilegious desecrations in the sight of God. In keeping with the clearly separated lives of men and women in their communities, however, male mourning patterns were apparently always quite distinct from those of women, involving emphasis upon suppression of emotion and a separate set of burial and mourning duties. Though in recent years men have forbidden the excesses they felt characterized female grieving practices, much more emotionalism has continued to be allowed to women than to men and male condolences reportedly always were given in a much more restrained and dignified manner: a man simply pressed his face to each shoulder of the bereaved repeating "It is God's will." It was permissible to weep briefly on arrival at the house of the deceased if the latter were a primary relative, but displays of grief afterwards were severely criticized as unseemly.

Nevertheless, breakdowns in emotional restraints apparently were not uncommon. We observed a Kenuz man in the village of Kanuba who was unable to restrain himself when his young wife died. He sobbed openly for several hours, much to people's distress, and women were heard speaking of him contemptuously. Men tried to restrain his outburst, both by gentle persuasion and sharp commands, but had no effect on him; and the story of his improper "feminine" behavior went around the village for at least a year after the event.

After giving condolence, males repaired to a special mourning area set up for them outside the house (*khayma* in Arabic, *tafe negr* or *tigīr* in Mahas), usually an enclosure constructed of palm branches and mats, though in recent times in some districts the courtyard of the mosque has been used. Inside the enclosure, visiting men sat on mats called *farsh* (Arabic) with turbans untied, thus demonstrating their support of the male members of the immediate family. In former times, they would remain for forty days. After the first three or seven days those most closely related to the deceased would again don their turbans, but would leave the ends hanging over their shoulders during the whole period. For the first fifteen days they were prohibited from shaving and could not re-enter their own houses. These restrictions have been gradually reduced in recent years, following the Nubian pattern of ritual numbers. Thus the time for sitting in the mourning enclosure or mosque became progressively reduced from forty to fifteen, to seven, in some districts to three, and in Kanuba at the time of the study, to one day. These reductions correspond to increasing pressures on men to return to urban jobs, and to a lessening dependence upon the agricultural way of life with its more flexible time schedules.

Burial

The burial itself followed patterns similar to those in other parts of the Muslim world. Interment took place as soon as expedient. If death occurred in the morning the funeral was completed the same day; if it occurred late in the afternoon or after sunset, burial was deferred until the following morning. One reason given for this was that in Old Nubia, because of prowling wolves graves had to be deep, and that at night it was often too difficult to dig sufficiently.

Certain specialists, usually older relatives of the same sex, prepared the body for interment. The most important preparations were washing the body and making the shroud. The corpse was placed on an *angarib* bed covered with palm fronds, under which had been placed three pots to catch the water. After the clothing had been removed the face and body were rubbed with henna, a cosmetic regarded as holy and said to be suitable for entering paradise because it was recommended by the Prophet Muhammad. Hot water and soap were used to cleanse the corpse as the washer chanted *"Yasin," "Tashahhod wa tawhid."* Perfume was sprinkled on the body and hair before a wrapping (*Tarha*) was put on the head. If the deceased was a virgin, this had to be white. When ritual washing was complete, a final purification with perfumed smoke and incense was made, and the shroud, sewn collectively in the mourning area by a group of older men, was put on and tied with three knots (at the feet, chest and head). The corpse was transferred to another *angarib* bed, which had been transformed into a bier by arching palm branches over it at the head and foot. When the deceased was a woman the arches were draped with red cloth, since it was felt that the feminine shape of a woman should not be visible to the crowd as the bier moved toward the cemetery. Green palm fronds were said to please the soul of the dead person, alleviate his suffering, and "light" his way; they also acted as a prayer to the spirits to allow the survivors to keep his house "open." While preparations of the body proceeded, some of the young men who had been sent ahead to the cemetery dug the grave, and lined it with flat stones.

When preparations were complete, four close male relatives of the deceased carried the bier, preceding the mourners in their procession to the graveyard (*torbah* in Mahas). Men led the procession while wailing women followed the bier. At the graveside, the body was wrapped in a cloth or blanket, taken from the bier, and lowered into position by two men, protecting it from the view of anyone except those carrying out the actual interment. The corpse was placed on its side facing Mecca, the three knots in the shroud were loosened and green cloves called *bartod* were dropped in the grave. The body was then sealed into the burial recess with flat stones and filled in.

An animal was sacrificed and left for the spirits (and birds) on top of the grave. Then men all listened as the imām, or some other wise and holy man, repeated verses from the Qur'ān, finishing with the *Fātiḥa*, while the wailing women continued to stamp out their funeral rhythm some distance away. When the grave was heaped up slightly with dirt, a flat stone was inserted upright into the earth at either end, and a pigeon was slaughtered and presented to the man who had recited the Qur'ān. Some grains of *durra* were planted on top, which would be watered for at least forty days thereafter. A clay bowl called the *kaway* (Mahas) was placed at one of the mound and filled with water, to be kept replenished for forty days.

After the burial everyone repeated the *Fātiḥa* and returned to the house of the deceased, where they were offered tea or cinnamon tea, after which all villagers but the closest relatives returned to their houses. At this time visitors coming from greater distances remained and slept at the house of the bereaved.

The *angarīb* bed upon which the deceased had been carried to the cemetery could not be taken back inside the house immediately because it would bring the destructive effects of *mushāhara* to the family. It was left outside in the street until the new moon, as "Every month comes with new events."

Post-burial Customs

The Nubian belief system contains a fatalistic notion that "God gives birth and life, and God takes them," as one informant put it. Also involved are beliefs that the soul (*shorti* in the Mahas dialect) of the deceased lingers around the grave for forty days before going to an interim place near either Heaven or Hell where it will remain until judgment day. It returns during yearly feasts or occasionally at other times to visit relatives and to receive offerings of water, palm leaves, and food.

During the forty-day period (and especially the first three days) after death, the spirit keeps a close eye on what is being done at his funeral. For example, a dead woman was said to reject the person who was washing her for burial; the third finger of one hand remained extended and could not be put in proper position until another person was called to do the washing. On another occasion, a dead woman's bier became so heavy that the pallbearers could not lift it to carry it to the cemetery. It happened that a certain man whom the *shorti* wanted to assist in carrying her had departed that morning for the city. Unaccountably impelled, he returned to the village, however, and when he helped lift the bier it immediately became very light and was borne quickly to the cemetery.

There is also the belief that after a future judgment day the soul will either ascend to paradise or descend to hell, according to one's deeds during life. A slow, painful, or lingering death is a sign that the person has been evil, that his guardian angels are not present, and that, instead, a demon *gour* (Mahas) is sitting next to him and causing him pain. But if he has been virtuous, his two angels will be by his side, permitting him to die quickly. After death in any case his spirit must be accompanied by the angel Israel to a waiting area where it remains until moving to its final destination, either to a large tree where it awaits ascent to Heaven, or to a well, where it awaits descent to Hell.

An unborn child or a baby less than forty days old were considered to be in severe danger when a death occurred, and menstruating women were prohibited from visiting graves and from encountering corpses, as well as from taking part in funeral activities, a custom stemming from belief in *mushāhara* dangers to fertility. Other close relatives refrained for a whole year from going to joyful occasions, such as weddings, cicumcisions, and the procession for the Small Feast (*'īd al-ṣaghīr*). Women of the family did not go to market for as long as forty days after a death and could not participate in wedding preparations. Families with very recent deaths were also exempt from making the ceremonial food that was distributed to the visiting men in their procession during the Small Feast, and households that had had a death in the family within the previous year served coffee to the procession instead of cinnamon tea.

Since the bereaved family was suspended from all productive activity during the mourning period, neighbors and close relatives were responsible for feeding both them and the guests who continued to come individually or in small groups from distant villages. Many of the guests stayed for three days, sometimes utilizing the situation to return visiting obligations or to transact business. The amount of food supplied by these neighbors and relatives was often a real economic burden, eased slightly by a prohibition against eating a mid-day meal before the third day of mourning.

The first three days after death were the most intense period of communal mourning. Women danced and sang as continuously as they were able, and between periods of dancing sat in groups talking quietly. The large water jar had to be filled each of the first three nights, for if the spirit returned and did not find water, it would kick the jar and break it.

The *khitma* was an important ceremony held on the third day after the death. For this a sheep was slaughtered to feed the people and special ceremonies for men and women were performed before everyone joined together in the evening for a feast. The male *khitma* ceremony began in the men's mourning area. Parts of the Qur'ān were read alternately by Sheikhs or religious leaders, and another procession was made to the cemetery. At the grave, the mound was leveled somewhat, and custom prescribed that the group chant "la ilaha illa Allāh" seventy thousand times, each time dropping a tiny pebble (called *rahama* in Mahas) on the mound. A distinguishing feature of Nubian graves is thus the mass of fine gravel piled upon them, visibly symbolizing the multitude of prayers the community made for the deceased.

Finally they sprinkled the grave with water, and the close male relatives ritually replaced their turbans, which had been tied around their waists, on their heads. However they still left them partially untied, the ends hanging down across their shoulders, to symbolize that they were still in mourning. Following the ceremony at the grave, the men returned to continue their mourning vigil. The ceremony was sometimes concluded by recitation of Qur'ānic verses in commemoration of the deceased, and sometimes a *dhikr* ceremony was performed by the men in the evening following the recitation. Both these customs appear to have been rather late introductions, however, and they were not universal even as late as the time of our study. During these days of confinement, details of the inheritance were often worked out, in addition to performance of mourning rituals.

The women's roles on the third day after death were even more elaborate than those of the men. The women of the bereaved family, accompanied by all those visiting for condolence, proceeded to the cemetery behind the men. After the male ceremony of counting the pebbles they distributed shares of dates and sweets to any children or non-village passersby who might be there. This was called *ṣadaqa* (Arabic), a traditional Islamic form of almsgiving.

The groups of women then trooped to the Nile with the clothing of the deceased, where they washed it and left it on the bank for any needy persons who might pass, such as poor people or traveling nomads. They also ritually washed their faces in the Nile and, in some districts, sat quietly together by the river for a period of time, for it was said that their washing their faces helped cool the face of the dead, while their resting had the effect of relaxing the body of the deceased in its grave. Some *sha'reya* and henna were offered to the water spirits, accompanied by the incantations of those *naqības* who had relationships with the "people of the river."

Returning from the Nile each woman picked a palm frond, carried it to the doorway of the house and, uttering the *Fatiḥa*, hurled it inside before entering. This action brought God's blessing and protection to the children, and dispelled lurking jinns. In some areas, another ritual was performed after entering the house: a mixture of *mahlab* and perfume had been prepared, and as each woman came in she dipped her little finger into the container, making contact with this protective symbolic material.

When both men and women had returned from these ceremonies, a feast of *fatta* made from the slaughtered animal was served, and the *walīl* was distributed, consisting of dates and other sweets served on Nubian flat basket plates, along with tea for the women and cinnamon tea for the men. This ritual was called "rolling up the *farsh*," since at this point the male mourning mats were ritually rolled up. Except for close relatives, who might stay till the seventh or fifteenth day, the guests from distant villages then began the return journey to their homes. People living within the immediate village and those from other villages in the same district were expected to visit the bereaved at least three times during the mourning period, while those from distant villages and districts were obligated to come and give condolence only once.

Women of the village, especially close relatives of the deceased, visited the grave every day for forty days after the death, though some stopped going after seven or fifteen days. For the first fifteen days, each took seven dates with her to the cemetery, which she either distributed to children there or left for passing strangers. Sheep were again slaughtered and ritual feasts called *atīgas* in the Mahas dialect (*atagas* in Kenzi) were given for invited guests on the seventh, fifteenth, and fortieth days after the funeral. If the deceased was a young adult or a respected sheikh, such commemorations were almost mandatory. The later rituals generally did not have the compelling obligatory force of the earlier ones, however, and in recent times these customs have become adhered to sporadically, as the tendency to reduce all life-cycle ceremonials has increased. The later ceremonies were also more likely to be performed if the family was well off financially.

Besides communal feasts and *dhikr* ceremony, the fortieth day (*gorgitti* in Mahas, *arba'īn* in Arabic) was marked by a ritual in which the women of the family again went to the cemetery. After placing three palm fronds (*tokadt* in Mahas) in the loose soil, one at each end and one at the center of the grave, they passed incense over it seven times and poured libations of water. At this time, the hovering soul was released to begin the journey to the tree in the sky (or the well), not to return again except on the occasions of *atīgas* in his honor or for the Small Feast.

If the dead person were highly esteemed, another communal feast might be held in his honor at the end of the year. As before, a sheep was slaughtered and a communal meal prepared for villagers and invited guests from neighboring communities. This ritual had some resemblance to the funeral proceedings of the third day: it involved reciting from the Qur'ān, but with only seven thousand repetitions of "lā ilāha illa Allāh" followed by a *dhikr*. If the family could afford it, or if the man's memory was extremely important to the group, such *atigas* might be repeated annually for several years after the death.

Nubian graves were unmarked with names, so that except for holy men or saints, the particular places where individuals were buried were forgotten in a generation or two. Burkhardt described the cemeteries as he observed them in 1813 as follows: "The Nubians place an earthen vessel by the side of every grave, which they fill with water at the moment the deceased is intered, and leave it there: the grave itself is covered with small pebbles of various colors, and two large palm leaves are stuck into the ground at either extremity" (1822, p. 32). This pattern is the same as that reported by Amelia Edwards several decades later (1891, p. 254) and as is evident from the description above, is identical to what I saw in 1963–1964.

In a recent comment on Nubian burial customs Cavendish remarks as follows: "Specially selected stones, usually of quartz, are prayed over and put in the grave over the body of the deceased. Water is poured over them and grain (durra) is made to grow, either directly in the form of actual grain planted on the grave, or indirectly, in the form of giving its growth to the children, who eat if off the top of the grave, above the quartz stones" (1966, p. 154).

Càvendish points out the similarities between the Nubian uses of the small stones and their use in rituals of fertility and rain-making among a Nilotic tribal group called the Bari, who live in the southern Sudan (155–6). It is also clear that the customs of offering food and putting water in pottery vessels at the foot of the Nubian grave go back at least to the period of the "C Group" people, who are dated at 2270–2600 B.C. (Emery 1948, p. 17). Such customs may be distinctive to this part of the world and seem not to be shared with other Islamic societies, but the use of the stones for multiple prayers or blessings for the deceased, rather than for rainmaking, seems an interesting syncretism with the Islamic tradition of counting prayers with beads (*sibha* or *misbaha* in Arabic). The storing of water and food for the ghost, of course, is early and ubiquitous in Africa and, along with many of the other funeral customs, such as the women's dance and the *mushāhara* taboos, seems to be a remnant of that pre-Islamic substratum of Nubian religion which has never been completely supplanted by Islam. It is not my intention to try to explain this persistence here, though it is undoubtedly related to the long relative isolation of the Nubian villages. I merely want to emphasize again the syncretistic character of Nubian ritualism and to remind the reader of the distinctive features that such beliefs and practices give to the Nubian "Little Tradition" of Islam.

The Social Repercussions of Death

The intensity of community interest and the mobilization of activity for any particular funeral ritual depended upon the age, sex, and social importance of the deceased. For children, many of the ceremonies were left out or abbreviated, and little expenditure was involved. For those under twelve years of age, the men did not sit in the *tafe neger* or perform the post-funeral rituals. At the other end of the age range, exceptionally elderly people also did not rate great elaboration in ceremony or expenditure unless they were famous, wealthy, and powerful. As Herzog comments: "When a man of high standing dies, his relatives, who are dispersed all over the country, hold mourning rituals in their homes" (1957, p. 102). More elaborate and complete funeral ceremonies were also held for young leaders and men in the prime of life who were supporting families. Young married women with children were also given large funerals. The way death overtook the individual was also a factor affecting the scale of ceremonial celebration, however, and the greatest funerals of all were for young married men (usually between the ages of twenty-one and forty-five) who had met a sudden or untimely end.

Besides the ceremonial requirements entailed by a death, numerous restrictions and obligations for many people were automatically in force for a long period thereafter. All relatives, friends and neighbors were strongly obligated to participate in the funeral if they were in the area, and if they were in the city, they were expected to telegraph or immediately to write to the family. When they returned, it was mandatory to visit the family of the deceased to give condolence. These obligations held indefinitely, and we observed cases in which people who had been absent from the village of Kanuba for ten and twelve years immediately sought out the families in which deaths had occurred in the interim and gave condolences. In each case, the full condolence ritual was repeated, no matter how many years had passed since the demise. Thus women had to cry and wail on the shoulders of the close relatives of the bereaved, as if death had only just occurred; all jewelry had to be removed, particularly if made of gold. Neglect of condolence was not only severely censured; it also incurred avoidance and the breaking off of reciprocal obligations on the part of the offended family, creating a powerful sanction for conformity.

The ceremonial complex surrounding death was thus an important force in Nubian society. The social obligations devolving upon every member of the village of the deceased, as well as upon all relatives and friends outside the village, were extremely compelling. Fernea's observation with reference to a village in the district of Ballana, in the Fadija area, is an accurate assessment:

The strength of these reciprocal obligations can hardly be overestimated. The failure of the obligated to oblige can result in an almost irreparable break in social relations between the families of those involved, making such negligent behavior unthinkable among kinsmen and neighbors. The entire community would participate in the censure of such deviance to the point that a migrant from Ismailia who fails to note the death of a kinsman neighbor in Ismailia is spoken of as being "dead," as socially he indeed is.

Obligations of relatives and neighbors were largely concerned with supporting the family and keeping the ceremonial process running for them. Neighborhood women collectively took the responsibility for caring for guests and cooking. Single girls were delegated these tasks. The supporting families co-operated in the expenses of feeding guests, who continued to come in groups, though in diminishing numbers, for most of the forty-day period.

Menstruating and pregnant women and those still in a state of sacred vulnerability due to birth, circumcision, or marriage, made the only legitimate exemptions from these obligations. Failure to perform expected roles led to retaliatory abstinences from ritual obligations to the offenders and to lasting enmities. Women of the immediate family of the deceased were prohibited, as we have noted, from going to the market for forty days following death. Anything they needed was brought to the house by families in the neighborhood.

The most astringent taboos and requirements were applied to widows, but many requirements also were placed on other members of the immediate family of the deceased and some even applied to more distant relatives. Some activities were prescribed for the community as a whole.

It was the women of the immediate family who were under the most severe constraints; female members of the families of procreation and orientation of the deceased had to wear black continuously for a six-months period, while the mother and sisters of a dead male wore it for a year. The widow theoretically symbolized her sorrow in this way for at least three years and might dress in mourning for the remainder of her life.

Though customs have changed somewhat today, widows in the past had a particularly severe set of taboos imposed upon all their activities. Their mourning role required them to remain in the house on a mat (agtah) for a period of four months and ten days. This long period of mourning was called edigo, meaning literally "take your hands off" in the Mahas dialect and was sometimes also observed by the mother of the deceased if he were a young man. The widow was also prohibited from braiding her hair for the entire period of mourning. Her head was shaved and for the first five days she was obligated to sit unmoving and to sleep in the same place upon the ground. After this initial period, she moved to the mat for the remainder of her confinement. It is reported that in the past a straw hut was constructed inside the house for the widow, making her separation from daily life even more complete.

For the first three days, the wife of the deceased could not eat, and for the first seven days she could not walk or change her clothing. The only exception was when she visited the cemetery on each of the first forty days. On each visit, she placed dates or grain on her husband's grave, sprinkled it with water, and changed the green palm fronds. On her second day visit, she sprinkled milk on the grave.

After returning from the cemetery to her *agtah* mat at home, the widow received condolences from those visitors who continued to come from other villages or from the city. The sleeping room (*diwani*) of the husband and wife, which had been decorated at marriage, was ceremonially stripped of the rolled-up mats, hanging bowls, pictures, and colorful basketwork plates that set it apart from other rooms of the compound. At the end of the four-month and ten-day *edigo* period, the widow was allowed to terminate her confinement by again going ritually to the Nile to offer her mourning mat to the *aman nūtū* river spirits. She also threw into the water the knife she had kept under her pillow to ward off dangerous supernatural beings.

Within the village itself, wedding or circumcision ceremonies that had previously been scheduled had to be cancelled if they fell with the forty-day mourning period, regardless of how much expense had been involved in their preparation. Members of the immediate family or lineage were expected to postpone such events much longer, and this requirement held whether they were living in the village, in the city, or elsewhere. Close relatives were prohibited, as we have noted, from attending any weddings, *mawlids*, or other festive occasions for one year. Other relatives, such as aunts and uncles, nieces and nephews, and in-laws, had more options in observing these restrictions; they could obey them according to their feelings of closeness to the deceased.

During a condolence period for a previous death, pregnancy, a menstrual period, or the forty-day confinement following the birth of a baby, a woman of the village was not allowed to take part in funeral ceremonies and was exempted from most of her obligations toward the family of the deceased. Dangerous spirits were regarded as threats to her fertility and health at these times.

Understanding Funeral Rituals

General explanations of death rituals fit into two broad categories, the psychological and the sociological. On the psychological side, the main explanatory ideas have come from Freud (1917). The most important of these conceptions is that human beings everywhere perceive the death of a person psychologically close not only as the loss of a loved object, but actually as a loss of a part of their own selves. This then sets off a series of emotional responses resembling the psychiatric state of agitated depression. The process, known as grieving, goes through a course of increasing intensity. Since Freud we have more clearly understood it as a process by which the bereaved individual is enabled to heal the wound to his selfhood by means of a "working through" of the powerful ambivalent emotions of fear, guilt, and incomprehensible deprivation that have been activated by the shock. Freud pointed out, for example, that much of the depressive pain of grief derives from the ambivalence of repressed wishes for the downfall of the loved one that have been harbored in the unconscious. These feelings are additional to the sudden stress, the feelings of unreality, and the threat to the orderliness of things stemming from the sudden removal of what was a dependable, feedback-giving part of the environment, and to the sudden threat to the working illusion of one's own immortality. Through mourning, interest must be transferred from the self and the dead love-object back to the living world.

On the psychological level, mourning rituals are thus often conceived of as a customary means for assisting the individual through a crisis of the self; they provide a framework of therapeutic meaning and action. The stages of funeral ceremonies in many parts of the world correspond rather closely to this pattern and are therefore usually interpreted as social responses built upon the psycho-physiological grief pattern, as functioning therapeutically to support and sustain persons suffering emotional loss. By this theory, ghosts and spirits constitute the transmuted guilt and repressed hostilities projected outward as personified threats.

Most modern students of bereavement have elaborated Freud's ideas and have generally agreed that the mourning process follows three main stages: an initial short period of shock, bewilderment, anger and high anxiety; a stage of violent despair, rumination on the past association and imagination of the dead, with some personality disorganization; and a final period of psychological reorganization (e.g., Klein, Bowlby, Lindemann, and Gorer). Ceremonies created to deal with the anxiety-producing forces of death have the effects of allowing catharsis of guilt and promoting therapy. So-called "primitive" mourning rituals are often cited by the psychoanalytically inclined as more effective means for performing therapeutic functions than the comparatively restrained customs current in Western societies.

In contrast with the psychological view, sociological explanations of these rituals, since Durkheim, have viewed them as shared customary mechanisms of the group developed to maintain its unity and solidarity in the face of the threat posed by loss of a member. In his monumental work on the rituals of the Australian aborigines, *The Elementary Forms of the Religious Life*, Durkheim interpreted funeral rites in terms of his idea that the origin of "God" derives from the group's reification of itself, i.e., of "society." Thus, he rejected the concept of mourning ceremonies as stemming from individual feelings of loss and attributed them instead to powerful norms imposed by the group.

> When someone dies, the family group to which he belongs feels itself lessened, and to react against this loss, it assembles. A common misfortune has the same effects as the approach of a happy event. Collective sentiments are renewed which then lead men to seek one another and to assemble together.... Not only do the relatives, who are affected the most directly, bring their own personal sorrow to the assembly, but the society exercises a moral pressure over its members, to put their sentiments in harmony with the situation. To allow them to remain indifferent to the blow which has fallen upon it and diminished it would be equivalent to proclaiming that it does not hold the place in their hearts which is due it; it would be denying itself (1965 (1915), p. 445).

One of the main features of native Australian mourning that led Durkheim to his interpretation of the funeral emotions as obligatory and as thus deriving from social rather than personal needs was the frequently reported fact that the weeping and mourning behavior was not genuine: people seemed to turn their weeping on and off at will according to the situation and some reported that they were forced either to mourn strenuously, even to lacerate themselves, or be punished by the ghost.

Other aspects of this functional theory of mourning rituals were added by Hertz, an associate of Durkheim. He theorized that conceptions of an afterlife and immortality are constructed on the paradoxical assumptions that culture is ongoing and immortal, but that it can only be manifest in individuals, which means that an individual death is a threat to the culture. He further argued that ritual elaboration of death is correlated with the social importance or cultural significance of the deceased, both to the group as a whole and to those tied most closely to him. Thus children are little mourned because they have not yet become a contributing part of the society and old people are similarly treated because they have retired from active social participation. Similar reasoning accounts for the fact that those socially closest to the deceased are generally under the severest restrictions, since they partake of his "impurity" according to their degrees of closeness, i.e., their relative social importance (Hertz 1960; pp. 51–52, 79–80, 84–86).

Modern anthropological studies of death ceremonies have generally assumed most of these notions and have concentrated upon accounting for some of the specific aspects of *form* found in a particular set of customs, attempting to show in detail how the ceremonies reflect and reaffirm a particular social order – the lineage system, the cultural values and so on.

For example, a paper by M. E. Opler on the Apache relates two opposite emphases in their death ceremonies to a structurally induced ambivalence of feeling created by the customs and socialization practices of the tribe. A strenuous public outpouring of grief is followed by attempts to wipe out all trace and memory of the deceased, even his name. These practices, with their opposed tendencies, are related to strongly taught obligations to support and defend relatives, and to equally strong stresses upon individuality and self-reliance. The exuberant outbursts of grief express emotional loss and dependency, while the customs of obliterating the traces and memories of the dead person stem from repressed hostilities and fears.

Carter's (1968) analysis of an Aymara funeral ritual shows the ways in which the particular set of funeral customs of this group is integrated with and reflects their secular life. Similarly, Orenstein's interesting study of Hindu death rituals delineates how the often implicit structural rules underlying pollution beliefs in India can enhance our understanding of Hindu practices and, at the same time, indicates how general functional theory may be translated at the level of a specific culture. Goody has written a whole book of finegrained description and analysis showing how the funerary customs and ancestor beliefs of two closely related groups of the LoDagaa tribe in Ghana likewise vary as a result of their differing lineage rules and inheritance customs.

An excellent analysis of this type is Goldschmidt's paper on Sebei mortuary rituals. He illuminates the precise mechanisms by which the personal motivations typical of this group are translated into the adaptive social processes that maintain social stability. The Sebei emphasis upon the defilement of death, their lack of interest in the ghosts of the dead, and lack of poignant grief, are shown to be related to the property advantages involved in a death, as well as to general customs and basic personality traits among the Sebei which impel individuals to seek personal advantage.

All of these analyses by anthropologists emphasize the cultural phrasing of the universal elements and functions of mortuary ritual. They show how rituals reflect the particular concerns, values, structural features, and local conditions of each particular society.

Conclusion

Let us review those areas where psychological and social theory are relevant to the Nubian material. In this case, the immediate supportive rush to the house where death took place, the collective condolences, the cathartic wailing, the self-defilement by the women, and other such actions correspond rather closely to what has been isolated as the universally human phase of shock in grief reaction. The rituals, gradually tapering off for the forty-day period, seem therapeutically tailored to the natural periods of despair, general disorganization, and psychological reintegration which have been described in the psychoanalytic interpretation of death reactions. During the whole process, great effort is devoted to defense against the disruptive forces of the demonic world. The psychological effect of Nubian ritual activities and taboos can be seen as not only providing defenses against the projected fears and guilts elicited by death, but also as obviously helping to enable the bereaved to "work through" his grief. They do this by keeping him busy, by showing him a solid front of human caring and support, and by dramatically enabling him to displace his own guilts, projecting them onto dangerous spirit entities which, as we have seen, constitute a real part of his world.

The activities of the Nubian bereaved and of those who are "sharing" their grief fall into distinct categories. People of each sex know their expected role patterns very well; they have watched and participated in many funerals from early childhood. Thus, though they are expressed irregularly, we may legitimately speak of "bereaved roles" in the strict role-theory sense. It may be remembered that Durkheim pointed out how much of the wailing and self-punishment of native Australian funerals did not spring from inner emotions of loss, but could be stopped or started at will, and were attributed by the people to fear of spirits, indicating to him that rather than being spontaneous inner responses to loss, these behaviors were the result of socially imposed norms.

It is important, however, to distinguish here between those persons most closely tied with affective bonds to the individual (including those regarded as most closely tied according to cultural definitions), and those more distant persons who, it is felt, *should* share the grief, though they may be regarded as without intimate affective involvement. Freud's concepts of mourning apply to the closely tied, while Durkheim's apply more to the less involved.

The point I want to stress, however, is that there are two categories of learned roles: one that allows cathartic expressions of inner grief, and one that compels social support of the grief-stricken. It is obvious that the second category of role-requirements is patterned upon "real" grief, yet allows much more flexibility.People can and do distinguish those who are not so closely tied, who are not expected to be so profoundly affected.

Thus, I hypothesize that the often-noted pro-forma grieving, which may be turned off and on at will, relates in most cases to a situation like that of the Nubians. Such grieving derives, that is, from a dual social pattern for death, which seems clearly to be built upon an implicit recognition of the psychological concomitants of bereavement and a powerful communal co-operation pattern. The resultant mourning system clearly divides the group struck by death into two categories which different sets of role prescriptions, even though the model of behavior for the category more removed from death is almost always derived from, and imitative of, the grief reaction itself. Those further away can, by implicit rule, stop their perfunctory wailing to gossip, perform tasks, and generally act in an ordinary manner. Many ethnographers apparently have thought that there was some kind of general lack of genuine feeling involved in groups exhibiting this behavior, but I would guess on the basis of the Nubian data that these observers simply did not know the situation well enough to distinguish the truly bereaved from the supporters. Thus they were led to make facile generalizations about "primitives" being "uncaring about human life."

Freud's ideas about mourning have shed a good deal of light on the origin and function of funeral ceremonies, and hypotheses derived from his theory should be field-tested. For example, we should expect a correlation of the degree of severity of mourning rituals with the degree of closeness of affective ties in a group. Casual comparisons, such as we may make of the Nubians, who have strong communal ties, with the Sebei (Goldschmidt 1973), who are much more individualistic, support the Freudian interpretation, but much more careful comparative research on such questions is needed. Single cases can only raise them.

Many features of the general sociological theories of death ceremonies are also confirmed by the Nubian ritual complex. For example, the differential ceremonial attention to children, the old, and the socially important, as well as the fact that the most stringent taboos and onerous requirements devolve upon those most closely tied to the deceased, clearly support the functional sociological theory. Certainly the solidarity of the group is strengthened by the Nubian rituals. Its members are all made aware of the lineaments of their society and are reminded of their own part within it as well as of whence their own support will come in time of need.

The Nubian case thus demonstrates that there need be no reason for a psychological analysis to invalidate or be "more true" than a sociological one, or *vice-versa*. They simply explain different levels or aspects of the same phenomenon. Even when they discuss the same feature the two approaches are not incompatible. When Hertz says that those individuals of less social importance, both to the group and to the individual, are given less group ritual attention and evoke fewer restrictions and taboos than socially close individuals, he is not contrary to Freud's concept that the embivalent emotions of envy, guilt, and love result in more stringent ritual requirements being imposed upon those tied by more close affective bonds to the dead person. Each kind of interpretation illuminates different aspects of the same behavior and they complement one another.

On the level of particular societal coloring and expression, as discussed in the other anthropological accounts, it seems clear that Nubian funerary rituals reflect the dominant concerns, values, and social situation of the group. When we examine the Nubian death ceremonies in the context of the total ceremonial pattern of this group, it is evident that these practices shared many features with the other life-cycle rituals. The general symbolism of green palms, ritually numbered days and activities, the taboo of *mushāhara*, the protective devices against spirits, the communal patterns of obligations, visiting, gifting and feasting — all these were general to the Nubian ritual system. On the other hand, there were a number of particular features, which seemed to derive from the fact that death is different from other, essentially joyful life-cycle events: death ceremonies omitted such regular Nubian ritual features as visits to saints' tombs and *dhikr* rituals, while elements added to the normal ceremonial pattern included special mourning dress, clothing restrictions, and the imposition of a somber, subdued mood upon community activities.

As in the other anthropological studies referred to above, the general conclusion drawn here from viewing death ceremonies within the larger Nubian ceremonial system is that they are consistent with it. Given the special circumstances that death imposes upon a group, they are part of an overall ceremonial pattern. All the Nubian life-cycle rituals had a certain irregular character in comparison with calendric or periodic rituals, such as Friday Prayer or annual holidays, but death ceremonies had, obviously, a more sudden and unplanned occurrence. Reflecting on this special element of funerals enables us to see more clearly an important element of the ritual system as a whole — the oscillation of Nubian social life between two distinct worlds of reality. One was "mundane reality," everyday life with its real-time scheduling of activities and its secular role expectations, while the other was a "ritual reality," a sudden shifting over from the mundane world to a pattern of expectations governed by a symbolic order, a supernatural set of assumptions, and ritualized time.

When the high-pitched *wigība* cry echoed through a Nubian village, the normal order of tasks and events was preempted by a set of higher priorities. The total regular life pattern of the community was suddenly shifted into another gear, in which another equally well-known set of interlocking role prescriptions prevailed. No matter what plans and desires were uppermost within individuals' priorities of action, each felt a powerfully sanctioned necessity to subordinate and defer them in favor of ritual obligations. Of course, the same ceremonial order was also activated by the initiation of wedding ceremonials, births, and circumcisions and to a lesser degree it prevailed at *zār* rituals and on feast days. But on none of these occasions was the change so clear-cut as at funerals. When the ritual "switch" had been thrown, as it were, each person knew what his course of activity would be for a prescribed number of days, with the precise period depending upon his social relatedness to the protagonists who were to be the focus of the ceremonial sequence.

These prescribed and proscribed activities were measured and spaced in time. They could not be hurried, changed, or delayed, though there were certain rules of exemption. Everyday activities and roles always have predictable time' and role expectations built into them too, but they also have a latitude and interchangeability, a sense of choice, and a quality of spontaneity that are quite foreign to the rigid sequence and pace of Nubian ceremonial reality.

The sharp dichotomy between defined social realities which I am emphasizing here may be difficult for those reared in a modern multireligious environment to comprehend. In Western societies, one becomes aware of the domain of the sacred when one enters a church or temple. But this slight voluntary contact with ceremonial reality is only a vestige of our medieval heritage, where the relative importance of the sacred domain was much closer to the conceptions and experience still found in some non-Western societies.

The Nubian life-cycle ritual series focused upon two concerns: (1) communal efforts to protect individuals believed to be rendered vulnerable by their life cycle states, and (2) cooperative efforts to show support to the threatened individual and his family. The Islamic Allāh was recognized in the reading of the Qur'ān at death and marriage, but the relevance of the abstract concepts of the Muslim faith were generally at a minimum. The basic core and stress of these crisis rites was non-Islamic, with emphasis upon the ritual manipulation of symbols and the acting of symbolic roles, which brought the community together behind one of their member families in the time of crisis. Each family unit realized that it must find itself in the same predicament at some time and each knew that it would then need reciprocal support. The compulsive rigidity of the ceremonial cycle was thus maintained by motivations of fear and anticipated need of social support.

Tangible evidence of that support and demonstrations of continuous readiness to act in full compliance with one's obligations at any time were made manifest during periods of ceremonial need. Funerals were simply the events of greatest loss, threat, and fear. Death also constituted a threat at the other times of life-cycle crisis, however, when fertility, virility and health were similarly endangered. In funeral ceremonies, these feelings of threat were made most real by the fact that death, the ultimate sanction, had actually been visited upon a number of the group. Thus, funerals most clearly and effectively activated and delineated the structural pattern of the entire community, illustrating the general sociological principle that the greater the crisis, the more powerful and positive are motivations to adhere to and to demonstrate public adherence to social obligations.

There is a sense, however, in which the intensity of acted-out social obligations following upon a death, and the communal sharing of grief, may be seen to dramatize a latent social structure, one that only emerges or exists in its concrete form at such times. It is a structure in which, for a time, people actually do cooperate and aid and respect one another, in a way that the value system prescribes as the ideal daily norm. The mythic "charter" of the society is thus at this time tangibly demonstrated. Such a temporary but absolutely required activation of the ideal model of social relations has the further psychological function of allowing all individuals, not simply those most bereaved, to purge themselves of guilts they have been harboring about the accumulated general failures of obligation that have occurred in daily life. (I am speaking here of those guilts apart from the intense familial ones concerning the deceased, which I discussed earlier.) This cathartic activity contributed in Nubia to the emotional intensity of the occasions and its benefit to many individuals undoubtedly helped to perpetuate and energize the customs.

The absolute requirement to suspend daily activities had a highly rewarding effect in itself, compounding the many ambivalences inherent in the situation. The often dull quietness of village routines had to be broken, and the heavy obligational load was compensated for by the excitement, the high density of social interaction, the feasting, and the activation of all the positive and protective symbols for the collective good of the Nubian community and family. At the same time, however, by the end of the long period of mourning, many people had been wearied by the enforced isolation and inactivity of the traditional pattern, were oppressed by the continued forced attention to death, with its intimations of mortality, felt burdened by the totality of expectations constituting the ceremonial role system, and wished to return to the activities and business of daily life. Several funerals in a short period of time could blight the life of a village for months at a time.

Many informants said that despite the loss of mutual sharing of grief that modern changes have brought to the Nubians, they were very relieved by the shortening of the periods of obligation and the abbreviation of onerous complexes of taboos. To Nubian men, particularly, the ceremonial complex, especially that part concerned with life crisis, has lost much of its compelling spiritual basis.

In a general sense it seems clear that Nubian funerary rituals were part of cycle of crisis rites and were consistent with the total belief system of the group. Identical symbols and ritual sequences are found throughout Nubian ceremonialism, and in each case they are related to the focal concern of communal sharing and mutual help, fertility, virility, and health. In each crisis-ritual complex, the same patterns of numbers, symbolic substances, spirit beliefs, feasting and sacrifice are found.

The impress of the universalistic religion of Islam is obvious, as the whole funeral is cast in the general Islamic mode, evidenced in the reading of the Qur'ān, in the rituals of washing and burial, and in the adherence to Islamic rules of inheritance. This latter feature makes the situation much different from the case in many societies in the anthropological literature. The standardization of procedure which Islamic law imposes eliminates most of the tension and haggling over the disposal of property that takes place in many societies. This does not mean that such disputes do not occur among Nubians; it only means that most of them are avoided, and that the remainder are disposed of according to legitimized and standardized means. Eliminated are the possibilities of the development of such idiosyncratic complexes of sacrifices as, for example, are found among the LoDagaa (Goody 1962) or the Sebei (Goldschmidt 1973), in which death rituals and beliefs seem to revolve around and reflect social conflict and problems of property transmission, including sexual rights over widows. Thus, a point I want to emphasize is one I have previously made several times. Death ceremonial, like all other ritual complexes of this group, must be understood as syncretism of Islam with ancient local customs—this fusion resulting in a unique system. It is in the rituals following a death that the ceremonial reality and the ceremonial role system, which was so sharply distinct from and so counterposed to the mundane reality and social order of the Nubians, can be most readily seen.

Bibliography

Adams, W. "Continuity and Change in Nubian Cultural History." *Sudan Notes and Records* 48 (1967), pp. 1–32.

Alexander, F. *Fundamentals of Psychoanalysis.* New York: W. W. Norton and Co., 1963.

Ammar, H. *Growing Up in an Egyptian Village.* London: Routledge and Kegan Paul, 1954.

Antoun, R. T. "On the Modesty of Women in Arab Muslim Villages: A Study in the Accommodation of Traditions." *American Anthropologist* 70 (1968), pp. 671–697.

Armbruster, C. H. *Dongolese Nubian, A Lexicon.* London: Cambridge University Press, 1960.

Barclay, H. *Buurri al-Lammaab: A Suburban Village in Sudan.* Ithaca, New York: Cornell University Press, 1964.

———. "Study of an Egyptian Village Community." *Studies in Islam* (1966), pp. 201–226.

Berger, M. *Islam in Egypt Today.* London: Cambridge University Press, 1970.

Bettelheim, B. *Symbolic Wounds.* Glencoe, Illinois: Free Press, 1954.

Blackman, A. M. "Some Egyptian and Nubian Notes." *Man* 11 (1910), pp. 25–29.

Blackman, W. *The Fellahin of Upper Egypt.* London: Harper and Row, 1927.

Blum, G. S. *Psychoanalytic Theories of Personality.* New York: McGraw Hill, 1964.

Bonaparte, M. "Notes on Excision." In *Psychoanalysis and Social Science.* Geza Roheim, ed., New York: International University Press, 1952.

Bowlby, J. "Processes of Mourning." *International Journal of Psychoanalysis* 42 (1961), pp. 317–340.

Brown, J. K. "A Cross-Cultural Study of Female Initiation Rites." *American Anthropologist* 65 (1963), pp. 837–853.

Burkhardt, J. L. *Travels in Nubia.* London: John Murray, 1822.

Callender, C. "The Mehannab: A Kenuz Tribe." In *Contemporary Egyptian Nubia.* R. Fernea, ed., New Haven: Human Relations Area Files Press, 1966.

———, and al-Guindi, F. *Life-Crisis Rituals Among the Kenuz*, Studies in Anthropology, No. 3. Cleveland: Case Western Reserve University, 1971.

245

246 BIBLIOGRAPHY

Carter, W. E. "Secular Reinforcement in Aymara Death Ritual." *American Anthropologist* 70 (1968), pp. 238–263.
Cavendish, M. W. "The Custom of Placing Pebbles on Nubian Graves." *Sudan Notes and Records* 14 (1966), pp. 151–156.
Cohen, Y. "The Establishment of Identity in a Social Nexus: The Special Case of Initiation Ceremonies and Their Relation to Value and Legal Systems." *American Anthropologist* 66 (1964), pp. 529–552.
Crawley, E., and Besterman, T. *The Mystic Rose*. New York: Boni and Liveright, 1927.
Durkheim, E. *The Elementary Forms of the Religious Life*. London: George Allen Unwin, 1915.
Edwards, A. *A Thousand Miles Up the Nile*. London: George Routledge and Sons, 1891.
Emery, W. B. *Egypt in Nubia*. London: Hutchinson and Company, 1965.
Evans-Pritchard, E. E. *Theories of Primitive Religion*. Oxford: Clarendon Press, 1965.
Ewalt, J. R., and D. L. Farnsworth. *Textbook of Psychiatry*. New York: McGraw-Hill, 1963.
Fahim, H. M. *Change in Rituals in Kanuba*. M.A. thesis, American University in Cairo, 1968.
———. "Change in Religion in a Resettled Nubian Community, Upper Egypt." *International Journal of Middle Eastern Studies*, (1963).
Fakouri, H. "The *Zar* Cult in an Egyptian Village." *Anthropological Quarterly* 41 (1968), pp. 49–56.
Fernea, R. "Integrating Factors in a Non-Corporate Community." In *Contemporary Egyptian Nubia*, R. Fernea, ed., New Haven: Human Relations Area File Press, 1966.
———, ed. *Contemporary Egyptian Nubia*, 2 vol. New Haven: Human Relations Area File Press, 1966.
———, and Kennedy, J. G. "Initial Adaptations to Resettlement: A New Life for Egyptian Nubians." *Current Anthropology* 7 (1966), pp. 349–354.
———, and Gerster, G. *Nubians in Egypt*. Austin: University of Texas Press, 1973.
Fortes, M. "Ritual and Office in Tribal Society." In *Essays on the Ritual of Social Relations*, Max Gluckman, ed., Manchester: Manchester University Press, 1961.
Frazer, J. *The New Golden Bough*. Theodor H. Gaster, ed., New York: Doubleday and Company, 1961.
Freud, S. "Mourning and Melancholia." In *Collected Papers*, vol. 10. New York: Basic Books, 1917.
———. "Totem and Taboo." In *The Basic Writings of Sigmund Freud*, A. A. Brill, ed., New York: Random House, 1938.
———. *Moses and Monotheism*. New York: Alfred A. Knopf, 1939.
Geiser, P. "Some Impressions Concerning the Nature and Extent of Stabilization in Nubian Society." In *Contemporary Egyptian Nubia*, R. Fernea, ed., New Haven: Human Relations Area File Press, 1966.
———. "Some Differential Factors Affecting Population Movement: The Nubian Case." *Human Organization* 26 (1967), pp. 164–177.

————. "The Myth of the Dam." *American Anthropologist* 75 (1973), pp. 184–194.

Gennep, A. van. *The Rites of Passage*. Chicago: University Press, 1960.

Gerster, G. *Nubien, Goldland an Nil*, Zurich and Stuttgart: Artemis, 1964.

Ghalioungui, P. *Magic and Medical Science in Ancient Egypt*. London: Hodder and Stoughton, 1936.

Gibb, H. A. R. *Mohammedanism*. London: Oxford University Press, 1969.

Gilsenen, M. "Some Factors in the Decline of Ṣūfī Orders in Modern Egypt." *Muslim World*, vol. 58 (1967), pp. 11–18.

Goldschmidt, W. *Man's Way*. New York: Henry Holt and Company, 1959.

————. "Guilt and Pollution in Sebei Mortuary Rituals." *Ethos* 1 (1973), pp. 75–105.

Goody, J. *Death, Property and the Ancestors: A Study of Mortuary Customs of the Lo Dagaa of West Africa*. Palo Alto: Stanford University Press, 1962.

Gorer, G. *Death, Grief and Mourning*. New York: Doubleday and Co, 1965.

Grauer, A. *Die Architektur und Wandmalerei der Nubier, 1963–1964*. Ph.D. dissertation, Albert Ludwig Universitat, 1968.

Guindi, al-, F. "Ritual and the River in Dahmit." *Symposiom on Contemporary Nubia*, Robert Fernea, ed., New Haven: Human Relations Area Files Press, 1966.

————. "The Internal Structure of the Zapotec Conceptual System." *Journal of Symbolic Anthropology* 1 (1973), pp. 15–34.

Harris, G. "Possession 'Hysteria' in a Kenya Tribe." *American Anthropologist* 59 (1957), pp. 1046–1066.

Hassan, Y. *The Arabs in the Sudan*. Edinburgh: University Press, 1965.

Hertz, R. *Death and the Right Hand*. Glencoe: Free Press, 1960.

Herzog, R. *Die Nubier*. Berlin: Deutsch Akadamie der Wissenschaften zu Berlin, Volkarkunliche Forschungen, vol. 2, 1957.

Heyworth-Dunne, J. *Introduction to the History of Education in Modern Egypt*. London: Luzac and Company, 1938.

Homans, G. "Anxiety and Ritual: The Theories of Malinowski and Radcliffe-Brown." In *Reader in Comparative Religion*, W. Lessa and E. Vogt, eds., New York: Harper and Row, 1965.

Honigmann, J. J. *Personality in Culture*. New York: Harper and Row, 1967.

————, ed., *Handbook of Social and Cultural Anthropology*. New York: Rand McNally, 1974.

Hussein, S. A. *Aus Meinen Leben*. Wiesbaden: Sudan Pionier Mission, 1938.

Junker, H., and Schafer. *Nubische Texte im Kenzi Dialekt*, 2 vol. Wien Schriften der Sprachen-Kommission, Akademie der Wissenschaften, 1921 and 1932.

Katsha, S. *The Impact of Environmental Change on the Marriage Institution: The Case of Kanuba Settlers*. M.A. thesis, American University in Cairo, 1969.

Keating, R. *Nubian Rescue*. London: Robert Hall and New York: Hawthorne Books, 1975.

Kennedy, J. G. "Occupational Adjustment in a Previously Resettled Nubian Village." In *Contemporary Egyptian Nubia*, R. Fernea, ed., New Haven: Human Relations Area File Press, 1966.

————. "Nubian *Zār* Ceremonies as Psychotherapy." *Human Organization* 26 (1967), pp. 185–194.

————. "Mushahara: A Nubian Concept of Supernatural Danger and the Theory of Taboo." *American Anthropologist* 69 (1967), pp. 685–702.

————. "Aman Doger, Nubian Monster of the Nile." *Journal of American Folklore* 83 (1970), pp. 438–445.

————. "Circumcision and Excision in Egyptian Nubia." *Man* 5 (1970), pp. 175–191.

————. "Cultural Psychiatry." In *Handbook of Social and Cultural Anthropology*, J. J. Honigmann, ed., New York: Rand McNally, 1974.

————. *Struggle for Change in a Nubian Community*. Palo Alto: Mayfield, 1977.

————, and Fahim, H. M. "Nubian Zikr Rituals and Cultural Change." *Muslim World*, 64 (1974), pp. 205–219.

Kiev, A. "The Study of Folk Psychiatry." In *Magic, Faith and Healing*, A. Kiev, ed., London: The Free Press of Glencoe, 1964.

Kriss, R., and Kriss-Heinrich, H. *Volksglaube im Bereich des Islam*, 2 vol. Weisbaden: O. Harrassowitz, 1960. 1962.

Kroeber, A. L. "Totem and Taboo: An Ethnologic Psychoanalysis." In *Reader in Comparative Religion*, W. Lessa and E. Vogt, eds., New York: Harper and Row, 1965.

Lane, E. *The Manners and Customs of the Modern Egyptians*. London: Dutton, 1908.

Levy, R. *The Social Structure of Islam*. London: Cambridge University Press, 1962.

Lindemann, E. "Symptomatology and Management of Acute Grief." *American Journal of Psychiatry* 101 (1944), pp. 101–144.

Massenbach, G. von. *Volkssagen aus der Gebiet der Kunuzi Nubier*. Wiesbaden: Mittelungen des Seminars fur Orientalische Sprachen 34, 1931.

————. *Nubische Texte im Dialekt des Kunuzi und der Dongolawi Abhandlungen fur die Kunde des Morgenlandes*. Deutsche Morgen Ladisehe Gesellsehaft, 34: 4: F. Steiner, 1962.

Mayer-Gross, S. Elliot, and Roth. *Clinical Psychiatry*. Baltimore: The Williams and Wilkins Co., 1960.

McPherson, J. W. *The Moulids of Egypt*. London: N.M. Press, 1941.

Merton, R. *Social Theory and Social Structure*. Glencoe: Free Press, 1957.

Messing, S. "Group Therapy and Social Status in the *Zār* Cult of Ethiopia." *American Anthropologist* 60 (1958), pp. 1120–1126.

Messiri, N. *The Sheikh Cult in Dahmit*. M.A. thesis, American University in Cairo, 1965.

————. "The Sheikh Cult in Dahmit Life." In *Contemporary Egyptian Nubia*, R. Fernea, ed., New Haven: Human Relations Area File Press, 1966.

Modarressi, T. "The *Zār* Cult in South Iran." In *Trance and Possession States*, R. Prince, ed., Montreal: R. M. Buck Memorial Society, 1968.

Nelson, C. "Self Spirit Possession and World View: An Illustration from Egypt." *International Journal of Social Psychiatry* 17 (1971), pp. 194–209.

Nicholson, R. A. *The Mystics of Islam*. London: Routledge and Kegan Paul, 1969. (first published by George Bell and Sons in 1914).

Norbeck, E. *Religion in Primitive Society*. New York: Harper and Bros., 1961.

————, "African Rituals of Conflict." *American Anthropologist* 65 (1963), pp. 1254–1279.

———. Walker, D. and Cohen, M. "The Interpretation of Data: Puberty Rites." *American Anthropologist* 64 (1962), pp. 463–485.

Opler, M. E. "An Interpretation of Ambivalence in Two American-Indian Tribes." *Journal of Social Psychology* 8 (1963), pp. 82–115.

Opler, M. K. "The Cultural Backgrounds of Mental Health." In *Culture and Mental Health*, M. K. Opler, ed., New York: The MacMillan Company, 1959.

———. *Culture and Social Psychiatry.* New York: Atherton Press, 1967.

Orenstein, H. "Death and Kinship in Hinduism: Structural and Functional Interpretation." *American Anthropologist* 72 (1970), pp. 1357–1377.

Prince, R. "Indigenous Yoruba Psychiatry." In *Magic, Faith and Healing* A. Kiev, ed., New York, London: The Free Press of Glencoe, 1964.

Radcliffe-Brown, A. R. *Structure and Function in Primitive Society.* Glencoe: The Free Press, 1952.

Redfield, R. *The Little Community, and Peasant Society and Culture.* Chicago: University of Chicago Press, 1960.

Reik, T. *Ritual.* New York: International University Press, 1958.

Reinach, S. *Orpheus.* New York: Liveright Publishing Corp, 1930.

Reinisch, L. *Die Nuba Sprache.* Wien: W. Braumuller, 1879.

Schäfer, H. *Nubische Texte in Dialekte der Kunuzi* (Mundart von Abuhor), Berlin: Verlag der Konigl, Akademie der Wissenschaften, 1917.

———. *Nubisches Franenleben.* Weisbaden: Mitteilungen des Seminars fur Orientalisohe Sprachen, 1935 and 1938.

Scudder, T. "The Economic Basis of Egyptian Nubian Labor Migration." In *Contemporary Egyptian Nubia*, R. Fernea, ed., New Haven: Human Relations Area File Press, 1966.

Seligman, B. "On the Origin of the Egyptian *Zār.*" *Folklore* 25 (1914), pp. 300–323.

Seligman, C. and Seligman, B. *Pagan Tribes of the Nilotic Sudan.* London: Routledge and Kegan Paul, 1932.

Shinnie, P. L. *Medieval Nubia.* Sudan Antiquities Service Pamphlet #2. Khartoum: Sudan Antiquities Service, 1954.

Smith, W. *Kinship and Marriage in Early Arabia.* Boston: Beacon Press, 1903.

Swan, G. "The *Dhikr.*" *The Moslem World* 2 (1912), pp. 380–386.

Trigger, B. *History and Settlement in Lower Nubia.* Yale University Publication in Anthro. 69, New Haven: Yale Univ. Press, 1965.

Trimingham, J. S. *Islam in the Sudan.* London: Frank Cass and Co., 1965.

Tylor, E. *Religion in Primitive Culture.* New York: Harper and Brothers, 1958.

Van Gennep, A. *The Rites of Passage.* 2nd rev. ed. Chicago: University of Chicago Press, 1960.

Westermarck, E. *Marriage Ceremonies in Morocco.* London: MacMillan and Company, 1914.

———. *Ritual and Belief in Morocco*, 2 vol. London: MacMillan and Company, 1926.

Whiting, J. W. M., Kluckhohn R., and Anthony, A. "The Function of Male Initiation Ceremonies at Puberty." In *Readings in Social Psychology*, E. Maccoby, et al, eds., New York: Holt, Rinehart & Winston, 1958.

Winkler, H. A. *Bauern, Zwischen, Wasser und Wuste*. Stuttgart: W. Kohlhammer, 1934.

———. *Agyptische Volkskunde*. Stuttgart: W. Kohlhammer, 1936.

———. *Die Reitenden Geister der Toten*. Stuttgart: W. Kohlhammer, 1936.

Young, F. W. *Initiation Ceremonies: A Cross-Cultural Study of Status Dramatization*. New York: Bobbs-Merrill, 1965.

Index

251

1

2

3

4

5

6

7

8a

8b

8c

8d

8e

9

10

11

12

13

14

15

16

17

18

19

20

21

22

23

24

25

26

27

28

29

30